Simone Panter-Brick is a renowned expert on Mahatma Gandhi's political thought and action. Her previous publications include *Gandhi and the Middle East: Jews, Arabs and Imperial Interests* (I.B.Tauris) and *Gandhi Against Machiavellism: Non-violence in Politics*. She holds a doctorate in Law and Political Science from the University of Nancy, France.

'Simone Panter-Brick's elegant new study attends to the stages and evolution of Gandhi's nationalism. Brimming with insight and written with a sure and fluid hand, Panter-Brick carefully navigates through and makes sense of the often dramatic turns in Gandhi's political vision and strategies for attaining independence.'

Karuna Mantena,
Associate Professor of Political Science,
Yale University

'Was Gandhi a nationalist? This engrossing and intricate study illuminates the thought and action of Churchill's "half-naked fakir" as he resisted anti-Indian legislation in South Africa in his younger days, accepted separation from the British Empire in middle age, and labored to prevent the partition of the subcontinent late in life. Any reader wishing to fathom just what India meant to Gandhi should read this book, the work of an author who understands "Gandhianity" and "Indianity" almost as well as the Mahatma did himself.'

Paul Jankowski,
Ray Ginger Professor of History,
Brandeis University

GANDHI *and* NATIONALISM

The Path to Indian Independence

SIMONE PANTER-BRICK

Foreword by
WM. ROGER LOUIS

Viva Books

New Delhi | Mumbai | Chennai | Kolkata | Bengaluru | Hyderabad | Kochi | Guwahati

First Indian Edition 2012

VIVA BOOKS PRIVATE LIMITED

- 4737/23 Ansari Road, Daryaganj, New Delhi 110 002
  E-mail: vivadelhi@vivagroupindia.net, Tel. 42242200
- 76, Service Industries, Shirvane, Sector 1, Nerul, Navi Mumbai 400 706
  E-mail: vivamumbai@vivagroupindia.net, Tel. 27721273, 27721274
- Jamals Fazal Chambers, 26 Greams Road, Chennai 600 006
  E-mail: vivachennai@vivagroupindia.net, Tel. 28290304, 28294241
- B-103, Jindal Towers, 21/1A/3 Darga Road, Kolkata 700 017
  E-mail: vivakolkata@vivagroupindia.net, Tel. 22836381, 22816713
- 7, Sovereign Park Apartments, 56-58, K. R. Road, Basavanagudi, Bangalore 560 004
  E-mail: vivabangalore@vivagroupindia.net, Tel. 26607409, 26607410
- 101-102 Mughal Marc Apartments, 3-4-637 to 641, Narayanguda, Hyderabad 500 029
  E-mail: vivahyderabad@vivagroupindia.net, Tel. 27564481, 27564482
- Beevi Towers, First Floor, SRM Road, Kaloor, Kochi 682 018, Kerala
  E-mail: vivakochi@vivagroupindia.net, Tel: 0484-2403055, 2403056
- 232, GNB Road, Beside UCO Bank, Silpukhuri, Guwahati 781 003
  E-mail: vivaguwahati@vivagroupindia.net, Tel: 0361-2666386

www.vivagroupindia.com

Published by arrangement with:
I. B. Tauris & Co. Ltd.
6, Salem Road, London W2 4BU
175 Fifth Avenue, New York NY 10010
www.ibtauris.com

ISBN : 978-81-309-2254-6

Published by Vinod Vasishtha for Viva Books Private Limited, 4737/23, Ansari Road, Daryaganj, New Delhi 110 002.

Printed and bound by Raj Press, R-3, Inderpuri, New Delhi - 110 012.

To Catherine and Mark

porque el amor da tal vida,
cuando más ciego va siendo

San Juan de la Cruz (1542–1591)

CONTENTS

ILLUSTRATIONS

FOREWORD

One of the virtues of Simone Panter-Brick's perceptive study of Gandhi as a nationalist is to make clear Gandhi's own view of nationalism in relation to his priorities. He was a nationalist 'of a sort.' The qualification is important. Nationalism was a subject on which Gandhi held relatively straightforward views. It could be understood, in his own definition, simply as India's quest for freedom. But 'freedom' itself meant different things to Gandhi, and went beyond mere liberation from colonial rule. His sometimes contradictory interpretations of the term and his ideas about the means to achieve freedom changed over time.

In the first period of his life, until his return to India from South Africa at the beginning of the First World War, he believed that equality and eventually independence could be achieved by keeping good faith with the British. He changed tactics in the inter-war years, with the famous non-violent resistance campaign that became known as *Satyagraha*. It is easy to forget how revolutionary Gandhi's strategy appeared to his contemporaries. One of the few Englishmen who came close to recognising the full significance of the spiritual as well as the political dimension of Gandhi's personality, Lord Halifax (or Lord Irwin as he was known at the time) remarked that it seemed as if Gandhi had been dropped off from a different planet. In the last phase of his life, from 1942 to his death in 1948, Gandhi reverted to seeking cooperation with the British as a way to prevent partition.

Keeping India unified was one of his foremost priorities. Ultimately, the national family with a common identity might be legally divided but still remain united on the principle of equality and the resolution of disputes by peaceful means.

Simone Panter-Brick's emphasis on 'his own brand of nationalism' helps to explain Gandhi's erroneous belief that Muslims and Hindus, Sikhs and other minorities, could live harmoniously after the British departure. Gandhi used to say that he was Hindu to his very core, but in fact he differed from most of those of his time in the way he absolutely regarded Muslims and others as equals. Yet neither Gandhi's tolerance, nor, for that matter, the principles of equality proclaimed by the Indian National Congress, could eradicate suspicion among Muslims that British withdrawal would lead to a Hindu Raj. It was this suspicion that in turn helps to explain the insistence of Jinnah and the Muslim League on Pakistan. Gandhi also differed from many of his fellow nationalists in the extent to which he was open to compromise. He rejected the two-nation idea and the demand for parity or the equal sharing of power by the Muslim League and the Indian National Congress. But he was quite prepared to work towards the possibility of a Pakistan province within an all-India federation.

He was even prepared to offer Jinnah the opportunity to become prime minister. The proposal to make Jinnah the head of a new, united federal state never had the remotest chance of being accepted by Gandhi's fellow nationalist leaders including Jawaharlal Nehru and Vallabhbhai Patel. But Simone Panter-Brick provides an historical corrective to many accounts by tracing the antecedents of the idea and the way in which Gandhi remained at the center of the debate. She further reveals a strand in what many have described as Gandhi's Machiavellian thought. Though Jinnah might in theory have become prime minister, he would still have been subject to the will of the Indian National Congress majority. And it is in regard to governance and stability that she makes perhaps her most original point in her account of the period before independence. There were no fixed ideas and no common agreement on the names for the successor states. It was commonly assumed that they would be Hindustan and Pakistan. Although Gandhi was by no means alone in thinking of 'India' as the successor state, the inspiration coincided with the pattern of his thought. India would inherit the British Raj. There would thus be a continuity of tradition and identity. Pakistan might be partitioned from India, but India itself would preserve the unity, integrity, and identity of the state.

Gandhi's nationalism was larger than the struggle for independence. Thus there is imaginative utility in Simone Panter-Brick's invention of the word *gandhianity* to refer to the whole of the Gandhian vision and the reasons for its enduring inspiration. His example of civil disobedience in the cause of equality motivated future generations, not only in India but also throughout the world. His sense of social conscience and tolerance is now more a global than an Indian phenomenon, above all as a moral shield for vulnerable minorities.

Wm. Roger Louis
Harry Ransom Humanities Research Center
University of Texas at Austin

INTRODUCTION

GANDHIAN NATIONALISM IN ONE SONG AND THREE CARTOONS

This book is about the world of Mahatma Gandhi, and its influence on Indian nationalism. It does not dwell at length on the non-violent campaigns for the liberation of India: it focuses mainly on the interludes and armistices between those campaigns. It observes how, during those periods, Gandhi changed his political opinions about nationalism in the Indian context – for which purpose I coin the word *indianity*, referring to a *prise de conscience* of the identity of the Indian nation. I group these meaningful changes into three periods. His nationalism was at first compatible with allegiance to the British Empire. He later rebelled against it. Last, he sought to save his country from partition – in a way reminiscent of the story of King Solomon judging over two claimants. He was one of these claimants, identifying his soul with the map of India, as illustrated so vividly in Figure 1.

Thus, the emphasis in this book is not on the concept of non-violence – well known to any reader – but on tactics and strategies used to achieve independence, and also on the consistent line of thought in apparently inconsistent decisions. Motives and goals are questioned, Gandhi's and those of his rival Jinnah, the second claimant for his part of India. Nobody is sure about the latter's political game. His nationalism, too, is assessed and scrutinised, especially as it affected Gandhi.

Figure 1: Gandhi as India

In the twenty-first century, nationalism has reverberated in so many traumatic creeds and experiences. The pursuit of nationalism usually begets violence. More rarely is it achieved by means of non-violence. An examination of Gandhi's nationalism shows the global relevance of his path to independence, the constraints on his political actions, the nefarious disruptions of violence, and, through it all, his indomitable faith in a better, Gandhian world: in what I shall call *gandhianity*, namely the world of Mahatma Gandhi.

Nationalism and the Mahatma

'Nationalism' has at least two meanings: 'devotion to one's own nation, patriotic feelings, principles or efforts' and a 'movement favouring political independence in a country that is controlled by another or is part of another.'[1]

The first definition fits the nationalism of Mahatma Gandhi like a glove. Devotion, fervour, patriotism, and a vocation to act accordingly in the political field were qualities that made Gandhi a politician early in his life. And the nation he was devoted to was, of course, India.

But nationalism in the second sense – which, in Gandhi's case, meant demanding India's independence from foreign rule – applied to only half of his political career. As a matter of fact, Gandhi, the leader of the movement that led India to independence, and that initiated the great current of decolonisation in the twentieth century, was not a nationalist in the sense of the second definition for most of his political life. Born in 1869, Mohandas Karamchand Gandhi became a nationalist and was dubbed a *mahatma* (great soul) as he was reaching his fifties, leading his first liberation movement in 1920.

Nationalism implies a belief in the *congruence of the nation and the state.* A nationalist movement therefore aims at liberation from a foreign yoke. Its leader, if successful, achieves the independence of all the territory belonging to the nation.

This was not Gandhi's initial objective. Love of his country made him work for the good of his nation as he saw it then. And he saw the good of his nation to lie in remaining part of the British Empire. He therefore identified not only with the Indian nation, but also with the British nation and, moreover, with the British state. As an Indian, he considered himself a citizen of the Empire.

When this allegiance to Britain foundered, Gandhi put his formidable energy in the service of rebellion, becoming a belligerent reformer, a skilled mediator, an advocate of lost causes, a political activist, and a self-made leader of his fellow Indians, in striking contrast to his previously unfailing loyalty to the Crown.

The nationalist dream of the last third of his life – liberation from foreign rule – failed, however, because independence was achieved for two nations, not for one, when Gandhi's India lost territory to new-born Pakistan.

The focus of this book rests on these three successive periods in the evolution of Gandhi's nationalism – loyalty to the British Empire, rebellion against it, and the demand for Pakistan – all of which shaped the evolution of Gandhi's politics in the independence movement.

Devotion, Illustrated in a Revolutionary Song

Devotion was the very marrow of Gandhi's political and religious life – the quintessence of his thoughts and deeds. In this sense, he was a nationalist to the core. Interestingly, the word 'nationalist' dates back to 1830, and the word 'nationalism' to 1798.[2] They were engendered by the political swing of French revolutions, in 1789 and 1830, and the Napoleonic wars in between. No wonder then that Gandhi's command of *do or die* at the start of his last campaign against British rule in 1942 echoed the sentiments of those French revolutionaries who sang poignantly of their burning love for the homeland:

Mourir pour la patrie	To die for one's country
C'est le sort le plus beau	Is the most sublime,
Le plus digne d'envie.	Most enviable destiny.
(Refrain)	(Chorus)
Par la voix du canon d'alarme	Raising the alarm by cannon roar,
La France appelle ses enfants.	France summons her children.
Allons, dit le soldat: aux armes,	Go, take up arms, the soldier calls,
C'est ma Mère, je la défends!	She is my Mother, her I defend.

The essence of nationalism – sacrifice and pride – is fittingly and forcefully conveyed in this revolutionary chant of eighteenth-century Europe. It calls to mind the startling opening sentence in Elie Kedourie's book *Nationalism*: 'Nationalism is a doctrine invented in Europe at the beginning of the nineteenth century.'[3]

If that is true, Gandhi, reared in the British courts of law, inhaled the sweet promise of the freedom of democracy from his days as a law student in London in the late 1880s. He felt exhilarated by the European winds of freedom until the end of his days.

Gandhian Nationalism, Sketched in Three Cartoons

Gandhi's nationalism, in the second meaning of the word, fostered different priorities in his political life. Three of them are selected here as being the most meaningful of his career, the most representative of his successive aims, and the driving force behind his strategy.

Let us invent three nationalistic Gandhis as a way to provide some insight into this exceptional statesman. They will add up to a list of what Judith Brown calls 'invented' Gandhis: 'To historians one of the most interesting aspects of the career of Mahatma Gandhi is the way he was, and still is, continuously "reinvented."'[4]

Let us describe them in a manner that will exaggerate the core of resilient features that compose Gandhi's nationalism. Let us imagine three political sketches that will convey the evolution of Gandhi's political thought – in the same way that a nationalist song can communicate the quality of Gandhi's patriotism. Let us conjure three cartoons of three Gandhis who embody Elie Kedourie's 'invented' doctrine.

The National Anthem Cartoon

The first sketch relates to the period before the end of the First World War, when our 'hero' joined in the singing of the British national anthem. The anthem was sung at the meetings of the Natal Indian Congress (affiliated with the Indian National Congress), which Gandhi had founded in May 1894. In spite of being in those days a keen defender of Indian interests, he never failed to proclaim his allegiance to the Queen – or King – as a citizen of Her Majesty's Empire: 'With careful perseverance I learnt the tune of the "national anthem" and joined in the singing whenever it was sung. Whenever there was an occasion for the expression of loyalty without fuss or ostentation, I readily took part in it.'[5]

Our first cartoon (Figure 2) depicts him singing, 'in the cumbersome clothes of a middle-class, conservative Hindu male from Kathiawar: a long cloak, a shirt under the cloak, a dhoti down to his ankles, and a heavy turban.'[6]

God save our gracious King,
God save our noble King,
God save the King.

Figure 2: The National Anthem

Send him victorious,
Happy and glorious,
Long to reign over us:
God save the King.

He has just disembarked from South Africa with his wife, and the boat is still steaming in Bombay harbour. Speaking in English, and on behalf of the reception committee, Muhammad Ali Jinnah, impeccably dressed in a Savile Row suit, welcomes him in the name of his friends, his admirers, and the party, to which both belong. He pulls a face for having been rebuked by Gandhi for not using their mother tongue.[7]

The contrast between Gandhi's and Jinnah's attire – both men were from Kathiawar – and the unsavoury remark of the former about the unsuitability of the language of the latter is the first clash between their personalities and a harbinger of things to come.

This is the first Gandhi, praised by the Congress for his work in South Africa, a hero firmly rooted in his allegiance to the British Empire.

The One-Year-to-Independence Cartoon

In the second cartoon (Figure 3), Gandhi is portrayed as a convert to the cause of independence from British rule. It shows him haranguing the Indian National Congress meeting at Nagpur in December 1920, when, on the spur of the moment, he unexpectedly came up with the promise of 'independence in one year' if the delegates would endorse his campaign of Non-cooperation against the British government. The Congress is seen responding with enthusiastic applause, but it also barracks Jinnah for opposing the Non-cooperation policy and heckles him for saying 'Mr. Gandhi' and refusing to say 'Mahatma Gandhi.' Shocked and shaken, followed by his young and pretty wife in dismay, Jinnah leaves the meeting, the Congress, and the party. He will later leave India as well, after another, even more painful rebuff from the Congress and from Gandhi in 1928; he will then board the boat waiting in Bombay harbour to take him to a London exile.

As for Gandhi, having won the day, he walks out of the Nagpur session as a rebel leader, and within nine months of the day, he will take

Figure 3: One Year to Independence

up his new role by discarding his clothes. Cap, shirt, and long dhoti are cast aside to reveal Gandhi in a loincloth.

This is the second Gandhi, adulated by the Indian crowds, not just a hero but an emblematic figure and, moreover, a rebel, a mass leader and reorganiser, a dictator, now in command of his party's strategy to dislodge the jewel from the crown of the British Empire.

The Solomon Cartoon

The third cartoon (Figure 4) depicts the 'great soul' – or Mahatma (Gandhi) – on April Fool's Day 1947. He is expounding to the Viceroy,

Figure 4: Solomon and Partition

Lord Mountbatten of Burma, his plan to hand over India to the 'great leader'– or *Quaid-i-azam* (Jinnah) – who returned from exile in the mid-thirties to prop up the failing Muslim League. It is Gandhi's final solution to the Hindu–Muslim problem.

This cartoon is inspired by *Le Jugement de Salomon* (1649), the famous painting by Nicolas Poussin.[8] Mountbatten appears as King Solomon on his throne, and Jinnah and Gandhi as the two claimants, fighting over the same baby. Infant India is about to be cut in two when Gandhi, as the desperate mother, tries to save him from the sword by offering him to the other woman. The offer saved the child's life in King Solomon's day; it did not save India from partition in Mountbatten's.

This sketch conveys not only a different aspect of Gandhi's nationalism, but also a change in circumstances. The Muslim question, which had been dealt with so successfully in 1920 with a show of political unity in the Non-cooperation campaign, had festered during the Second

World War until it became a running sore, one that could be excised only with partition in 1947. Jinnah had become Gandhi's *bête noire.* This third Gandhi gives priority to the unity of India. He is reported to have said in January 1947: 'Should the evil I apprehend [partition] overtake India and her independence be imperiled, let posterity know what agony this old man went through thinking of it. Let not the coming generations curse Gandhi for being a party to India's vivisection.'[9]

Thus three Gandhis dominate this book. Critical studies of Gandhi's politics abound. But this one will focus on these three insights into Gandhi's nationalism.

Along with the Three Gandhis, Three Jinnahs

The three Gandhis are shadowed by three Jinnahs, indispensable keys to understanding the plot of the story of Indian independence. The first Jinnah shared the first Gandhi's brand of nationalism: a desire for Hindu–Muslim unity and for a united India within the British Empire through British sponsorship.

The second Jinnah opposed the second Gandhi's policy openly in what was then their common party, the Indian National Congress, and when he was unpleasantly spurned, he left the Congress and even politics for a while. He did not abandon his belief in Muslim–Hindu unity – on the contrary, when he came back to politics after a self-imposed exile in London, he resumed his efforts in the Muslim League to promote cooperation and to solve amicably the Muslim problem.[10] But at this stage, both men differed on the use of non-constitutional means to attain independence.

As for the third Jinnah, he is an enigma. On 14 August 1947, on the eve of independence, Jinnah confided to his aide-de-camp that he had never expected to get Pakistan in his lifetime: 'I never thought it would happen.'[11] This is generally understood to mean that his beloved utopia had come true in a flash of destiny (seven years only!). It could simply mean, however, that Pakistan, to Jinnah, had never been seen as a utopia, but was, rather, a device contrived for political gain, one that took on a spontaneous and unexpected life of its own – the well-known story of the sorcerer's apprentice overwhelmed by his work.

The third cartoon shows clearly how the enigma posed by Jinnah can be solved: two mothers want the same baby, India. In this reading, Jinnah wanted India, not Pakistan. Although this view has been expressed by some political analysts, it has not ousted the entrenched belief that Jinnah's fundamental dream was an independent Pakistan.

This cartoon explains why, when Jinnah was offered Pakistan by Mountbatten, he demurred and showed reluctance to accept. Years later, the Viceroy recalled this crucial interview with Jinnah on the eve of his announcement of partition in June 1947:

> I can't allow you [he remembered telling Jinnah] to throw away the solution you worked so hard to get. It's absolutely idiotic to refuse to say yes. The Congress has said yes. The Sikhs have said yes. Tomorrow at the meeting, I shall say I have received assurance from the Congress Party, with a few reservations, that I am sure I can satisfy and they have accepted. The Sikhs have accepted. And I had a very long, very friendly conversation with Mr. Jinnah last night, we went through every point and Mr. Jinnah feels this is an absolutely acceptable solution. Now, at this moment, I will turn to you and you will nod your head in agreement, and if you shake your head (to indicate disagreement) you will have lost the thing for good, and as far as I am concerned, you can go to hell.
>
> I didn't know [after Jinnah left him] whether he was going to shake his head or nod his head the next morning. [So the next day, announcing partition,] I said, 'Finally, Mr. Jinnah has given me his personal assurance that he is in agreement with this plan,' and turned to him and he went like that. (Mountbatten nodded his head imperceptibly.)
>
> Now I can tell you that if he had shaken his head, the whole thing would have been in the bumble pot. To think that I had to say yes for this clot to get his own plan through, it shows you what one was up against. This was probably the most hair-raising moment of my entire life. I've never forgotten that moment,

> waiting to see if that clot was going to nod or shake his head. He had no expression on his face. He couldn't have made a smaller gesture and still accepted.
>
> The funny part is that the others, I knew, guessed that Jinnah was being difficult. And I think they realized the only hope for them to get a transfer of power quickly was to agree, and I think they allowed me to get away with it. They could have absolutely had me by questioning Jinnah, but they didn't. They knew pretty well what was going on.
>
> You can't make too much of that, that dramatic moment when this great clot was about to throw everything away and I don't even know why. I can't imagine. He was the Muslim League and what he said, they did. He knew he'd got the last dreg....
>
> But isn't it fascinating that the whole thing should have depended on which way he was going to shake his head.[12]

The Solomon cartoon gives one plausible answer for Jinnah's attitude: Jinnah was after power in a unified India, and was playing war games to get it. Pakistan was a 'bargaining counter' – to quote Ayesha Jalal.[13] It left Mountbatten puzzled: 'I don't even know why, I can't imagine,' commented the Viceroy. Solomon, in his wisdom, knew. The Viceroy did not.

The Concept of Indianity

We shall now approach Gandhi's nationalism from a different angle – that of indianity. At times, this word has been used to refer to the identity of the Indian diaspora. This book, however, introduces the concept of indianity within the political context of India: it specifies the kind of nationalism expressed in Gandhi's thoughts and actions.

'Indianity' has yet to find a place in current dictionaries. Gandhi never mentioned nor thought of it, and neither did his interviewers, commentators, and biographers. Yet the concept has analytical strength. We know that the suffix *-ity* expresses 'quality or condition . . . or degree of this.'[14] Quality, indeed, is inherent in the concept 'indianity.' Like Christianity, for instance, it is comprehensive as well as many sided. There are numerous examples of the usefulness and of the importance of such conceptual frames as creativity, sensibility, originality – and of the impact and drive of slogans like 'Liberty, Equality, Fraternity' (from the latin *liber, aequus, fraternus*) at the birth of modern nationalism and up to this day. Indianity, therefore, refers to the awareness and consciousness of the identity of the Indian nation.

Indianity opens a world of its own. To outsiders, indianity is rather like an Aladdin's cave. Once discovered and entered, by chance or design, the cave offers stupendous riches and contrasts. In September 1888, young Gandhi resolutely stepped out of the cave, by sheer tenacity, and left for Victorian England: 'The difficulties I had to withstand [to go to England] have made England dearer to me than she would have been.'[15]

Globalisation has blurred the significance and consequences of this voyage. Gandhi lost his caste when he crossed the seas for England. That was a harsh penalty. But the knowledge of the two worlds, the Victorian and the European, proved of great significance for his career, when India became the focus of his work. He must have had a premonition of this when he left his schoolmates at the Alfred High School in Rajkot in order to study at the bar in London. He said a few words in answer to their good wishes. And what did he mutter (at the time, he was very shy and reluctant to speak in public) in his first recorded speech (4 July 1888)? 'I hope that some of you will follow in my footsteps, and after you return from England you will work wholeheartedly for big reforms in India.'[16]

Thus, his first recorded speech speaks out in favour of reforming his Indian world. In the same vein, Gandhi's first real job, in a Muslim South African firm, offered him the opportunity to develop further his devotion to the concept. Indianity had to be preserved at all costs if Indians were to survive in the racial atmosphere of South Africa. *Coolies* (Asians) had to be kept separate from *kaffirs* (Africans) in Gandhi's political endeavours so that Indians could distance themselves from the downtrodden black natives and hold fast to the glory of their ancient civilisation. Thus, indianity justified then, in Gandhi's eyes, the claim for the higher social status of the white population.[17] Single-handedly, the 'coolie-barrister,' as he was then known, focused on fusing the strength of the divided Indian community: the Muslim merchants, the Hindu traders, the Christian clerks, the indentured and outcastes. Not only did they have in common their indianity, but indianity was also immediately recognisable in their African environment.

Later on, back in India, Gandhi pursued the same purpose of unification that had worked so well in Natal and the Transvaal. He built up a new India. Indianity offers a convenient word for the kaleidoscopic mix of peoples, languages, religions, and customs. His nationalism created a melting pot for a new nation. Although he shifted his attitudes and his recipes for non-violent action, his goals were always centred on the nation India. The successful Salt Campaign of 1930 illustrates his consistency of purpose. In February 1891, forty years before the defiant old man marched to the sea to pick up a handful of salt, he had written in an article for *The Vegetarian* while studying in London: 'They [the poor Indians] live on bread and salt, a heavily taxed article... even in a poverty-stricken country like India.'[18]

Gandhi's nationalism makes no sense severed from India. Indeed, he was mesmerised by India as a nation – a common nationalist feature. But his method was unique. He gained international repute by the way he cared for his country and his countrymen. International affairs were left to others to handle. From the 1930s, Nehru was solely in charge of his party's foreign policy. The Mahatma's world related fundamentally to Indians, and his constructive work consisted of making India a nation. Gandhi loved India, British-made. Gandhi loved Britain that had made India.

The concept of indianity can be used to describe the matrix of British India under direct rule, and of a sizeable Princely India, which was autonomous in internal matters. Indianity equally applies to the India of previous conquerors, with its shifting shapes and frontiers. And although Gandhi admired the indianity of old and was bent of clearing from it the taint of untouchability, among other undesirable elements, he politically adhered to India as shaped by British hands.

Political consciousness in India was still nebulous before the First World War, resting in the hands of middle-class lawyers and businessmen. In the hands of Gandhi, indianity served as the constructive base on which to build a nation.

The historian Judith Brown reported that at the time Gandhi launched his first liberation movement, and while he was serving a prison sentence in India (1922–24), 'he reflected, too, on the identity of the Indian nation.' Moreover, in her concluding chapter, on the Non-cooperation movement of the 1920s, she drew attention to the developing consciousness of Indian politics: 'India was not yet a nation in actuality, but in the process of self-definition and self-creation. Nowhere was this clearer than in the matter of communal relations. Gandhi had deliberately attached himself to the Khilafat movement [in the defence of the Ottoman Caliphate]... But the campaign [of Non-cooperation] deepened Indian awareness of community.'[19] The consciousness of nationalism in India and the consciousness of nationalism in Gandhi were, indeed, intertwined. They grew together in an interdependent and indispensable relationship.

Gandhianity and Its Global Relevance

Let us now push the analysis a significant step further and look at indianity in the context of the work of Mahatma Gandhi. In the vast folder that covers the concept of indianity, let us insert a sub-file relevant exclusively to the Mahatma and give it the name 'gandhianity.'

As an analytical device, the concept of 'gandhianity' has two meanings, much like the key concept of *satyagraha* – or 'adherence to truth' – a composite of two Indian words woven together by Gandhi. In the first sense of the word, *satyagraha* means non-violence as a way of life. In the second sense, *satyagraha* refers to the weapon of non-violence and non-violent campaigns. Gandhianity, likewise, relates firstly to an inner conviction expressed in the way of life as pursued by the Mahatma and his disciples, and secondly, to Gandhi's political work and nationalism. Lifelong dedication to an ideal prevails in the first sense, opportunism and tactics inform the second. And as is the case with *satyagraha*, the second meaning of gandhianity is used more often than the first. But in both cases, non-violence sits at its heart and is necessarily associated with both meanings. Non-violence is the core of gandhianity as both a way of life and a political method.

Consequently, in the first sense, gandhianity offers a doctrinal and comprehensive way to look at the world and to live one's life. Seen from that wholesome and exacting angle – from that challenging utopia with its core of non-violence – gandhianity hangs on the beliefs of Mahatma Gandhi. His world – indeed his two worlds, the Victorian and the Indian – can simply be described as one, as Gandhian. Therefore, in this first sense of the word, gandhianity is akin to a derivative of the adjective *Gandhian*, joining *Gandhi* and *-ity*. It suggests, therefore, the quality attached to the Gandhian way of life as promoted and lived by the Mahatma. As he said: 'My life is my message.' It is well to remember that widespread use of the adjective 'Gandhian' postdates the death of the Mahatma, and the word is not found in the early biographies of the great man, or analyses of non-violence. It is difficult to date its belated appearance,[20] which was probably due to Gandhi strongly objecting in his lifetime to any 'Gandhism.'[21]

> We say that we are devoted to non-violence. If so, we must reveal in our lives the force of non-violence. Unless we can reveal its force in our lives, we will not be true Gandhiites. In fact, there is no such thing as Gandhism. If anything, it is non-violence that deserves to be called an ideology.[22]

In the second sense of the word, from a political angle, gandhianity takes a different meaning. Instead of suggesting a Gandhian quality to a way of life as in the first sense, it joins, politically and philologically, Gandhi and indianity, the man of action with the field of his nationalism, by contracting the two substantives into one word. Like *satyagraha*, it is a composite of two words. Gandhianity depicts the reciprocal, interlocking, and creative influence of Mahatma Gandhi on his nation, and of the nation on the Mahatma. It includes the Mahatma's ideas and experiences in fields such as politics, economics, and social work – realms bearing Indian names difficult to translate, like *swadeshi* (self-sufficiency) or *sarvodaya* (welfare of all). India is the

Mahatma's domain of action and the love of his days, with the heartfelt belief that his imprint on non-violence will benefit the whole world by osmosis. Thus, gandhianity creates the proper environment for studying Gandhi and nationalism, in spite of the fact that Gandhi was not a theorist[23] but a man of action.

Indeed, gandhianity can be best compared to a basket from which one can pick and choose any desired Gandhian item, and wilfully neglect the others. The basket is a convenient, practical and useful container to gather the Gandhian crop. The item most in demand concerns the strategies of non-violence. Most items bear Indian names with special connotations, starting with *swaraj* (independence). Some, like Gandhi's attachment to *dharma* (duty) and the four *varna* (*Brahmins* being the first), or the protection of the sacred cow, have no attraction to non-Hindus. Education is another specificity of gandhianity. Cleanliness is more of an Indian issue. As for *brahmacharia* (chastity), it has little personal appeal, but a great fascination as far as Gandhi is concerned. *Charkha* (spinning wheel) is a symbol that inspired the Indian flag, and *nai talim* refers to basic education re-visited. *Sarvodaya* (the welfare of the poor and downtrodden) is with *ahimsa* (love for one's neighbour) attracting the good will of many. These are examples of items gathered in the basket, for selection by the humble or the great.

Although gandhianity as a way of life is specifically Indian in the making, it is adaptable to other places. It is an exportable commodity, and like young Gandhi, it crossed the waters to unfamiliar European surroundings. Let us take the example of Lanza del Vasto (1901–81). He founded a rural community in France at the end of the Second World War, ten years after discussing the idea with the Mahatma in 1937–38. Members of the Community of the Ark have been living the Gandhian way of life to this day. [24] The son of Mahadev Desai, the trusted secretary and confident of the Mahatma, visited the main community two decades ago and testified to the Gandhian authenticity of this 'best' of Gandhian *ashrams*.[25]

Lanza del Vasto had discussed with Gandhi the idea of establishing a foundation in Europe. However, he had to wait for the end of the war to give it a try. His enterprise was Gandhian in several aspects. He spoke eloquently of a doctrine that would tie together Gandhi's teachings. He published many books, including a best seller, *Return to the Source* (1973) about his stay in India. He adopted practices favoured by Gandhi: sitting on the floor, meditation, hand carding, hand spinning and hand weaving, no electricity or machinery, a vegetarian diet, manual labour, handicrafts like pottery and carpentry, recitation of morning and evening prayers from other religious faiths, and also a profound appreciation of artistic beauty in the environment, reflecting inner spirituality. Moreover, non-violence was present in his political choices and tactics. Thus the Community of the Ark was at the forefront of meaningful experiments in civil disobedience undertaken with other non-violent associations. Interestingly, these exercises of *satyagraha* were not concerned with nationalism, but with the defence of rights: protests against torture in Algeria (1957), against nuclear armament (1958), against the internment of suspects in camps (1960), against the eviction of farmers in the Larzac plateau (1972–81), against nuclear reactors (1976), and, after the founder's death, resistance to the introduction of genetically modified seeds.

Many great men, indeed, have been attracted by some of the contents in the basket and made their fame from the Gandhian connection. Martin Luther King, Nelson Mandela, the better known of a long list of names, put their hands in that basket. They selected the items they liked or found useful for their work. Likewise, many scholars and admirers have concentrated on some aspects of gandhianity. Books keep coming out to satisfy the thirst for the Mahatma, his experiments and pronouncements in so many fields of life.

And what is true of great men is true of great movements. To this day we wonder at the great impact – in ways it was impossible to forecast – of non-violence across the Arab world, tainted by violence. Was India's independence not so? Given time, these movements will be analysed and their non-violent relevance dissected. This exercise has already been performed in regard of the undoing of the vast Soviet Empire. In France, Jacques Sémelin, at the turn of this century, studied the fall of the iron curtain and its Gandhian inspiration.[26] In England, Adam Roberts and Timothy Garton Ash recently edited *Civil Resistance and Power Politics, The Experience of Non-violent Action from Gandhi to the Present*,[27] a book devoted to the study of leading cases of non-violent action throughout the world – demonstrating the global relevance of gandhianity. For his part, David Hardiman undertook a survey of *Gandhi's Global Legacy* outside India, beginning with the American lawyer Richard Gregg (1885–1974) and ending with Petra Kelly (1947–92) of the German Green Party. In the authoritative volume of *The Cambridge Companion to Gandhi*,[28] his essay elicited the following conclusion from the editors Judith Brown and Anthony Parel, regarding Gandhi's legacy:

> In his lifetime, he was most significant in India itself, but perhaps ironically after his death, his insistence on spiritual values and his practice of nonviolence has made his influence even more of a global phenomenon than an Indian one.[29]

Truly, gandhianity fits Gandhian ideology and style like a glove. It denotes a substance, an ethos, and a set of beliefs that can be put into action, timelessly and internationally.

***

This book, also, grasps the concept of *swaraj* from the Gandhian basket and unfurls the path to independence. Steeped in indianity, one after another, the three Gandhis sketched in the three cartoons change the political scene of India in idiosyncratic, Gandhian ways (Part I). Those ways are laid down as stepping stones to the goal of Indian independence (Parts II–IV).

Herein, Gandhi is seen fighting, year in and year out, the kind of nationalism that takes the form of violence, intolerance and sectarianism. While the Mahatma keeps firmly to the side of non-violence and tolerance, Jinnah assumes, progressively and unwillingly, the role of leader of a darker shade of nationalism to get his share of power. This book is a new assessment of the roles played by these two statesmen, strikingly similar in their upbringing and political ends, but driven apart by political means and clever manoeuvres. Domineering the nationalist saga of the partition of India, Muhammad Jinnah and Mohandas Gandhi act out their roles in a dramatic scene reminiscent of the Judgment of Solomon's painting by Nicolas Poussin.

PART I

NATIONALISM AND INDIANITY

Figure 5: Indianity (stamp based on a cartoon by Ranga)

1

SWARAJ, THE OBJECTIVE

Mahatma Gandhi saw his life as a succession of 'experiments with truth' – the title of his autobiography. This is equally true of the expression of his nationalism: it was a succession of experiments with independence. It ran through his series of endeavours to build a new India with his novel 'weapon' of non-violence. They could just as well be called experiments in indianity, with *swaraj* at the heart of it all.

Swaraj was this political objective and his preferred word for independence. However, his idea of *swaraj*, even in the strictest political sense, had an uncertain, evolving connotation, and may have meant different things at different times. For this reason, three main phases have to be considered at length. In the first, loyalist period (1893–1920), the independence asked for was perfectly compatible with the colonialism of the British Empire. This was not so in the rebellion phase, which followed: the campaigns for the liberation of the country from British rule (1920, 1930, and 1942) were fought and lost in the name of *swaraj*, and against the British Empire. In the end (1947), the final, negotiated push to independence achieved *swaraj*, but did not sever the British connection. Self-government emerged in a new, refashioned Commonwealth, British nonetheless.

Thus, Gandhian *swaraj* was a well anchored notion, but one which had a rippling effect, moving with tide and current, like algae on the seabed. Not only was the notion of *swaraj* elusive, but for Gandhi, it embraced politics, economics, social reforms, and religious and spiritual achievements. Furthermore, it was not static, but stretchable, malleable, expandable. This is why 'independence' does not render the full flavour of the Hindi word as understood by Gandhi. The great man himself had some unexpected definitions for this key slogan and objective.

This chapter is structured around the comprehensiveness of Gandhi's *swaraj*, around his political tool – the Indian National Congress – and then around the three phases of his political exertions, from allegiance to rebellion and then to Commonwealth membership.

The Comprehensiveness of Gandhi's *Swaraj*

'*Swaraj*' is formed of two Sanskrit words: *swa* (self) and *raj* (rule). Thus, it can be construed either as rule over the self – the spiritual assertion of every person – or as self-rule – participation in the political affairs of the nation as citizens fully conscious of their rights and duties. For Gandhi, it was both.

On one hand, rule over the self gives a person the ability to rein in passions, to enlighten the mind, to strengthen the spirit, and to shake off the encumbrances of materialism. In other words, it is self-control, a basic virtue and a personal reward. *Swaraj*, for Gandhi, was a feeling, an ideology, and a will. It was a state of mind to be experienced, desired, and conquered. Thus, independence, for Gandhi, was first and foremost self-reliance. It did not necessarily entail anti-British sentiment. On the other hand, self-rule was the capacity to control the environment and one's relationship with others. It was the freedom of Home Rule as against foreign rule. The emphasis was social and political. Social work was not to be divorced from politics. Self-reliance was also expressed by a craving for self-sufficiency in economic matters as well as by a demand for political autonomy.

Every person was to be involved in this egalitarian and democratic society. On the social side, Gandhian independence involved care for all and the extension of benefits to the last in the land. Hence, three Hindi words are associated with Gandhi's work: *swaraj* (political *raj*), *swadeshi* (economic sufficiency), and *sarvodaya* (social uplift). The core of Gandhian teachings is inspired by the well-known injunction:

> I will give you a talisman. Whenever you are in doubt, or when the self becomes too much with you, apply the following test. Recall the face of the poorest and the weakest man whom you may have seen, and ask yourself if the step you contemplate is going to be of any use to him. Will he gain anything by it? Will it restore him to a control over his own life and destiny? In other words, will it lead to *swaraj* for the hungry and spiritually starving millions?
>
> Then you will find your doubts and yourself melting away.[1]

Bound together, *swaraj*, *swadeshi*, and *sarvodaya* operate through non-violence – the core belief given the name 'satyagraha' by Gandhi himself. This word, which means 'clinging to loving force,' is as comprehensive or as restrictive as *swaraj* itself, because it is the means to an end. Thus, all these concepts shelter under the main umbrella of another Gandhian keyword, *Rama-raj*, the Kingdom (*raj*) of God (*Rama*), to be realised on this earth. Independence in its extended sense fits into a cosmic dimension.

This earthly *raj* of heavenly dimension should be perceived as an enlightened state, both anarchic and democratic, and as a vision. It is a utopia out of reach because it describes perfection – in this case, an idealised village, self-governing and self-sufficient. Self-realisation through the attainment of rule over the self explains the anarchic component, and democratisation through self-rule flowers into a vision of village republics.

Hence 'enlightened anarchy' is the purposeful insight 'in which each person will become his own ruler. He will conduct himself in such a way that his behaviour will not hamper the well-being of his neighbours. . . . In an ideal State there will be no political institution and therefore no political power. That is why Thoreau has said in his classic statement that that government is best which governs the least.'[2]

Next to the anarchic strain, the rural content of *swaraj* was made prominent in an article titled 'Independence,' which Gandhi wrote in his journal *Harijan* (28 July 1946). It is a forceful utopia of village republics:

> Independence must begin at the bottom. Thus, every village will be a republic or panchayat having full powers. It follows, therefore that every village has to be self-sustained and capable of managing its affairs... Thus, ultimately, it is the individual who is the unit...
>
> In this structure composed of innumerable villages, there will be ever-widening, never-ascending circles. Life will not be a pyramid with the apex sustained by the bottom. But it will be an oceanic circle whose centre will be the individual always ready to perish for the village, the latter ready to perish for the circle of villages, till at last the whole becomes one life composed of individuals, never aggressive in their arrogance but ever humble, sharing the majesty of the oceanic circle of which they are integral units.
>
> Therefore the outmost circumference will not wield power to crush the inner circle but will give strength to all within and derive its own strength from it. I may be taunted with the retort that this is all Utopian and, therefore, not worth one single thought. If Euclid's point, though incapable of being drawn by human agency, has an imperishable value, my picture has its own for mankind to live. Let India live for this true picture, though never realisable in its completeness.[3]

Swaraj and the Indian National Congress

Gandhi's political party, the Indian National Congress, did not share these views. Many Congressmen disliked the *swadeshi* flavour of *swaraj* with its emphasis on spinning. Many were ambivalent about non-violence as a political weapon, and were therefore critical not only of the aims, but also of the means selected by the Mahatma for their acceptance. 'He thus formulated a vision of *swaraj*,' comments Judith Brown,

> that was to be markedly at odds with the vision of political independence held by most of his colleagues in the Indian National Congress and in the country at large. For him *swaraj* was not a matter of Indians ejecting the British and stepping into their shoes and seats of power... It was a great enterprise of moral regeneration of a whole people and a transformation of their society, a righting of the wrongs and weaknesses that had made colonial rule possible, and ultimately a transformation of the processes of governance.[4]

Gandhi preferred the word *swaraj* to that of *independence*, 'a word employed for European consumption.'[5]

The clash between these views – amplified by the pull between the left and the right of the party – fed the saga of Indian independence. In confrontations with his party, Gandhi often suffered defeat. But in the contest between pragmatism versus utopia, pragmatism won the day. Gandhi pushed his point as far as he could to prevail, but in the end, he knew when to concede defeat and how to compromise in the interests of Indian nationalism. He always stopped short of dividing his party and did not hesitate to support demands he disapproved of, for the sake of India's unity. He was a very astute politician. Thus the quest for political independence made the Congress and Gandhi interdependent and cooperative in spite of misgivings and discord. The Congress agreed with him on one formula: 'Let us understand what nationalism is. We want freedom for our country.'[6]

Whatever the differences, Gandhi could not do without his party, while nearly up to the last years of the nationalist fight, the Indian National Congress could not do without Gandhi. In the long list of his experiments with *swaraj*, Gandhi used the Congress as a tool – indispensable, however blunt – against British rule.

Gandhi's political *swaraj* has to be appreciated against the steady background of imperial power. Its adaptability has to be measured by taking into account the stiffness of constitutional progress. Because the unwilling British Raj was slow to react favourably to Indian nationalism, granting too little too late, the content of political *swaraj* hardened with the failure of timely agreement.

Pro-British Empire *Swaraj*

In the loyalist period, political independence fitted in with Gandhi's attachment to the British Empire. Not only did he take it for granted, but he also rated it highly. Indeed, India was then 'a country where there was no internal coherence beyond that provided by the state.'[7] India was British-made through commerce and conquest. Administered by a well-trained and capable Indian Civil Service – a training ground for promising British careers – and enjoying the Pax Britannica provided by the Indian Army under British officers, the nation was tied politically together, under direct rule in the case of British India, or by the Empire's paramountcy over the autocratic Princely States.

However, *swaraj* was no stranger to the romance with the British lion, which turned into some kind of love–tease (rather than love–hate) relationship, because while Gandhi loved and admired the British nation, he also fought its representatives with amazing determination when Indian rights were encroached: 'If man will only realize that it is unmanly to obey laws that are unjust, no man's tyranny will enslave him. This is the key to self-rule or home-rule... Real Home Rule is possible only when passive resistance is the guiding force of the people. Any other rule is foreign rule.'[8]

So it was unlawful disobedience to unjust enactments that launched Gandhi on a nationalist path after he settled in South Africa and was provoked by anti-Asiatic legislation. The first skirmish in Natal (1894) regarding disenfranchising the few Indians on the electoral roll was conducted through legal channels of resistance, and failed. The second started in the Transvaal (1906) as a civil disobedience movement in all but name.[9] Thus was born the first non-violent campaign (1906–14).

However, this defiant step, this time unlawful, did not change the favourable lip-service Gandhi paid to the British Empire, which lasted up to 1919. And yet, the strain on his loyalty to the Empire was already showing, not only in his disobedience of anti-Indian laws, but also in a book he wrote in 1909, which gave a grim critical assessment of the forces arrayed against him. The title of the book, *Hind Swaraj,* is a statement on Indian independence.

First published in Gujarati in November 1909, *Hind Swaraj* was translated by Gandhi into English. Interestingly he chose the title *Indian Home Rule*, thus coordinating the longing for independence and the attachment to the British Empire. But he did not, and indeed could not, have forecast that the 'Hind' qualification of *swaraj* in the title of his book was rather unfortunate, since the main Muslim claim in the 1940s pointed to the difference between Pakistan and *Hindu*-stan.

In the book, Gandhi refers to Muslims, praising the capacity of India to absorb waves of invaders: 'The introduction of foreigners does not necessarily destroy the nation. A country is one nation only when such a condition obtains in it. That country must have a faculty for assimilation. India has ever been such a country.'[10]

Hind Swaraj, written on a boat journey after unfruitful canvassing in London, reveals a strong anti-Western bias and a longing for the golden age of Indian civilisation. It expresses a strong distaste for the materialism, modernity, and violence of the West, which Gandhi shared with Tolstoy, with whom he corresponded. It describes the ills and evils of Western civilisation, including oppressive technology, in no uncertain terms. *Hind Swaraj* is an indictment of Western civilisation and a rejection of terrorism – not of British rule, even if parliamentary institutions suffer some abuse. It is an extraordinary statement on machinery, on railways, on hospitals, on consumerism, and on the Western way of life. Simple life and non-violence should be – and were, he thought – the Indian way to Home Rule.

Rajmohan Gandhi, his grandson and biographer, explains the book as a 'warrior's manifesto' and concludes: 'We may see *Hind Swaraj* as an assertion of Eastern identity in a world and an age dominated by the West, and Gandhi's assertion of himself before an India that could only petition or throw a bomb here and there.'[11]

Although Gandhi very much softened this approach with time, he never denounced the views of his book as erroneous. He said, however, twelve years later:

> I would warn the reader against thinking that I am today aiming at the swaraj described therein [in *Hind Swaraj*]. I know that India is not ripe for it. It may seem an impertinence to say so. But such is my conviction. I am individually working for the self-rule pictured therein. But today my corporate activity is undoubtedly devoted to the attainment of *parliamentary* swaraj in accordance with the wishes of the people of India.[12] (Emphasis added)

It ought to be stressed that the kind of *swaraj* Gandhi was after had an uncommon feature: he did not so much want a change of rulers as a change of rule (which was not the approach of his party). He aimed at reverting to the kind of age aspired to in *Hind Swaraj*: 'It is my deliberate opinion that India is being ground down, not under the English heel, but under that of modern civilization.'[13]

Indeed, the British connection was used to advantage. Throughout his fight in South Africa, Gandhi looked up to the support of the British Government, which could withhold the Royal Assent necessary to enact colonial legislation. Simultaneously in India, he sought and won the active support not only of the Congress party, but of the incumbent Viceroy, Lord Hardinge – a move that helped resolve his eight-years conflict with General Smuts. The General was sent a parting gift when Gandhi left for India on the eve of the First World War, after the satisfactory Indians Relief Act (1914): a pair of sandals he had made in prison for his foe.

For another ten years after writing *Hind Swaraj*, Gandhi clung to the belief that India's best interests were served by the British connection, and, indeed, that this was the best way to Indian Home Rule – never mind the bickerings with the authorities, never mind the book's harsh criticisms. What counted for him was the means to the end, deploying non-violence to reach *swaraj*. The relation between means and end, between independence and the means to achieve it, was comparable to the connection between the seed and the plant, the fruit and the tree.[14]

But the above statement also had its limits. An incident concerning an early argument with Jinnah is illustrative of the strength of Gandhi's conviction and the intricacy of his thought. As late in the loyalist period as mid-1918, at a time when he was actively organising mass support against the Rowlatt Bills, which prolonged the anti-terrorist powers of the wartime Defence of India Act, Gandhi engaged Jinnah, who was then a leader in the Congress party as well as in the Muslim League, in a controversy on recruitment for the war. Gandhi was for recruiting, Jinnah was against. 'Can't you see that this is the best way to home rule?' was Gandhi's argument. Jinnah had a different sense of priorities. Before recruiting Indians for the war, there had to be 'action and immediate deeds.'[15] To persuade him to join the recruiting drive, Gandhi sent 'Dear Mr. Jinnah,' a letter in which he referred to a quote in the Bible: 'I do wish you would make an emphatic declaration regarding recruitment... "Seek ye first the recruiting office and everything will be added unto you." ... I know you will not mind my letter.'[16]

True to his word, in July and August 1918, Gandhi trod the hot countryside as a recruiting agent for the Raj, ruining his health in the process. But this disagreement between the two Congress leaders had been laid aside by the end of the war. Jinnah seconded Gandhi's resolution at the December session of the Indian National Congress at Amritsar in 1919, which accepted the Reforms Act and its constitutional advances, albeit as an 'inadequate' step and a 'disappointing' reward for India's support in the war. Both men were still treading the same constitutional path towards a similar *swaraj*, upholding the same goodwill for Hindu–Muslim unity, and devotion to the oneness of India.

Anti-Empire *Swaraj*: The First Step

Gandhi's nationalism entered a new phase, when his loyalty snapped under unexpected stress from the enactment of anti-terrorist legislation, while unexpected strength was gained from an unlikely Muslim alliance. In 1920, Gandhi stood on the verge of rebellion against the British Raj. His leadership attracted the audible approval of the Khilafatists, the vocal Indian Muslims pledged to save the Ottoman Caliphate from extinction in the aftermath of the war. Their cause, however, left the Hindus unimpressed and reluctant – in spite of their own grievances about the recent Jallianwalla Bagh massacre and martial law in the Punjab – to join the Gandhian-Muslim scheme of non-cooperation. Strong opposition was at work in the Congress party to prevent the adoption of the proposed campaign of non-violence in India.[17]

Counting the odds, Gandhi decided to present his party with a *fait accompli*, launching his Non-cooperation campaign on 1 August 1920 with his Muslim allies. Then he stormed the special Congress session at Calcutta, convened for September, and won the day against his opponents, including Jinnah – thanks, some say, to the vote of train loads of Khilafatists sent from across the country to support Gandhi.

The support at Calcutta had to be confirmed three months later at the Nagpur regular session before becoming definite. As a precautionary step to forestall a possible negative outcome, Gandhi secured the presidency of the Home Rule League when he was invited to chair a meeting in Bombay on 3 October 1920. There he changed the name of the association to Swaraj Sabha – not 'Home Rule' any more, but an 'Association for Independence' – and, most significantly, pruned its creed of '*swaraj* within the Empire' to a bare '*swaraj*.' Jinnah, who was one of the former presidents and had followed Gandhi from Calcutta to Bombay, dissented publicly with the programme and methods of the new chairman, and consequently resigned from the association in protest. But Gandhi argued with him that the change 'left open the question of India's link with the Empire, which could be retained or broken as needed.'[18]

For Gandhi, this political move was a temporary measure destined at securing a political base for his non-violent strategy in case the Congress refused to endorse his policy of non-cooperation at Nagpur in December. But his charisma won the day in Nagpur, as it had in Calcutta, so much so that he heard himself promise to enthused followers that he would not just demand redress of the 'Khilafat and Punjab wrongs,' but also achieve '*swaraj* in one year.'[19]

Accordingly, the Congress copied the move of the Swaraj Sabha by erasing 'within the Empire' from its aim, *swaraj.* Its constitution did away with the encumbrance of 'constitutional' means. It reorganised the party, opening it to a wider membership, and improving its efficiency with the creation of the All-India Congress Committee and the smaller Working Committee, composed of fifteen executives. Jinnah, hissed and booed for opposing Gandhi, left the Congress. The Viceroy, Lord Chelmsford, responded disparagingly to 'the most foolish of all foolish schemes.'[20]

The Non-cooperation campaign launched at Nagpur was lost before it reached the stage of non-payment of taxes – Gandhi suspended it without consulting his co-workers and Muslim allies after some twenty policemen in Chauri-Chaura were murdered. Then Gandhi was arrested for inciting disaffection towards His Majesty's Government and sentenced to six years imprisonment, though he was freed in 1924 on medical grounds. The rebellion had burned itself out, the mood in the country quietened down. Jinnah watched the collapse of the campaign with some satisfaction.

Purna Swaraj, or the Rejection of Dominion Status: The Second Step

The Government anticipated the next constitutional step set by the Reforms Act of 1919 and nominated a Parliamentary Commission for the purpose of constitutional advancement (1927). Unfortunately, because this Simon Commission was all white, it was boycotted by the Indian political parties. The next political upheaval started in earnest, strikingly like the previous one: by a show of Muslim and Hindu unity as to recriminations and protests.

Jinnah, too, putting his resentment aside, sought Congress cooperation. While Motilal Nehru hammered out the 'Nehru Report,' which was intended to undermine the future Simon Report, Jinnah, who was against the Nehru Report, drew proposals for a rapprochement between Muslims and the Congress, which, had they been accepted, would have re-created a Muslim-Hindu alliance in the 1920s.

But neither Jinnah nor his ailing Muslim League impressed the Congress leaders, who were only too aware of the weakness of the League and of the divisions in Muslim ranks caused by strong provincial affiliations. These Congress leaders, including Gandhi, failed, in December 1928, to seize the opportunity to do away with separate electorates, which Jinnah was ready to concede, and which would be the cause of the future disruptions that led to partition. They refused to grant a third representation (33 per cent) at the centre, which the Muslims asked for, and offered instead a quarter (27 per cent). Jinnah was seen leaving, upset and tearful.

The Nehru Report (August 1928), trying to upstage the Simon Report, asked for Dominion status. But young and radical Congressmen pressed for full independence – *purna swaraj*. At their head was Jawaharlal Nehru, whose father, Motilal Nehru, had authored the report. The young Nehru got a resolution on complete independence passed by the Madras Congress at the end of 1927, in Gandhi's absence. Unimpressed, Gandhi derided the resolution as coming from 'prisoners in chains spitting frothy oaths only to provide mirth to their gaolers.'[21]

However, he was churning up in his mind the concept of *swaraj*. In January 1928 in a statement entitled *Independence v. Swaraj,* he insisted on the special significance of *swaraj:*

> I defy anyone to give to independence a common Indian word intelligible to the masses. Our goal at any rate may be known by the indigenous word understood of the three hundred millions. And we have such a word in 'swaraj' first used [in 1906] in the name of the nation by Dadabhai Naoroji [a founder of the Indian National Congress]. It is infinitely greater than and includes independence. It is a vital word. It has been sanctified by the noble sacrifices of thousands of Indians... It is a sacrilege to displace that word by a foreign importation of doubtless value...
>
> Personally, I crave not for independence, which I do not understand, but I long for freedom from the English yoke. I would pay any price for it. I would accept chaos in exchange for it.[22]

At the next annual Congress session (Calcutta, December 1928), the two Nehrus, father and son, voiced their opposing views on Dominion status. Gandhi, bent on action as well as on words, suggested a compromise:

the British Government had two years to agree to Dominion status for India; if not, a campaign of civil disobedience would fight for the new goal of *purna swaraj*. The young Nehru replied he would not wait two minutes, but he was persuaded to agree to the arrangement when the delay was cut down to one year. Thus, *purna swaraj* became the political aim of the Indian National Congress (the Viceroy having not responded favourably to the request for Dominion status), meaning undiluted independence outside the British Commonwealth. This was a considerable step for the Congress party; but Gandhi remained ambivalent and ready to compromise. One year later, he declared to the Second Round Table Conference in London (1931): 'Time was when I prided myself on being, and being called, a British subject. I have ceased for many years to call myself a British subject; I would far rather be called a rebel than a subject. But I have aspired, I still aspire, to be a citizen, not of the Empire, but in a Commonwealth.'[23]

This he said in 1931 between the first and second round of the Civil Disobedience campaign, which was fought for the sake of complete independence outside the Commonwealth. However, *purna swaraj* remained the objective of the Congress up to the eve of independence in 1947, through peace and war, constitutional reforms, the Quit India campaign of 1942, and the decolonisation policy of the new Labour Government after the war. On 2 September 1946, when the first Interim Congress Government was formed, Gandhi declared that the door to *Purna Swaraj* had at last been opened.

It was now up to the Congress to walk out of the Raj. So why did India join the British Commonwealth?

The last Viceroy, Lord Louis Mountbatten, had taken great care not to press the Congress leaders to join what was then a 'white' Commonwealth; he knew that no would have been the answer. But he was manoeuvring for them to change their mind, waiting for a propitious occasion to herd India into the Commonwealth fold. The minutes of the Viceroy's staff meetings on 9 May 1947 report that: a request by India to remain in the Commonwealth would be of paramount and overriding importance. The Congress, however, was adamant in its resolve to sever all ties with the British Empire. But then why did the Congress ask for India's Commonwealth membership when finally granted independence?

Swaraj in the Commonwealth: The Last Step

The Civil Disobedience campaign (1930–34) had petered out after the initial, worldwide acclaimed success of the Salt March and the Gandhi-Irwin Pact (1931). Gandhi took the decision to retire officially from the Congress (1934), but he remained its *éminence grise*, taking on the role of negotiator and decider for a party to which he did not officially belong. He held that role to the great displeasure of Jinnah, who thought that the Mahatma played on the uncertainty and ambiguity of this position: sometimes Gandhi was representative of his party, sometimes he said he was not.

Up to 1938, Muhammad Ali Jinnah had behaved as an 'Indian first,' a 'Muslim second.' He had steadily worked for Hindu–Muslim unity. He had sought an alliance with the Congress party. But all this was to change after the elections of 1937, which came in the wake of the Government Act of 1935, the upheaval of the Simon Commission, the Round Table Conferences in London, and the Civil Disobedience campaign.

Jinnah, after his own relative electoral success in 1937, asked the Congress for a share of power in some provincial governments, and was told by Nehru that there were 'only two forces in the country, the Congress and the Government,' to which Jinnah replied: 'There is a third party in this country and that is the Muslims.' Nehru just pushed him aside and, moreover, tried to win over the Muslim League electorate by a mass contact campaign.

From then on, a vengeful Jinnah became a foe of the Congress and surreptitiously copied its tactics: mass contacts with the electorate, a nominal membership fee in order to increase numbers, enlistment of an active network of co-workers, a devoted Working Committee, and last but not least, a president – himself – to decide everything, represent every Muslim – in brief, a distorted Muslim replica of the Mahatma. He would be the *Quaid-i-azam* (great leader), acclaimed as such for the first time at the annual meeting of the Muslim League in December 1938. His dress, too, would proclaim his new creed, like the loincloth of the Mahatma. He now often wore a Punjabi sherwani long coat and a Persian lamb cap – seen in public for the first time on 15 October 1937 – and the traditional Punjabi pyjamas. There would be a 'Jinnah cap' to rival the 'Gandhi cap.' Just as Gandhi claimed to represent the whole nation from the centre of Indian politics, Jinnah would likewise speak for his people at the centre of the old Muslim empire and, step by step, gain painstakingly the support of Muslim provinces: Baluchistan, Sindh, the North-West Frontier Province and the two provinces of Punjab and Bengal, where the Muslims formed just more than half the population.[24] He spoke for them all, albeit in English, for he was not versed in Urdu. But this was no hindrance. His enthused audience approved anyway, and the world then could hear what he had to say. And he could speak, uninterrupted, for two hours at a stretch, in a language that most of his listeners did not comprehend.

What creed did he preach? Reluctantly, it had to be the cry of 'Islam in danger.' Given the parochial interests of the various provinces, the Hindu scare alone could submerge all the scattered controversies of the Muslim fold. Within two years, the Muslim League was transformed into a large political party, submissive to its president, on a par with Gandhi's party and hoping to snatch from it, with the nation of Pakistan, the glory of undivided India.

To make credible the threatened encroachment of Pakistan on India's territory, Jinnah used a trump card in the defence of his Muslim nation. He was going to force his way into the Commonwealth. He told Sir Stafford Cripps in 1947 that there was no precedent for forcing parts of the Empire to leave against their will.

On 26 April 1947, Jinnah and the Viceroy, Lord Mountbatten, had this verbal exchange, after the former mentioned

> that Pakistan would wish to remain within the Commonwealth. I [Mountbatten] corrected him and said, 'No, you told me that, if the Pakistan Government was formed, its first act might well be to ask to be admitted to membership of the British Commonwealth.' He corrected me and said I completely misunderstood the position. He said that Mr. Churchill had told him, 'You have only to stand firm and demand your rights not to be expelled from the British Commonwealth, and you are bound to be accepted. The country would never stand for the expulsion of loyal members of the Empire.'

Strangely enough, the territorial definition of Pakistan's jurisdiction remained elusive to the end – like the definition of *swaraj*. Independence was feted on 15 August 1947 in two countries undivided by a line of demarcation, since it was kept a close-guarded secret until that day was over. Just as the flexibility of Gandhi's conception of *swaraj* had contributed to the success of his movement, the elusiveness of Pakistan had attracted general Muslim acclaim. The deliberate vagueness of Muslim territorial claims had contributed enormously to the attractiveness of partition, since it drew the support of a variety of Muslims for distinctive, contradictory, or erroneous reasons. (Not the least among the enthusiasts were Muslims from the old part of the Mughal Empire, who were cut off from the western part of Pakistan and marooned in what became the Union of India.)

Right up to the end, in early June 1947, the Congress leaders, Nehru and Patel, asked unsuccessfully for a viceregal assurance that if India left the Commonwealth, Pakistan would have to leave it too. But delaying tactics at this point would have meant either the postponement of independence or the promotion of the sole Pakistan as a new Dominion. The leaders chose the lesser evil: they, too, asked for Dominion status.

In the end, Nehru's belated acceptance of Commonwealth membership served his country well, since the Viceroy helped tremendously in the integration of the Princely rulers into the two Dominions. Independence was to be *swaraj* within the Commonwealth: not as an interim arrangement (as it was sold to the left wing of the Congress), but as a definite move towards the greater enhancement of that British institution.

Nehru had built a strong friendship with the Mountbattens. On the night of 14 August 1947, he became Prime Minister and the Viceroy Governor General of the Union of India. The new Prime Minister handed Lord Mountbatten the list of his Government. When the Governor General opened the envelope, he found a blank sheet of paper. Some commentators think it was an oversight in the rush of the day. Some suspect spiteful intent. It was more likely to have been some kind of joke, a relevant bit of humour.

2

THE VOICE OF INDIA

Our analysis of Gandhi's nationalism will now focus on the recipients of his solicitude. Who were those he was prepared to sponsor? His nationalism governed his political choices of resistance. He championed his fellow Indians in an exclusive, passionate way. The soul of India lay, he thought, in every Indian, whether in his home country or abroad. The nobility of the Indian soul, he said to his countrymen in South Africa, 'consists in realising that you are yourself India. In your emancipation is the emancipation of India. All else is make-believe.' Gandhian nationalism was truly embodied in a growing awareness of indianity.

The Geographical-cum-Political Frame of India

In the search for a common link between these emancipated souls, noble and otherwise, we ponder on the contingency of national status. For, to quote Ernest Gellner: 'In fact, nations, like states, are a contingency, and not a universal necessity.'[1] What sort of a contingency was Gandhi's India? And the answer is: it was politically British-made India.

India was cast in a mould shaped by the East India Company and British armed forces in the eighteenth and nineteenth centuries. The 'jewel' of the British Empire was encased in a well-defined geographic frame, which gave its inhabitants the label of 'Indians,' and its ruler the title of 'King-Emperor.' Burma and Ceylon, appendages to that south

Asian continent, and also ruled by Great Britain, fell into another category and were excluded from the Indian map. This sub-continent included numerous autonomous Indian States – Princely India – as well as British-administered India.

This unity of India was very precious to Gandhi. It excluded for him any possibility of balkanisation. No Pakistan was allowable, no defaulting Indian princedom, no Kashmir truncated, no independent Bengal – in short, no 'vivisection,' in Gandhian terminology.[2] Only the North-West Frontier Province could have been given the green light to form its own state, because it could have been a friendly Muslim 'Pashthunistan.' There, the 'Frontier Gandhi,' Abdul Ghaffar Khan, and his brother Dr. Khan Sahib, politically in charge, stood guard as indefatigable allies of the Indian National Congress – in a region that was ferociously non-violent, independent, and 99 per cent Muslim.[3]

The geographical-cum-political boundaries of India had been set by the British for all generations to come, in spite of the persistent incursion threats on its unruly Afghan borders. The British conquerors had resurrected the forgotten boundaries of a golden age of old, and thus fed the dream of a lost paradise that predated centuries of division and strife: a political unity that the Muslim conquest had not managed to complete. That India was Gandhi's India, an indivisible political unit, a receptacle of his culture and mores, the visible shell of indianity.

The Diaspora in South Africa

The first beneficiaries of Gandhi's political life, however, were not Indians from the sub-continent, but South African Indians from the diaspora.

For India's sons and daughters were soon in great demand in British possessions overseas as an alternative to slave labour in mines and sugar-fields. The indenture system – a nineteenth-century form of serfdom on a three-year contract basis – fed on Indian labour and emigration. Thus, India's arms extended overseas. The case of the Crown Colony of Natal is of special interest because Indian traders had followed the indentured, and Gandhi happened to be hired on a court case by a Muslim firm for one year (1893).

As the sole Indian barrister – however inexperienced at first – available at that time to this illiterate community, he took charge of the defence of Indian interests in the Crown Colony of Natal and, after the Boer War, in the defunct Republic of the Transvaal. Thus the notion of nationalism rested solidly for him on the legal concepts of *jus sanguinis* – parentage – as well as on *jus soli* – birthright citizenship for those born and reared on Indian soil. Himself an Indian by blood, and a settled South African by his place of legal work, he made sure from the start of his political life on the African continent that the Indian nation in British India would not forsake the diaspora Indians, nor forget their plight, and that India should procure help and assistance for her children in need.

And how did he propose to do that? He had three strings to his bow: London was the first seat of power, Delhi the second, and the third was the main political party in India, his party of choice, the Indian National Congress. And he would be the voice of the Indians in South Africa.

This devotion to his fellow nationals was the positive side of Gandhi's nationalist coin in South Africa. There was also a negative side, which eschewed interference in the political concern of other communities in the land. Hence, interestingly, Gandhi disconnected his fight against racism in South Africa from non-Indian grievances. For example, he kept his distance from another Asian community also affected by the same colour prejudice and legislation, the Chinese diaspora – and apparently rightly so, because the Chinese resistance soon collapsed, when its leader absconded with funds.

With a sense of realpolitik that never left him, Gandhi abstained also from interfering on behalf of the local African population, again for political reasons. As he once explained, 'I had the privilege of often advising them ... But it was not possible to amalgamate the two causes. The rights and privileges – if any could be so called – of the indigenous inhabitants, are different from those of the Indians. So are their disabilities and their causes.'[4]

Whatever he thought these disabilities were, he seemed to feel and claim – at least in the first years of his South African stay – a sense of superiority as an Indian, worthy therefore, of a better status than the *kaffir* (native). In a petition in 1899 he said that Indians 'were infinitely superior to the Kaffirs.'[5]

Entry into Politics: The Fight for the Indian Franchise, 1894

How did these political constraints start to operate? And why was Gandhi drawn into politics? Was this due to providence, circumstances, or temperament? All three factors contributed to the making of the politician, as we shall now see.

In 1894, the legal case in South Africa for which Gandhi had been hired as a legal counsel by a Muslim firm the previous year had been satisfactorily concluded, and the departing barrister was celebrating his return to India with colleagues and friends, mostly Muslims. At that farewell party, he happened to glance at a newspaper, where the caption 'Indian Franchise' drew his attention. No Indian present, including him, knew anything about the bill to disfranchise Indians in Natal, as was reported in the paper. At the request of the guests, he accepted delaying his departure for a month, and as he recalled in his autobiography, 'The farewell party thus turned into a working committee.'[6]

The current Indian franchise accorded with the general franchise law of the Crown Colony. Adult males were placed on the voters' roll, if they owned £50 of immoveable property or paid an annual rental of £10. (The Natives, who numbered 400,000 in 1896, had a special franchise law.) In 1894, very few Indians reached that required financial standard. While 9,309 out of 51,000 European voters were qualified to vote in Natal, only 251 out of 50,000 Indians could do so – hardly a threat to the European community. If some Indian traders bothered to register for the electoral roll, it was not out of interest in politics, but as a move in the interest of promoting their trading. Before Gandhi's arrival, they had had to rely solely on European legal advice, and one of their counsels was Natal's Attorney General, who then needed their votes to get re-elected.

But the proposed Disenfranchisement Bill, which forbade the enrollment of more Asians, was due for a second reading at the Natal Legislative Assembly. Within two days, Gandhi managed to send a petition to the Assembly, asking for the postponement of the vote – which was granted. In two weeks, Gandhi obtained ten thousand signatures to his petition to the Secretary of State for the Colonies, and copies were sent to the press not only in Natal, but in India (where it raised interest) and in England.

Lessons and Benefits from the Franchise Experiment

The effort ended in failure. The bill became law. The failure was apparent, but the gain nonetheless real, and the impact on Gandhi's nationalism was decisive. Suddenly, he had been promoted to be the voice of Natal Indians. He had defended a basic democratic right. He had had his first taste of politics, had discovered his gift for political work and for leadership as well as the benefits of stirring the passivity of the Indian community. The beneficiaries of his first inroad in politics had been an elite group (markedly Muslim), but he had also relied successfully on Natal-born Christians from formerly indentured parents – the literates of the community, educated in missionary schools. He was now keen to extend his political base to the poorest of the community and to bill himself as the champion of the Indian cause. He shouldered the responsibility in the knowledge that he was 'the only available person who can handle the question.'[7]

Hence, he decided to settle in Natal, next door to the Attorney General, and to bring the family that he had left behind in India, to live 'in a style usual for barristers.'[8] The month that was to be devoted to the cause of Indian rights in South Africa lasted twenty years.

Gandhi had also gained a political point against racial discrimination:

> Fortunately the fight for the franchise had resulted in a decision to the effect that no enactment might be passed against the Indians as such, that is to say, that the law should make no distinctions of colour or race. The language of the [later] bills . . . made them applicable to all, but their object undoubtedly was to impose further restrictions on the residents of Natal . . . We appealed to the Colonial Secretary, but he refused to interfere and the bills became law.[9]

Gandhi's dedication to British constitutional practices had been clear from the start. Referring to the main argument of the petition he then presented to the Legislative Assembly of Natal (June 1894), he added persuasiveness to win his point: 'My argument centred round a principle and an expedience. I argued that we had a right to the franchise in Natal as we had a kind of franchise in India. I urged that it was expedient to retain it, as the Indian population capable of using the franchise was very small.'[10]

In his first political fight, he had followed normal legal procedures of redress. He did not bend the rules of political engagement. Rather, he tested cleverly the strength of home support in affiliating his Natal Indians with a ten-year-old, but significant, political party in his home-country. On 22 May 1894, the Natal Indian Congress was founded as a branch of the Indian National Congress.

The INC had been created at the end of the nineteenth century under British auspices with a British Committee set up in London, and in India, under the secretary-ship of Allan Octavian Hume. It responded to events in Natal with the desire to help 'His Majesty's Indian subjects, resident in the South African Colonies.' In Madras, 1,163 delegates passed a resolution on the 'Indians in South Africa,' demanding the vetoing of 'the Bill of the Colonial Government disfranchising them.' Practically every subsequent Congress session would protest against the disabilities of the 'Indian Settlers in South Africa.'[11]

This sounds like a very impressive achievement. Resolutions, however, before the First World War, were moved and passed by a show of hands, those of delegates as well as those of visitors who happened to move among them. Unanimity was not uncommon, and the sponsorship of a well-known political figure – such as Gopal Krishna Gokhale, who handled Gandhi's case – helped the spontaneous consensus. In Gandhi's own words (1901):

> In those days there was hardly any difference between visitors and delegates. Everyone raised his hand and all resolutions passed unanimously. My resolution also fared in this wise and so lost all its importance for me. And yet the very fact that it was

> passed by the Congress was enough to delight my heart. The knowledge that the imprimatur of the Congress meant that of the whole country was enough to delight anyone.[12]

Gandhi's voice, in his very first political experiment, had been raised and heard across the sea in the heart of the main political party of his homeland. His stature as the leader of Indians in South Africa continued to grow. In India, he was acclaimed as the hero and representative of the whole South African Indian community.

The First Campaign of Non-Violence in South Africa, 1906–14

The fight against disfranchisement had been an impromptu exercise in canvassing political support, but not in *satyagraha* – a political weapon yet to be discovered. The beneficiaries had been his fellow nationals from the Crown Colony of Natal. The next step in Gandhi's nationalism – the reliance on the new political weapon of non-violence – came in the aftermath of the Boer War (1899–1901), which put an end to the Boer Republics of the Transvaal and the Orange Free State.[13]

Two notable characteristics mark this period. First, the recipients of his political work would include the Transvaal Indians from Johannesburg, where he now settled in answer to their call for help.[14] The later inclusion of the Transvaal, the Orange Free State, Natal, and the Cape into the Union of South Africa (June 1910) earned Gandhi the distinction to speak for all Indians in South Africa. His work also had the exceptional merit of embracing all social categories of Indians and uniting into a single fight the fissiparous tendencies in the Indian social fabric, with its castes and religions, regional contingencies, and categories of employment and social status.

Second, rather than accept the stalemate of his previous political fights in Natal, Gandhi openly defied the Transvaal government by breaking laws he objected to, but non-violently. He forged his new weapon of non-violence in fights against the compulsory registration of Indians in the Transvaal, against immigration policy, against the levy of the £3 tax, and against the non-endorsement of Indian marriages.

His fight ended satisfactorily with the Indians Relief Act (Act 22 of 1914). His main adversary, General Smuts, then Interior Minister, seeing Gandhi sail away from South Africa, commented: 'The saint has left our shores, I sincerely hope for ever.'[15]

His wish was granted.

Because Gandhi managed to use the context of South Africa to assemble his people behind him, he gained the feeling and the belief that he could do the same for Indians in India – nay, that it was his vocation to do so. He now knew that he could win with non-violence. He now believed that he could unite his people in a common fight. His passion for Hindu–Muslim unity had become a tenet of his creed.

When he returned to India at the outbreak of the First World War, he was eager to prove himself right, and ready to reiterate the experiment in non-violence on his home ground. Consciously or unconsciously, he would look forward to represent all the Indians of India, as he had represented all the Indians of the South African diaspora. So confident was he that he ventured boldly into the minefield of international politics.

An Experiment in International Politics

The next campaign, in India this time, gave a new twist to his nationalism. He engaged in a fight for the sake of a religious group of Indians called Khilafatists. Oddly enough, the religious claim concerned not India, but the Middle East and the Ottoman Empire. The Indian Muslim desire to save the Caliphate from infidels allowed him to embrace his Muslim brethren, even if they were led by firebrands like the brothers Mohamed and Shaukat Ali. In Gandhi's eagerness to back their cause, he asked them to eschew violence in action, even if not in words: 'So long as our people did not go beyond words I paid no attention to what they said. I remained indifferent to violence in speech. Later it became a habit and I even stopped taking notice of it.'[16]

Gandhi dismissed as irrelevant the fact that the Ali brothers' cause concerned India's nationals, but not the nation of India. At this stage, he was ready to embrace the cause of Turkey in the Middle East in order to prevent the carving-up mandated by the Treaty of Sèvres. Moreover, he did not attach importance to the fact that only Muslim Indians were really frustrated by the dismemberment of the decadent Ottoman Empire and by the end of the temporal power of the Caliph of Turkey. Gandhi was only too ready to jump on the Alis' bandwagon, and for the sake of Hindu–Muslim unity – so precious an achievement – he would try to save for their sake pre-war conditions. He had to persuade the Hindus to join hands with the Muslims, and he knew how to touch the right chord: 'We, both Hindus and Muslims, have now an opportunity of a lifetime. The Khilafat question will not recur for another hundred years.'[17]

This opportunity, soon offered by Gandhi to the Indian National Congress, forged an alliance that would push India on the road to independence like nothing else. The Non-cooperation campaign, in an extraordinary show of Hindu–Muslim unity, was launched in 1920 to safeguard the jurisdiction of the Turkish Caliph over Jerusalem, with an added sweetener for the Hindus – the redress of the excesses of martial law in Punjab and, for good measure, the call to reject foreign rule in India.

Thus, Gandhi embraced the Muslims' cause not because it was of national concern, but because it concerned India's nationals. He was the one who made this issue a national cause: 'If I were not interested in the Indian Mahomedans, I would not interest myself in the welfare of the Turks any more than in that of the Austrians or the Poles.'[18]

However, the new Turkey, led by Ataturk, did away with the Caliph and the Caliphate, and the Mahatma had little recompense for his work with the Khilafatists. In the end, the Ali brothers turned against him. This taught Gandhi a harsh lesson: do not embark on the unfathomed waters of the international scene; keep to the chartered sea of indianity. Consequently, he would later leave to the well-travelled Jawaharlal Nehru the exclusive handling of foreign affairs.

But he was tempted twice to infringe on his self-imposed rule that the beneficiaries of his social and political work should be his fellow nationals only. Rules, as is well known, suffer exceptions. This rule was infringed twice.

Tentative Intervention in the Middle East, 1937

The rule in question was definitely broken in 1937, when Gandhi was tempted to again play an international role in Muslim politics. He planned a comeback in the same fraught area that he had tackled in 1919 – the road to Jerusalem – and again for the sake of friendship, but of Jewish friendship this time. His interference in the Arab-Jewish conflict took place just before the start of civil war in the region in September 1937.

Unlike the first, this second inroad in the affairs of Palestine remained a well-guarded secret for decades. The handful of people in the know kept silent to their graves, since the attempt to mediate the Arab-Jewish conflict failed to materialise. The opening of archives and the belated discovery of a treasured correspondence between Gandhi and his best South African friend, Hermann Kallenbach, at last shed light on this secret episode in Gandhi's life.[19]

Kallenbach had been Gandhi's right hand in the South African fight against General Smuts. He had planned to return with Gandhi to India and to settle there to help him as his right hand in his work. Accordingly, they boarded the same ship in 1914. Before the ship docked in London, the First World War started. Kallenbach was refused entry in India, and because he was travelling on a German passport, he was arrested and detained on the Isle of Man. He was shipped to Germany in 1917 in an exchange of prisoners. After the war, he did not join Gandhi in India, but went back to South Africa, helping raise funds for his co-religionists. When the Jewish Agency in Jerusalem became aware of his connection with Gandhi, it was decided to enlist his help. As they told him: 'You are in a unique position to help Zionism in a field where the resources of the Jewish people are so meagre as to be practically inexistent.'[20]

Kallenbach was persuaded, and he eventually proceeded first to Jerusalem, then to India. He stayed with Gandhi for an emotional reunion of six weeks. There he preached Zionism to his friend, who was ignorant about it, although he had had many non-orthodox Jews working with him in his South African days.

Before leaving India in July 1937, Kallenbach managed to persuade his friend – for the sake of friendship – to offer, in great secrecy, to mediate the Arab-Jewish conflict on behalf of the Jewish Agency. Gandhi had contacted Jawaharlal Nehru (notably pro-Arab) and Maulana Abul Kalam Azad (the Muslim president of the Indian National Congress) for preliminary consent. He then waited for the green light from the Jewish Agency, but since he received no response before the Palestinian conflict took a violent turn in September 1937, the proposed mediation between Arabs and Jews came to nothing. However, it is fascinating to hear, after so many years, of this Gandhian attempt at solving the (then soluble?) conflict between Arabs and Jews.

Aborted Attempt in Europe, 1938

Undiscouraged by the turn taken by events in the Middle East, and eager to counteract Hitler's 'Gross Deutschland' expansion, Gandhi looked forward to taking him on in Europe. But time did not allow that intervention to materialise.

Gandhi had been considering non-violent action in Czechoslovakia in 1938. Again, he was not thinking of going there in person, but of leading the resistance by proxy. The responsibility would have been shouldered by his 'daughter' Mirabehn, or Madeleine Slade, the daughter of a British Admiral, who had left family, friends and estate in England (and also her passion for Beethoven) in order to be with Gandhi.[21]

On 15 October 1938, Gandhi published an article in *Harijan* entitled 'If I were a Czech,' advising on a non-violent course of action. On 5 November 1938, he wrote to Mirabehn, accepting her offer to go to Czechoslovakia, and sent another letter to his secretary, informing him that 'her going can do no harm at all. While she has to suppress herself with me, in the West she can work independently.'[22] To Mirabehn, he had written: 'Evidently you had the call perhaps at the same hour that I felt you will have it. As far as my recollection goes, I wrote to you also that if you felt the urge I would let you go . . . We will discuss ways and means.'[23]

Circumstances prevented discussions from leading anywhere. Almost simultaneously (20 November 1938), his advice to the Jews in Germany to resist persecution non-violently raised a world outcry. Henceforth, he would advocate non-violence strictly for the benefit of his own people, although he did not refrain from advising others about its efficacy, whether in India or elsewhere.[24] Whether the aborted attempts to intervene in Palestine and in Czechoslovakia – however hushed up – were indications that he was ready to enlarge the circle of recipients of his political work, one will never know. Gandhi might well have been encouraged to do so, had he met with some success. Since he had not, the rule was left unchanged: he kept clear of the Middle Eastern and European killing fields and looked after his own sheep. Instead of setting his views in an international context, to fit his international stature, he adhered firmly to the hope that in his person, he could somehow embody the wholeness and non-violent-ness of the Indian nation.

The Voice of India and the Sore Issue of Representation

The Mahatma wanted to represent all Indians, but not all Indians accepted that claim. He was too democratic for the autocratic princes and their vast estates. He looked too Hindu to the Muslims, too unorthodox to the Brahmins, too anti-class-war to the Communists, too pro-landowner to the Socialists, and even in his party, too leftist to the right, too secular to some, too religious to others... and too non-violent to the politicians.

However, the Mahatma's credentials were unrivalled. Two main political achievements made him unique. He had turned to Muslim collaboration – there were slightly less than one hundred million Muslims in India in 1920. And he had reached out to the three hundred million beyond the grasp of the middle and professional classes, and in response they supported the Congress, which he reorganised as a mass party in 1920. The beneficiaries of the new political drive were that seething mass of illiterate humanity found in the countryside as well as in the sprawling slums, including even the Untouchables.

From then on, Gandhi wanted his party anchored in rural India. He wanted to represent all Indians in his person, and made that claim at the Round Table Conference in London in 1931. The charismatic figure of Gandhi in his shawl and loincloth – sometimes spinning at the meetings – faced many other delegates from the princedoms and the other political parties and pressure groups as the sole representative of the Indian National Congress and the voice of India's 350 million people. He said: 'All the other parties at this meeting represent sectional interests. Congress alone claims to represent the whole of India, all interests... Its message penetrates the remotest village of India... A nation of 350 million people... needs simply a will of its own, an ability to say "No", and that nation is today learning to say "No".'

But the Mahatma could not breach the wall of opposition to his diplomacy. The Princes, the Muslims (Jinnah among them), and the Untouchables (led by Bhimrao Ambedkar, himself an Untouchable) objected to Gandhi or to the Congress speaking for all India, and the Conference ended in discontent.

The Princes clung to despotic rule and past privileges and feared a future Federation with a democratic British India. Their inertia sealed their doom. The Muslims at the Round Table thought Gandhi's pretence preposterous. They were fast drifting away from the Hindu–Muslim alliance of the Non-cooperation days, fearful of perverse Congress ambitions. The Untouchables won their point, relying on the strength of their numbers and their demand for separate electorates. The British Government decided to allow the Untouchables a separate franchise, since the Muslims already had theirs. Gandhi reacted strongly against the British award by starting a fast unto death. Ambedkar generously saved the Mahatma's life by keeping the Untouchables in the Hindu fold.

Years later, the backlash of Gandhi's claim at the 1931 Round Table Conference to represent all Indians hit him hard in two ways. On the one hand, following the Mahatma's example, Jinnah had relentlessly striven to represent all Muslims at the centre, and for his Muslim League to dominate the strong Muslim provincial parties after the implementation of the 1935 Government of India Act, granting provincial Indian governments. The League was transformed from a small organisation to a powerful and influential political party. On the other hand, Jinnah tried to cut the Congress party down to size. In the negotiations of April 1942 with Sir Stafford Cripps, he even contested the right of the Congress to represent anybody but the Brahmin caste: 'We maintain that the Congress does not represent not only the Mussalmans of India but even a large body of the Hindus, the Depressed Classes, the non-Brahmins and other minorities.'

When it suited him better, the Mahatma softened his claim of representation. In September 1944, for instance, when, after the war, he tried for a week to reach an agreement with Jinnah, Gandhi insisted that he represented only himself in the negotiations, although he hoped to represent all Indians. In response, Jinnah upbraided him:

> When you proceed to say that you aspire to represent all the inhabitants of India, I regret I cannot accept that statement of yours. It is quite clear that you represent nobody else but the Hindus, and as long as you do not realize your true position and the realities, it is very difficult for me to argue with you and it becomes still more difficult to persuade you, and hope to convert you to the realities and the actual conditions prevailing in India today.

The war had profoundly renewed the *donnée* of the game, and the trump cards had changed hands. Because of his non-violence, Gandhi's authority was severely tested and contested in the Congress, and he often disengaged himself from its politics by using a claim of non-representation to distance himself from his party. He played on the fact that he had left the party in 1934, when he did not renew his membership.

This policy had hidden benefits. For instance, when the Viceroy Lord Wavell, hoping for a peaceful transfer of political power, asked Gandhi in 1945 to attend the leaders conference at Simla, the latter agreed to come, but not as representative of the Congress, thus leaving that role to the president of his party, Maulana Abul Kalam Azad, a Muslim plainly disliked by Jinnah. Gandhi was thus making a point: the Congress was led, like the Muslim League, by a Muslim and, therefore, was entitled to represent Muslims – a counter to the claim made by Jinnah.

Gandhi persevered in playing the ambiguous role of non-representative representativeness at later conferences as it suited him: present, but not representing, yet actively involved and influential in the outcome of the discussions. Jinnah responded and accentuated the pressure by refusing him and his party any Muslim nominations in the Interim Government.

Times were changing. With the end of the war, Gandhi began loosening his grip on the party's decisions in extremely stressful circumstances. At the most crucial moment (8 March 1947), when the decision was taken by the Congress Working Committee to accept the partition of the Punjab, and therefore the partition of India, Gandhi was sidelined and unrepresented. These leaders well knew the Mahatma's opposition to partition on a communal basis, and they were obviously aware that voting for the partition of the Punjab meant accepting the partition of India.

The momentous decision was surreptitiously taken in his absence – he was in Bihar – and without his knowledge: 'No emissary was sent to brief Gandhi or obtain his views. The Working Committee's momentous decision on partitioning Punjab [and Bengal] was thus taken without his knowledge or input.'[25] He read about the resolution on partition the next day in the morning papers.

3

THE DEFENCE OF INDIANITY

At first, mild nationalism fitted the yet underdeveloped coherence of Mother India. Later, and by contrast, the robust nationalism of the 'Quit India' rhetoric better suited the traumatic departure of the British Raj. We shall therefore consider, in appropriate stages, the interlocking dependence of the concepts of nationalism and indianity through the policies and methods used against British rule – in the 'means' adopted to achieve a nationalist 'end.'

The Gandhian concept of 'means and ends' is very basic and crystal clear. Means should blend harmoniously with the ends. The political end should only be reached by non-violent means. Machiavellism has no place in gandhianity. It is, therefore, of interest to examine how Gandhi fashioned a pervasive ideology and an efficient tool. He did it in several stages.

The Notion of Right and Duty: The First Stage, 1893–1907

Gandhi's entry into politics sprang from the firm belief that a citizen has rights and duties, and that he, as an Indian, had a duty to perform. This Indian conception of one's life task is best expressed in the word *dharma*, or righteous performance of one's duty in life. As an Indian, Gandhi had assimilated the notion of duty from his younger days, but in his own personal way, linking 'right' to the previous performance of 'duty.'

He gave *dharma* a twist in politics. Duty at first made his nationalism take the form of loyalty to the Empire, but later commanded his rebellion: 'The proper question is not what the rights of a citizen are, but rather what constitutes the duties of a citizen.'[1]

Up to 1907, he behaved as a willing and irreproachable citizen of the British Empire, ever ready to do his duty – to do 'the right thing' – a willingness that outlived his South African period and nearly cost him his life in 1918, before he threw his loyalty to the winds. The First World War left a moribund Gandhi recovering from exhaustion after tramping through the hot Indian countryside to drum up recruits for the British Armed Forces.

The emphasis, then, was on duty rather than on rights as 'the right way' to tackle political problems. Loyalty to the Empire was conceived of in basic terms: 'Begin with a charter of Duties of Man and I promise the rights will follow as spring follows winter. I write from experience.'[2] Judith Brown comments on the importance Gandhi attached to individual duty rather than to a holistic vision of rights: 'For him recognition of individual duty and social and moral interdependence were the foundation of an authentic human existence,' and not 'the device for protecting core values and attributes of individual and group life, *vis-à-vis* the forces of state and society.'[3]

Gandhi's ambition then, was twofold. On the one hand, nationalism – home-made, India-made – burnt fiercely in his heart and revealed itself in the active pursuit of assistance to his fellow countrymen, and to his fellow countrymen only, as privileged recipients of his endeavours. On the other hand, being conscious that he also had or should have the rights necessary for the exercise of citizenship, he focused his political work on fighting anti-Indian legislation in Natal and in the Transvaal in the hope of gradually obtaining a status of equality within the British Empire.

Love of his country and love of the Empire were, however, uncomfortable bedfellows in the peaceable partnership that was part of the late nineteenth-century Indian tradition. In a statement he made in court in March 1922, he told the judge:

> My public life began in 1893 in South Africa in troubled weather. My first contact with British authorities in that country was not

> of a happy character. I discovered that as a man and an Indian I had no rights. More correctly I discovered that I had no rights as a man because I was an Indian.
>
> But I was not baffled. I thought that this treatment of Indians was an excrescence upon a system that was intrinsically and mainly good. I gave the Government my voluntary and hearty co-operation, criticising it freely where I felt it was faulty but never wishing its destruction...
>
> In all these efforts at service I was actuated by the belief that it was possible by such services to gain a *status of full equality in the Empire for my countrymen*."[4] (Emphasis added)

This confident belief in the goodness of the British connection lasted for nearly half of his political life – even if the second part of that life was spent in shaking it off. He saw himself politically as an Indian and as a citizen of the British Empire, and was proud of the fact.

> Hardly ever have I known anybody to cherish such loyalty as I did to the British Constitution. I can see now that my love of truth was at the root of this loyalty.... Not that I was unaware of the defects of British rule, but I thought that it was on the whole acceptable. In those days I believed that British rule was on the whole beneficial to the ruled.
>
> The colour prejudice that I saw in South Africa was, I thought, quite contrary to British traditions, and I believed that it was only temporary and local. I therefore vied with Englishmen in loyalty to the throne...
>
> Never in my life did I exploit this loyalty, never did I seek to gain a selfish end by its means. It was for me more in the nature of an obligation, and I rendered it without expecting a reward.[5]

Although at the time of the Boer War, at the turn of the century, Gandhi's sympathies had shifted to the Boer camp, his moral judgment did not interfere with his political adherence to British rule: 'I held then that India could achieve her complete emancipation only within and through the British Empire.'[6]

Therefore, the path forward, the political path, was a plain although chaotic constitutional and democratic venture, aiming at equal rights and duties for Indian nationals and extending the benefits thereof to the South African diaspora under British control. Involvement in the political life of the country meant working for the full implementation of these rights through legal and democratic channels.

Law-Breaking versus Law-Abiding: The Second Stage, 1907–18

The moment Gandhi's nationalism stepped over the line dividing legality and illegality, a new world of resistance opened to him. He called the resistance 'civil,' in the sense that it was not criminal. Moreover, the resistance was called 'non-violent,' which was then a new concept in politics and which would, in his time and age, make of him a political leader different from any other. Non-violence in politics had the freshness of a word not heard of before Gandhi. It is the translation of an Indian word, *ahimsa*, or no-harm, or love.

The overwhelming impact of *ahimsa* on Gandhi's nationalism was triggered by his reading of the New Testament; thus he Christianised the meaning of the word and gained a sympathetic audience of Christians throughout the world. But Gandhi solidly anchored the Christian injunction in the Hindu tradition.[7]

Ahimsa and nationalism in the garb of civil resistance gave birth to a new concept and word coined by Gandhi. '*Satyagraha*' is the name he gave to his weapon of political non-violence and, incidentally, to the 'way of life' he thus promoted. *Satyagraha* was born in the following circumstances.

Legal channels allowed and offered some correctives to abusive and repressive measures, and resistance to the abuse of power is an integral part of the democratic process. But the South African channels of redress were restricted, and proved to be inefficient in the Indian case. A dilemma soon faced the barrister – not yet a saint. The dilemma had two horns: law-abiding and law-breaking. He eventually embarked on the last.

From 1906, Gandhi was faced with a series of measures in the new Crown Colony of the Transvaal (established after the Boer War), which he found most objectionable. The Asiatic Registration Act (1906) counted Indian and Chinese heads, and came with a thumb-printing obligation (a practice then required only of criminals) – a bad omen portending their expulsion back to their countries of origin. A complementary piece of legislation (the Immigration Act, 1907) sought to prevent the arrival of more Indian settlers. Later still, the indentured labourers in the sugar cane estates and coal mines went on strike for the repeal of the £3 annual tax that would be levied on each member of their family if, at the end of their indenture, they chose to settle in South Africa.

As in the 1894 fight for the franchise, the outcome of representations to authorities, petitions, and lobbying in India and London were to no avail. Although the Royal Assent was at first denied, it was then granted, because, at the end of 1906, the Transvaal was given self-governing status. The Indian position became even more precarious after May 1910 in the newly formed Union of South Africa.

In 1906, Gandhi pressed Indians not to register their names. This was a first, modest step into illegality, since they were bound legally to do so. After making a deal with General Smuts, he advised his community to proceed with registration; however, the 'Black Act' was not repealed as promised, and Gandhi – forcefully, this time – defied Smuts by burning the registration certificates in public. Illegal crossings between Natal and the Transvaal defiantly broke the new immigration law. Strikes and the breaking of indentured contracts by leaving places of work spread in Natal, with the Indian community – including women – taking its share in defying of the law.

A cluster of Europeans were helping Gandhi; two were even arrested and sentenced with him as accomplices. One was Henry Polak, who worked in Gandhi's office. The other, Hermann Kallenbach, organised and supervised the Natal-Transvaal March from the coal mines to the farm he had bought for Gandhi's self-sufficiency experiments in the Transvaal. Tolstoy Farm, untouched to this day, still bears witness to the event. It was used to house the destitute Indians who were neither arrested nor sent back to their work places under guard.

As he considered this new and inventive strategy in illegality, Gandhi made it absolutely clear that no violence should ever be used by the resisters and that no other piece of legislation should be defied, but only the one in question, with the obvious exception of any new statutes designed to break the Indian resistance. The deliberate entry into illegality in order to force the repeal of the Asiatic Registration Act engendered *satyagraha*. Born in 1906, and born without a name, it was referred to as 'passive resistance' in the press; but Gandhi objected, since he wanted an aggressive and open resistance, one that was non-violent, but neither passive nor weak. He therefore asked for suggestions in his journal, *Indian Opinion*, and finally settled on '*satyagraha*': adherence to the truth, or the force of truth, or force of love. The term was in use by 1908.

This force for truth was indeed aggressive, with its bonfires of legal documents, strikes, and illegal crossings of the Natal-Transvaal frontier. It never extended into breaking any other objectionable laws or supporting other labour disputes. It focused its strategy on a clearly defined and specific outcome, in a kind of mirror response to the government's specific abuse of power. It seemed as if the concept of the 'just war,' along with its restrictions, had been adapted to a 'just,' non-violent resistance.

Thus, means and ends blended on a moral high ground and made *satyagraha* something very special, a weapon that Einstein admired as the great discovery of the century, on a par with that of the atomic weapon.

Inciting Unrest on an All-India Scale: The Third Stage, 1918–20

Next to *dharma*, *ahimsa*, and *satyagraha*, *hartal* is a key word for the period following the First World War. This old Indian concept inspired and gave an incredible force to Gandhi's nationalism in 1918. *Hartal* means the cessation of work, the closure of all business for a day of protest and demonstrations. If successful, *hartal* entails the mobilisation of huge crowds and poses the problem of controlling them to keep them non-violent.

Satyagraha in South Africa had been a special case because Gandhi had, fortunately, not faced violence in the *satyagrahis*' ranks. Crowd control was dealt with satisfactorily. In spite of ups and downs in the movement's fortunes, the whole community could be said to fully support Gandhi in his non-violent ways. The importance of this should not be minimised, since during the next *satyagraha*, in India, the reverse situation confronted him, posing a problem that proved intractable. Violence raised its ugly head among his supporters in spite of his admonitions.

Gandhi had embarked for India with Kallenbach, his right and able hand, both men full of hope as well as certainty in their vocation to continue in India what they had started in South Africa. The weapon of non-violence lay in its sheath, ready for use. But the war stopped Kallenbach in London. The German–South African was interned as a hostile alien, and Gandhi thought him dead.

Taking a breath after twenty-one years of African experience, and missing Kallenbach, Gandhi was ready in 1917 to try his weapon in provincial disputes. In Champaran, he led peasants in a successful resistance against indigo exploitation (April to the end of 1917). In Ahmedabad, he advised strikers in an industrial dispute in the cotton mills (1918). In Kheda, he confronted the local government on the question of rising taxes in a no-tax campaign (January–June 1918).

Fairly confident in his role as an intermediary, and familiar by now with the Indian scene, Gandhi then launched an all-India political protest in March–April 1919 on the no less familiar question of law-breaking and law-abiding. The storm against the enactment of the Rowlatt Act (18 March 1919) had been brewing since April 1918, after Sir Sydney Rowlatt studied in India the lapse of the Government of India Defence Act (1915).

Thus, almost simultaneously in April 1918, Gandhi led the no-tax campaign in Kheda, watched the birth of the Rowlatt Bills, and engaged himself in war recruiting. Was there a connection linking the success in Kheda in June 1918 and Gandhi's recruitment in the same Kheda for the Indian Army in July? Here are the comments of Anthony Read and David Fisher:

> Even while he was concluding the campaign in Ahmedabad he was presented with a perfect opportunity [the refusal of the

> peasants to pay the taxes]...By June 1918, they [the peasants] were almost exhausted, and Gandhi later admitted that he was 'casting about some graceful way of terminating the struggle,' when he learned that because of the government's need for calm and support during the war, it had secretly instructed local officials not to collect tax from those who really were too poor to pay. There was to be no public announcement, which might jeopardize the entire revenue system, but since the outcome was more or less what Gandhi had been demanding, he called a halt to the *satyagraha*.[8]

In April, Gandhi had been corresponding with the Viceroy, making no secret of the fact that his collaboration with the war effort had to bring some tangible rewards. Thus, the link between helping the war effort and constitutional advancement was stressed in his letter to the Viceroy dated 30 April 1918:

> I recognize that in the hour of its danger we must give, as we have decided to give, ungrudging and unequivocal support to the empire of which we aspire in the near future to be partners in the same sense as the dominions overseas. But it is the simple truth that our response is due to the expectation that our goal will be reached all the more speedily on that account – even as the performance of duty automatically confers a corresponding right.[9]

Gandhi chose to help recruitment in Kheda, where he had organised the campaign against the local authorities. The response was minimal and unfriendly. He had to stop by August, his health greatly affected. Then the Rowlatt Bills revived him.

These two bills were to replace the Defence of India Act (1915), operating during the war to tackle terrorism – an endemic problem in India since 1907, which Gandhi had criticised in his book *Hind Swaraj* (1909). Gandhi re-enacted – in his well-trained South African way – the whipping-up of opposition to the Rowlatt Bills. Having no political base, he formed the Satyagraha Sabha to channel the forces unleashed by the insult to India's loyalty. Consequently, one of the bills was dropped. The other was put on the statute book for three years.

The vote on the Rowlatt Act in March 1919 was greeted by protests, strikes, and the closure of shops – the traditional *hartal* – and violence. But the actual breaking of the law was rendered impossible because, to be applied, the Rowlatt Act needed first to be enforced, if and when the political situation warranted it – and this was not the case. Despite unsubsiding agitation, the Rowlatt Act was never used; instead, it lingered in comatose ambiguity for the three years of its duration on the statute book. The situation thus differed from that of 1906 in the odd fact that no law-breaking was possible, since there was no law to break. (Law-breaking was thus confined ineffectively to selling forbidden literature.)

But violence had struck, and Gandhi was taken aback. It was the last thing he wanted. He suspended the movement. A 'Himalayan mistake,' he confessed, must have been made, leading to the violence. The Rowlatt Act was allowed to rest in peace. But the *hartals* had shaken India on a national level for the first time, and made a national leader of Gandhi.

Thus, Gandhi won his point: no prosecution followed in the wake of the Rowlatt Act. He also won fame and glory. He moved the soul of India. The Government's lack of sagacity, rather than Gandhi's unpreparedness, deserved being described as a 'Himalayan' miscalculation. Not only did the Rowlatt Act prove just a scarecrow, but this episode under Gandhi's aegis and under the *hartal* formula also paved the way for a nationalist rebellion.

In the Imperial Legislative Council, Jinnah had been taking a similar posture of protest against the Rowlatt Bills and had led the unanimous opposition of the Indian members. He wisely warned the Government of the pitfalls ahead if it clung to what he called 'this Black Act': 'If these measures are passed, you will create in the country from one end to the other a discontent and agitation the like of which you have not witnessed, and it will have, believe me, a most disastrous effect on the good relations that have existed between the Government and the people.'[10]

No doubt can be raised about the fact that Bapu ('father,' as Gandhi was now fondly called) and the 'Father' of the Pakistan-to-be – then better known as 'the ambassador of Hindu–Muslim unity'[11] – were on the same side of the fence, both entrenched in leading positions in the Indian National Congress. The next stage was going to change this fortunate alliance between the two Congress leaders.

Rebellion and Compromise: The Fourth Stage, 1920–39

The 'practical idealist' – as Gandhi saw himself – was not a theoretician. His argumentation was no theory, but an explanation of his conception of nationalism, and a justification of his behaviour. He reacted first, theorised later. He believed in compromise that did not sacrifice principles.

Gandhi's loyalty to the Empire was so well anchored that it survived the upheaval of the Rowlatt agitation in 1918, even if it took a dent. Hence, he supported, even as he criticised, the Montagu-Chelmsford Reforms, marking the next constitutional step for India, defending them in December 1919 at the annual session of the Indian National Congress. This was to be the last manifestation of his unquestioned loyalty to the Empire.

A few months later, by August 1920, Gandhi had cast this loyalty to the winds and demanded *swaraj*. For what reason, one might ask? Had Gandhi crossed the Rubicon?

A controversial but plausible answer to the first question is that the rebellion of 1920 was launched for the sake of the Caliphate, a religious institution – or rather, for the benefit of Indian Muslims, who would later support the demand for a religious state, anathema to Gandhi. Thus, the Mahatma paradoxically became a rebel for a religious reason that proved to be the seed of partition.

To the second question, the reply must point to the fact that Gandhi, a man of compromise and a resourceful diplomat, crossed, and re-crossed, the demarcation line evoked by the Rubicon – sometimes he was a rebel, sometimes a loyal citizen. After the failure of the first *satyagraha* campaign against the Raj (1920–22), 'he repeated that it would be possible to have *swaraj* and a British connection, and as the demand for total political independence began to grow among a section of Congressmen, Gandhi warned them to be careful of playing with words and to be realistic in their aims.'[12]

In the role of rebel, Gandhi manipulated two concepts: non-cooperation and civil disobedience. These gave their names to two campaigns on an all-India scale (1920–22 and 1930–34). Both tactics were inspired by Western thought. So much so that Gandhi could not think of a Hindi translation for the word 'non-cooperation' when the idea of non-cooperating with the government struck him at a meeting with the pro-Caliphate Muslims. As for civil disobedience, it owed its inspiration to Henry David Thoreau (1817–62), an American who 'invented' the idea in his book of the same name.

The first campaign, based on non-cooperation with a 'satanic' government, according to Gandhi, resorted to the indigenous tradition of boycotts which were best suited to indianity. Gradual non-cooperation extended from the return of honorific titles and medals to the boycotting of schools, law courts, elections, foreign cloth, liquor shops, serving in the army, and paying tax. This led to the setting of a semblance of parallel institutions in schools and universities; to a stimulation of the production of indigenous cloth; to a loss of government revenue on textile imports and alcohol; to a problem of disaffection in the Indian Army. The final refusal to pay taxes would have tested the Government even further, but for its cancellation a few days before it was due to start.

The second campaign refashioned anew the concept of law-breaking. It introduced the idea of focusing on a soft target unconnected with the causes of the conflict. The salt laws became that easy target for law-breaking in 1931. Picking up a pinch of salt on the seashore or boiling it from sea water made you a civil resister. Civil disobedience was praised as a right as well as a duty. It was resorted to not only on a wide scale and by a large number of people, but also in the full glare of the media. The success story ended with the Gandhi-Irwin Pact (1931), when Gandhi, offered a drink by Lord Irwin, the Viceroy, naughtily drew a pinch of salt from his pocket to add to the beverage. (The success turned sour when the campaign was resumed and resistance was crushed by a new Viceroy.)

Both campaigns failed to achieve independence, but they greatly increased the political consciousness of the nation, the intensity of nationalism, and the potency of the claim for an Indian state.

Thereafter, and only three years after winding up the campaign of civil disobedience, Gandhi, in a major turn-around, found a way to compromise with the Raj. He re-crossed the Rubicon.

It happened in 1937, during the elections that followed the Government of India Act of 1935, which granted self-ruling powers to the provincial governments. Non-cooperation had proved difficult to operate and sustain in the past. The Government had enticed Indian politicians to ignore the boycott and to contest elections. The non-cooperation ideology had been defeated with calls to 'let us strike the Raj from the inside.' The Indian National Congress, repeating the previous U-turn, suddenly changed tack in order to contest the 1937 elections – with tremendous success. It was able to form the majority of the provincial governments, with Gandhi changing his stance and persuading the recalcitrant Nehru to cooperate with the unexpected change of tactics.

The Congress provincial governments functioned fairly satisfactorily under the strict – and unwelcome – party discipline of the newly formed Congress High Command. The party entered the serious and studious phase of learning how to run a state at provincial level.

This first political experience in government administration was still running well when the Second World War broke out. But because the Viceroy declared India to be at war, without consulting the Indians, all the provincial Congress ministries resigned when ordered to do so by the Congress High Command. In the political void, Jinnah stepped in.

The Communal Quagmire: The Fifth Stage, 1940–47

After the 1937 elections, Jinnah and his Muslim League had been refused by the Indian National Congress a share in some provincial ministries and had been left out in the cold. The war declaration came to their rescue. The Muslim League, celebrating the resignation of the Congress provincial governments, rejoiced in a 'day' of thanksgiving, and by offering support for the war, Jinnah edged into a position of being granted a virtual veto of unwelcome political decisions. At the same time, he built the Muslim League into the main pro-governmental party. Now, from a position of strength, he hit hard at the Congress and its leadership. The blow came in March 1940, when the Muslim League endorsed the 'Pakistan resolution.'

Yet, did the 'communal' problem have to be solved by the dismemberment of India? Did Jinnah really want the partition of India? If the answer to both questions is no, as we think it is, we shall have to search for evidence of a hidden agenda behind the screen of Pakistan, an agenda that Jinnah had no time to bring to a satisfactory conclusion.

Jinnah clouded and tore at Gandhi's vision of India. Did he ever regret it? We would be well advised to listen to Jinnah's first address to the new Pakistan Constituent Assembly, three days before independence. The 'father of Pakistan' seemed to be daydreaming aloud, appreciating the wondrous achievement and singularity of his plan, but strangely reflecting and referring to another plan he had had in mind, which had stayed out of reach and had had to be put aside.

That plan he referred to would have retained the unity of India. His listeners heard him say, and conclude, that Pakistan had to come into being because there could not be a United India:

> The question is, whether it was possible or practicable to *act otherwise than what has been done*... A division had to take place... In my judgment there was no other solution and I am sure history will record its verdict in favour of it. And what is more it will be proved by actual experience as we go on that that was the only solution... Any idea of a *United India* could never have worked. (Emphasis added)

His biographer, Stanley Wolpert – who draws his own personal conclusions from Jinnah's speech – rightly wonders at the significance thereof: 'He seemed unable to move his mind from that awesome question. For the first time he openly challenged his own judgment... as though he had been transformed overnight once again into the old "Ambassador of Hindu–Muslim Unity."'[13]

Indeed, Jinnah went on in his discourse to tell his listeners what the minorities of the new Pakistan were to expect in the future.

> You are free; you are free to go to your temples, you are free to go to your mosques or to any other place of worship in this State of Pakistan... You may belong to any religion or caste or creed – that has nothing to do with the business of the State... We are starting in the days when there is no discrimination, no distinction between one community and another, no discrimination between one caste or creed and another. We are starting with this fundamental principle that we are all citizens and equal citizens of one State.

And Wolpert comments further: 'What was he talking about? Had he simply forgotten where he was? Had the cyclone of events so disoriented him that he was arguing the opposition's brief? *Was he pleading for a united India – on the eve of Pakistan... ?*' (emphasis added). But Jinnah ended his discourse in the same vein: 'You will find that in course of time Hindus will cease to be Hindus and Muslims would cease to be Muslims, not in the religious sense, because that is the personal faith of each individual, but in the political sense as citizens of the State.'

This was his message to the new Pakistan: citizenship with equal rights, privileges, and obligations. This had been Gandhi's belief since his South African days; the two positions were not that far apart. Can we now infer that the political game Jinnah was playing prevented him from revealing his hand too soon, and that history did not give him time to finish the game to his satisfaction? These questions have the merit of raising our awareness of a hidden agenda that Gandhi could rightly sense in Jinnah.

Indeed, Gandhi had his own doubts about Jinnah's tactics. He guessed the presence of a secret scheme under the cloak of the current negotiations. He felt that his rival wanted time, not a settlement: 'My impression is that he does not want a settlement till he has so consolidated the League position that he can dictate his terms to all the parties concerned including the rulers. I do not blame him for having taken up that position, if he has. But with this impression it is useless for me to approach him.'[14]

We are thus reminded of the puzzled Viceroy, amazed at Jinnah's frowning when granted Pakistan. Let us remember also our third cartoon (Figure 4), drawn after Nicolas Poussin's masterpiece *Le Jugement de Salomon*, showing the dead baby lying at the feet of the mother (Jinnah) who was claiming half of the living child. Why does she consent to the 'vivisection' of the latter? It is only because her own baby, her own dream of a baby, is dead. As for the real mother (Gandhi), she would rather give the whole infant to the other woman than have it cut in two.

Hence the tentative suggestion that both statesmen desired the same newborn India, an hypothesis that will be brought later in this book to a rightful conclusion. On this note, we bring Part I to an end and tread Gandhi's cautious path to Indian independence.

PART II

NATIONALISM AND ALLEGIANCE

Figure 6: Gandhi and Allegiance

4

WAR AND NON-VIOLENCE

Gandhi trod carefully the stepping stones on the path of loyalty to the British Empire. Perhaps no step was more difficult to take than the confrontation with war. How was he to solve the contradiction, being a non-violent man?

> I do believe that where there is only a choice between cowardice and violence I would advise violence. Thus when my eldest son asked me what he should have done, had he been present when I was almost fatally assaulted in 1908, whether he should have run away and seen me killed or whether he should have used his physical force, which he could and wanted to use, and defended me, I told him that it was his duty to defend me even by using violence.[1]

Thus did Gandhi solve the problem. Now, if we substitute the beleaguered British Empire for the assaulted father, and the loyal Indian called Mohandas Gandhi for the helpful son, we understand that Gandhi's faith in non-violence will confront him with a similar choice in case of war. Should he interfere on the side of the state or disown responsibility? Choose disaffection and cowardice rather than violence? Eschew the duty of a citizen to contribute to the defence of his homeland rather than enlist for the killing fields? The Augustinian concept of a 'just war' has, not yet, outlived its usefulness.

This dilemma faced Gandhi several times in his loyalty period, and the response he chose in a wartime situation was, undoubtedly, in favour of war rather than *ahimsa* (non-violence). But the choice was heartbreaking for the apostle of non-violence. *Himsa* means harm – it is violence. The prefix '*a*' has the same negative function as the Greek prefix '*a*,' meaning 'not' or 'without,' as in 'a-gnostic': one 'without gnosis, or knowledge.' Thus the antithesis of *himsa* is *ahimsa*, or harmlessness, non-violence, love.

Steadfastly, Gandhi chose to enter wars even when he did not have to. Nobody asked him to put on an army uniform. In fact, it was not that easy to have his services accepted by the Army. But the point was not whether he liked it or not, but whether this was or was not his duty.

Logically, when the bond of allegiance snapped, *ahimsa* prevailed. In 1940–41, in spite for his 'non-violent support' for Britain's fight, he launched a non-violent campaign to state his (or rather India's!) opposition to war. It was a kind of revenge, a way to atone for past behaviour: a protest by select people standing on a street corner and shouting a slogan against helping Britain, after duly notifying the authorities of its time and place.

Gandhi was perfectly aware that he had reacted differently to war in different periods of his political life. But he tried to explain himself. He blamed the difference on circumstances in order to account for the compromise between non-violence and war in the loyalty period and to make intelligible his evolving conception of duty. Overlooking the years when he responded positively to active service in the British armed forces and when, in *Hind Swaraj*, he countered the logic of terrorism, he said in 1939: 'The situation today is radically different for me from what it was at the time of the Boer War or the War of 1914. On both the occasions I was a believer in the Empire . . . though I was against war at that time as I am now.' The journalist to whom he was speaking had questioned his attitude: 'In South Africa you supported an alien Government in its war against the Boers, although it was at that time oppressing the Indians; again in 1914 you supported the British Government in its war against Germany.' 'On both the occasions,' Gandhi answered, 'I was a believer in the Empire. I thought that in spite of its lapses the sum total of its activity was beneficial to the world.'[2]

But interestingly, he also pointed to another reason, which had nothing to do with loyalty, but with status and political clout. He mentioned a difference of status that he did not have then but had now, one that made the same compromise between war and non-violence possible then but not later: 'I had no status or strength to refuse to participate in war. I suppressed my private judgment in favour of the duty of an ordinary citizen. My position is wholly different now.'[3]

Pursuing his argument further to show why his position had 'wholly' changed after the First World War, Gandhi argued that he was opposed to a war of independence in his own country because of a deeper personal commitment to *ahimsa,* a commitment that he now wanted to be seen as such: 'I have become by force of circumstances a teacher of non-violence. I claim to enforce my teaching in my own life to the best of my ability and I feel that I have the strength to resist war in my own person.'[4]

This kind of analysis during what was, after all, an impromptu interview at a non-descript railway station would be an unfair dissection of a moment of Gandhi's thoughts and words only if it had not brought out also the essential point of his explanation: 'I have [now] the strength to resist war in my own person.'

The importance of these few words reaches beyond the historical moment when they were uttered. They allude to his consciousness of a great interior impulse, of a state of grace, of an adherence to the power of love, to faith in *satyagraha.*

The experience of God's cosmic presence led him to say: 'I have the strength . . . ' Furthermore, he believed that this strength was equally available to others. He would at times, therefore, advise people to stand singly or in groups against overpowering violence, thereby shocking most of his listeners into disbelief. The most famous instances of this are his letter 'To the Jews' (26 November 1938), which raised Jewish protests and a furore, and his letter 'To Every Briton,' written after the fall of France (6 July 1940).

Do not fear death, act non-violently, and others will (may?) follow was his message, however frightening the words he used to the Jews of Germany:

> If the Jewish mind could be prepared for voluntary suffering, even the massacre that I have imagined could be turned into a

> day of thanksgiving and joy that Jehovah had wrought deliverance of the race even at the hands of the tyrant. For to the God fearing, death has no terror. It is a joyful sleep to be followed by a waking that would be all the more refreshing for the long sleep.

And to the Jews of Palestine:

> They can offer *satyagraha* in front of the Arabs and offer themselves to be shot or thrown into the Dead Sea without raising a little finger against them.[5]

And to the Britons:

> You will invite Herr Hitler and Signor Mussolini to take what they want of the countries you call your possessions. Let them take possession of your beautiful island, with your many beautiful buildings. You will give all these, but neither your souls, nor your minds.[6]

The Viceroy, who had forwarded this suggestion to His Majesty's Government on Gandhi's request, gave him the response four days later: '[His Majesty's Government] do not feel that the policy which you advocate is one which is possible for them to consider, since in common with the whole Empire they are firmly resolved to prosecute the war to a victorious conclusion.'[7]

When Gandhi described himself as a 'practical idealist,' he put his finger on a duality within: on the one hand, his idealism, expressed so airily in his advice to the Jews and Britons, and on the other, the practice of it, which necessarily leads to compromise. If we observe how he participated in the Boer War, we note that he did not walk into a recruiting office to register as a volunteer, but announced his intentions in a striking manner. He recruited eleven hundred Indians himself, and taking advantage of his experience in nursing, offered their services under his leadership as an Indian Ambulance Corps. A deal was made with the military authorities, and Gandhi was promoted to the rank of sergeant–major and put in charge of his Indians. He then asked to work on the front lines, retrieving the wounded. This is how Winston Churchill and Gandhi found themselves on the same battlefield against the Boers in South Africa.

Nevertheless, the 'practical idealist' showed his mettle in the fealty period with a very down-to-earth approach to the war problem. Having decided to do his duty, he did so in his own way and on his own terms.

The Boer War, 1899–1902

Let us resume the bundle of relevant facts from 1899 and stress that Gandhi's legal mind was perfectly aware that he was not legally bound by conscription of any sort. No South African Indian was expected to take part in the Boer War. No Indian was asked to enlist in the British Army. Besides, Gandhi hated war and violence and, as an Indian, had no preference for the British side of the conflict. He remembered: 'When the war was declared, my personal sympathies were all with the Boers.'[8] Yet Gandhi voluntarily, without any outside pressure from friends or foes, participated in a war he did not believe in.

He had spent only about six years in South Africa when the war broke out. He had no intention of settling there and had postponed his return to India only because of unforeseen circumstances – the 1894 protest against the Disfranchising Bill in Natal. Moreover, his experiences of life in Natal and in the Transvaal were hardly conducive to engendering sympathy for white racism, whether Boer or British. He had a great many European friends, who treated him as an equal and who were attracted to his personality, but he was amazed and shocked in 1893 to discover the depths of humiliation and the extent of the restrictions imposed upon the 'coolies' in ordinary life.[9] One personal experience was especially unbearable: he had been thrown out of his first-class compartment at the railway station of Pietermariztburg (and there was a similar incident later on a stagecoach). He recalled the night ordeal thus:

> It was winter, and the winter in the higher regions of South Africa is severely cold. Maritzburg being at a high altitude, the

> cold was extremely bitter. My overcoat was in my luggage, but I did not dare to ask for it lest I should be insulted again, so I sat and shivered. There was no light in the [waiting] room. A passenger came in at about midnight and possibly wanted to talk to me. But I was in no mood to talk.
>
> I began to think of my duty. Should I fight for my rights or go back to India, or should I go on to Pretoria without minding the insults and return to India after finishing the case?[10]

This humiliating incident was a decisive moment in Gandhi's life: it made Gandhi. It steeled him against adversity. It gave him the necessary frame of mind to think in terms of duties and rights, not likes and dislikes. It sent him back to work.

But work was now coloured by that intolerable experience What Gandhi called the 'colour bar' applied on a white-to-non-white basis, and Boers were included in the white batch. Boers, in fact, were harsher on Indians than the British, so much so that the improvement of the Indian condition had been accepted by the British side as being one of the aims of the Boer War. Natal, then a Crown Colony, had been granted responsible government in 1893, and the Transvaal was a Boer Republic. Gandhi's 'sympathies' for the Boers remained superficial. Their treatment of Indians seemed rooted in and justified by their brand of Christian theology, while it seemed to Gandhi 'quite contrary to British traditions.'[11] 'Race' had no confrontational connotation for him, no abhorrence. He used the word freely to describe his nationalist ties and those of his compatriots.

Consequently, he did not appreciate the war situation in a narrow, local context, but took a much broader view of the conflict. He did not consider himself a permanent resident of either the Republic or the Crown Colony, instead seeing himself as a citizen of the British Indian Empire, and he entered the Boer war as such: 'My loyalty to the British rule drove me to participation with the British in that war. I felt that, if I demanded rights as a British citizen, it was also my duty as such, to participate in the defence of the British Empire. I held then that India could achieve her complete emancipation only within and through the Empire.'[12]

The Indian Ambulance Corps – 1,100 men strong – was operative for six weeks on the battlefield, served gallantly in the line of fire, and was mentioned in a dispatch; Gandhi, the sergeant-major in charge, was rewarded by a medal for his war services.

The Zulu Rebellion, June–July 1906

After the Boer War, Gandhi and his family settled comfortably in Johannesburg in the Transvaal, mindful of new Indian grievances in the wake of the constitutional changes brought about by the defeat of the Boer Republic. The thirty-three-year-old barrister built a flourishing practice and a reputation in his community that made him self-assured. Four years later, circumstances put him – and his nationalism – to another test he could easily not have submitted to.

Another war was afoot in Natal, the Zulu Rebellion. Gandhi, although residing and practising law in the Transvaal, responded thus: '[I] felt that I must offer my services to the Natal Government on that occasion.' Gandhi explained what kind of help he was thinking of. Rather than a 'Stretcher-Bearer Corps,' he would favour a 'Volunteer Corps' bearing arms, which would make of the volunteer a 'civilian soldier.'

> There is much difference. The Stretcher-Bearer Corps is to last only a few days. Its work will be only to carry the wounded, and it will be disbanded when such work is no longer necessary. These men are not allowed to bear arms. The move for a Volunteer Corps is quite different and much more important. That Corps will be a permanent body; its members will be issued weapons, and they will receive military training every year at stated times . . . If the Indians are given such a status, we believe it would be a very good thing. It is likely to bring in some political advantage. Whether or not any advantage is to be derived, there is no doubt that it is our duty to enlist.[13]

In the previous war, Gandhi had sympathised with the Boers: in this case, he 'bore no grudge against the Zulus.' But the same reasoning that made him enter the Boer War in the Transvaal applied to the Zulu Rebellion in Natal, although by that time he was settled in the Transvaal.

> I had doubts about the 'rebellion' itself. But I then believed that the British Empire existed for the welfare of the world. A genuine sense of loyalty prevented me of even wishing ill to the Empire. The rightness or otherwise of the 'rebellion' was therefore not likely to affect my decision... I considered myself a citizen of Natal, being intimately connected with it.[14]

In this state of mind he gave up his home, 'the house... so carefully furnished' in Johannesburg, and took his family to Natal. There he formed an Ambulance Corps of twenty-four Indian volunteers. He looked mainly after Zulu casualties for the short duration of the campaign, his 'heart [being] with the Zulus.'[15]

On his long marches in Zululand – some covering forty miles a day – Gandhi reflected on making beneficial changes in his life in order to improve his spiritual enrichment and his growing social dedication to his community. There and then he decided on a life of greater simplicity and dedicated celibacy (*brahmacharia*) in order to increase his strength and commitment to his work.

The experience made Gandhi consider the unpleasantness of his position in the punishing exercise in Zululand, and he started questioning his decision to help crush the Rebellion. He still did not doubt the appropriateness of supporting the British Government in its wars, but he hated this 'man-hunt':

> The Boer War had not brought home to me the horrors of war with anything like the vividness of the 'rebellion' did... But I swallowed the bitter draught, especially as the work of my Corps consisted only in nursing the wounded Zulus. I could see that but for us the Zulus would have been uncared for. This work, therefore, eased my conscience.[16]

Thus, the conscience problem was left in abeyance until the declaration of the First World War. His nationalism, however, was not, because during that eight-year interval, he led his first non-violent campaign against the Government, regarding the constitutional changes leading to the Union of South Africa. Inescapably, Gandhi's nationalistic perceptions and conclusions were challenged by the major event in his life – mainly the discovery of *satyagraha* on the fateful date of 11 September 1906.

He went from the experience of Zululand to his first non-violent political confrontation within the space of a couple of months. The four weeks he spent helping the Empire were followed by eight years of selectively breaking its laws.

The Indians Relief Act of 1914 gave Gandhi the measure of success he wanted, and it put an end to his South African sojourn. Having sent his family directly to Bombay, he embarked with his wife and Kallenbach – they had become inseparable – in July 1914 for India via London, where he was to meet the ailing Indian Congress leader, Gokhale, whose protégé he was.

The First World War: The London Episode, August–December 1914

Both friends disembarked in London as the First World War had been declared. Gandhi reacted as he had done twice before. He decided to recruit and organise – for the third time – an Ambulance Corps, asking no question but the one he had put to himself – and had answered himself – in his journal *Indian Opinion* (April 1906), two months before the Zulu Rebellion: 'What is our duty in these calamitous times in the colony? It is not for us to say whether the revolt of the Kaffirs is justified or not. We are in Natal by virtue of British power. Our very existence depends upon it. It is therefore our duty to render whatever help we can.'[17]

Gandhi, now in his forties, would have to rely on the enthusiasm and goodwill of Indian residents in London. Kallenbach, who had been worth his weight in gold for Gandhi in South Africa, was now powerless, indeed useless. He had to be left out because his German passport made of him an enemy alien. Gandhi tried to get him a visa for India, but in vain. So Kallenbach, who had thought of absconding to some neutral country, waited in London, only to be interned on the Isle of Man. Thus the experience of again helping the Empire in its wars started on the wrong footing.

Previously, Gandhi had solved any contradiction in his involvement in war and adherence to non-violence by choosing ambulance work. This was also the acceptable solution for objectors of conscience. Nonetheless, Gandhi was not convinced that by doing so, he was exonerated from the culpability attached to the monstrous killings about to be unleashed. He questioned the excuse that a distinction should be made between inflicting wounds and healing them. He further doubted that ignorance of firearms practice was an asset for his countrymen. It made for cowardice, he thought, for the 'emasculation of a race.' There was some ambivalence in his attitude because he so much admired courage, bravery, discipline, recklessness, all the warrior qualities he associated with the bearing of arms, which could turn cowards into heroes. Non-violence was made of that stuff. And he would actually see, with 'boundless joy,' this dream come true in 1929 in the Khudai Khidmatgars, the fierce 'Red Shirt' Pathans turned non-violent on the Afghan border.

With Kallenbach cruelly sidelined in the hour of need, Henry Polak, his other dear friend, who had fought the South African *satyagraha* with Gandhi and Kallenbach, and who had been arrested and sentenced to prison with them, objected to Gandhi's decision as soon as he heard of it. From South Africa, where he had taken charge of Gandhi's office, he sent a cable to London to stress the inconsistency of a believer in *ahimsa* joining this war. Like others, he had assumed that the campaign of *satyagraha* (1906–14) had changed Gandhi's outlook and views on war. But Gandhi squarely faced the charge of being inconsistent.

> As a matter of fact the very same line of argument that persuaded me to take part in the Boer War had weighed with me on this occasion. It was quite clear to me that participation in war could never be consistent with *ahimsa*. But it is not always given to one to be equally clear about one's duty....
>
> I had hoped to improve my status and that of my people through the British Empire. Whilst in England I was enjoying the

> protection of the British Fleet, and taking shelter as I did under its armed might, I was directly participating in its potential violence. Therefore, if I desired to retain my connection with the Empire and to live under its banner, one of three courses was open to me: I could declare open resistance to the war, and in accordance with the law of Satyagraha, boycott the Empire until it changed its military policy; or I could seek imprisonment by civil disobedience of such of its laws as were fit to be disobeyed [as in the campaign in the Transvaal and Natal]; or I could participate in the war on the side of the Empire and thereby acquire the capacity and fitness for resisting the violence in war. I lacked this capacity and fitness, so I thought there was nothing for it but to serve in the war...
>
> Even today I see no flaw in that line of argument, nor am I sorry for my action, holding, as I then did, views favourable to the British connection.[18]

Gandhi also met opposition from Indians in London, but on different grounds. It was not the kind of opposition he had had to face from his people at the time of the Boer War or the Zulu Rebellion. Those Indians were mostly uneducated, which was not the case in England. He dismissed Indian objections that help was unwarranted because of the discrepancies of status in the British Empire. He 'thought that England's need should not be turned into our opportunity, and it was more becoming and far-sighted not to press our demands while the war lasted.'[19]

Thus, he proceeded to gather some eighty recruits for nursing work and to offer them for training in the Armed Forces. But unforeseen difficulties came his way from the very quarters he sought to help. He wanted to keep the Indians under his personal command, an expectation the British Army would not satisfy. He and his volunteers, therefore, objected to the authority of the non-Indian Commanding Officer and his 'non-elected' section commanders – who took that objection as a breach of discipline. Gandhi complained to no less than the Secretary of State for India. The Under-Secretary of State personally called on

Gandhi, and they reached a compromise for the Indian Corps. It came too late for Gandhi, who was struck by an attack of pleurisy that put an end to the matter as far as he was concerned. He left the Army, the winter, the fog, Kallenbach and England for India. 'Suffice it to say,' concluded Gandhi, 'that my experience was of a piece with the experiences we live daily in India.' The prized Indian-British connection had shown cracks in South Africa, and now in England as well, when Gandhi engaged in a skirmish with the military authorities – a resistance certainly unjustifiable in military terms, but grounded in some nationalist feelings of outrage. (He called his resistance to the authority of the Commanding Officer a 'miniature *satyagraha*.')[20]

The First World War: The Indian Episode, April–11 August 1918

Gandhi had taken 'part in the war as a matter of duty.'[21] The incident with the military authorities in London and the compromise reached – thanks to the intervention of the Under-Secretary of State for India – showed that he understood the word 'duty' as the duty not of a citizen of the British Empire, but as the duty of an Indian citizen of the British Empire. Indian nationalism made him the obligatory – though unofficial – representative of the Indians. And duty called again in 1918, in altogether more difficult circumstances.

His faith in *ahimsa* had grown stronger, and modern warfare as such was now a real problem of conscience. Gandhi had by now more practice of *satyagraha*, from his local campaigns in Champaran, Ahmedabad, and Kheda, all in 1917 and the first half of 1918. He was fast becoming a first-class leader, at a time when victory was still undecided and Great Britain needed more men and support – his own included.

Gandhi was invited by the Viceroy to attend a War conference in Delhi in April 1918.[22] C. F. Andrews, another of Gandhi's dearest friends, objected to Gandhi going to the War Conference, on the same moral grounds cited by Henry Polak in 1914. However, Gandhi ignored the warning. Loyalty still prevailed over *ahimsa*, in spite of the doubts now assailing Gandhi in earnest.

A month before the Conference, he had confessed candidly (and very privately) to Mahadev Desai, his secretary: 'My mind refuses to be loyal to the British Empire and I have to make a strenuous effort to stem the tide of rebellion.' But, added Gandhi, 'a feeling deep down in me persists that India's good lies in [the] British connection.'[23]

Unhappy, constrained, and hesitant, Gandhi went nevertheless to the War Conference. There he found an ingenious way to soothe his scruples. He asked the Viceroy's permission to speak in Hindi, and this unusual nationalist request was granted, provided he spoke in English as well. The speech took one sentence: 'With a full sense of my responsibility I beg to support the resolution.'[24] It was the first time anybody had used an Indian language at a similar meeting, a matter of nationalistic pride and congratulation.

The resolution, however, was about recruiting soldiers for the war. Other Indian leaders opposed his move, people he knew, like Annie Besant, the president of India Home Rule, and M. A. Jinnah. In the correspondence that ensued between Gandhi and Jinnah, the former argued that the success of the recruiting campaign would ensure the coming of *swaraj*. But the latter thought otherwise and would not be convinced. Neither would the former be dissuaded. Gandhi, however, made his aim absolutely plain to the authorities.

A letter to the Viceroy set out the hope of Dominion status overtly and expressed the nationalist requirement of aspiring 'in the near future to be partners in the same sense as the Dominions overseas.' And there was a threat attached to the letter (29 April 1918):

> We are today outside the partnership. Ours is a consecration based on hope of better future. I should be untrue to you and to my country if I did not clearly and unequivocally tell you what that hope is. I do not bargain for its fulfilment, but you should know that disappointment of hope means disillusion.[25]

With that hope, Gandhi proceeded to raise about one hundred Indian soldiers for the war in Kheda. It was a hard-going and disappointing experience. He had chosen the place of his recent *satyagraha* campaign about the land tax, but the simple folk who had suffered from the imposition of the tax were less than keen to enlist. He met indifference and resistance. Finding lodgings, food, and transport was an unexpected problem. Gandhi's health suffered, and he collapsed on 11 August after a ten-week ordeal. But he had sent a list of one hundred names to the Viceroy, with his own at the top of the list, desperate to state that he was 'willing to stride up to German guns in France or wherever, but he would not carry a weapon.'

His grandson Rajmohan Gandhi adds the pertinent remark that the list did not include any of his sons, ages thirty, twenty-six, twenty, and eighteen, even though the youngest, Devadas (his father), 'seemed willing to enlist.'[26] But it had many names from the *ashram*, Gandhi's place of retreat – always a reserve of manpower in times of need.

The performance of duty in the summer of 1918 had broken Gandhi's health. He had undertaken the recruiting task with a clear expectation of India's rights to self-governance inside the Empire, and that to be achieved 'speedily.' The emphasis on duty was clearly fading out, the insistence on non-negotiable rights was coming to the fore. His nationalism would soon reach a point of no return. Gandhi had gone the full length of the loyalty exercise. Non-violence had taken a backseat, contributing to his physical collapse in the summer heat. By September 1918, England was winning the war, so no more soldiers were required, but Gandhi's allegiance to the British Empire was ebbing away.

5

VOLTE-FACE

Introspection highlights the decisive moments in our lives, when fortune and misfortune hang in the balance while we are making our choice. One such occasion happened to Gandhi when he was rudely thrown out of his first-class compartment onto the platform of Pietermaritzburg station because a 'white' man would not share it with him. The insufferable racial humiliation made a nationalist out of him, a nationalist of a sort, since he did not react against 'white' rule. The question to be considered now is whether there were, after the end of the First World War, some similar circumstances that tipped the scales of loyalty in favour of rebellion. When and why did his nationalism and his loyalty to Britain go their separate ways?

The Timing of the Volte-Face

Let us first call to mind the political developments that might have caused Gandhi's volte-face, in order to eliminate irrelevant, inconsequential, or tributary events.

The previous chapter could lead one to expect that yet another conflict would have turned the tide after the Great War, when Gandhi's bitter cup of ethics had been filled to the brim. But rebellion did not have to wait for the next war. Indeed, the problem of violence in war and the ensuing dilemma of conscience recurred in 1939 (the declaration of war), 1940 (the threat of a German invasion after Dunkirk) and 1942 (the threat of a Japanese invasion in India after the loss of

Burma) and were solved in a new way, which had, however, no bearing on his volte-face in 1920.[1]

The volte-face must have happened soon after Gandhi's experience of recruiting soldiers for the Army, sometime between August 1918 and 1 August 1920, the starting date of his first liberation movement.

By the time Gandhi recovered from the extreme exhaustion of his recruiting tour, political India was seized by a nationalist frenzy against the Rowlatt Bills and the unsatisfactory political reforms announced as early as July 1918. The nationalist agitation against the Rowlatt Bills provoked a sudden and sharp aggressiveness in Gandhi's political agenda from the end of 1918.

Indeed, after two months' recovery from being near death's door, Gandhi was fiercely agitating in a field where he had some experience: disobedience to objectionable legislation. His recovery had even possibly been accelerated by the confrontation: one tends to repeat and enjoy successful patterns of past behaviour, and Gandhi's pattern of defying tyrannical laws had so far not only been satisfactory, but also consistent with his allegiance to the British Government. The Rowlatt political exercise in organising demonstrations was simply a repeat performance of the South African experience on an all-India scale (even if, because of the short time available to the organisers, most of India remained unaffected).

Moreover, despite the agitation, there were no law to transgress. If Gandhi 'shook with rage'[2] in February 1919 on reading the two Rowlatt Bills, which prolonged the powers of the wartime Indian Defence Act, there was no way he could infringe the Rowlatt Act, which, like martial law, needed a state of emergency in order to become operative. The Rowlatt Act remained a ghost statute in the political armoury of the Government, safely locked away for the three years of its existence.

Nevertheless, when the Viceroy signed the Rowlatt Act on 22 March 1919, Gandhi did not take the provocation lying down. He had set up his own organisation, the Satyagraha Sabha, because the Indian National Congress had its doubts about his policies and did not support his quaint determination. Thus, he was able to organise a *hartal* (suspension of all business) on short notice in Delhi on 30 March and in the rest of India on 6 April 1919. In the Imperial Legislative

Council, Jinnah had done his bit for Indian nationalism by remonstrating loudly against the Act and then by tendering his resignation in protest.

The *hartal* was a great success, of a kind not seen since the Mutiny of 1857. However, while in South Africa no violence had spoiled the agitation – because of the comparatively small numbers of participants, the unity and cohesion in their ranks, and the respected dominance of their non-violent leader – rioting marred the nationwide protests, especially in the Punjab. A week after the *hartal*, on 13 April 1919, General Dyer, in a show of strength at Amritsar, massacred the peaceful demonstrators assembled in the walled Jallianwalla Bagh in defiance of martial law (379 killed, 1,000 wounded).

On 18 April 1919, Gandhi suspended the movement. He acknowledged a 'Himalayan miscalculation.' But the mistake in question, he thought, did not concern his misplaced trust in the Empire, but the unpreparedness to cope with outbursts of violence from his people. As for his reaction to the gory execution of a defenceless crowd at Amritsar, Gandhi was prepared to wait for the results of two enquiries: one, non-official, led by himself, which took three months, and the other by the Hunter Commission (September 1919 to May 1920).

Rebellion, obviously, was not yet in the cards – but it was unobtrusively in the making. As had happened before with the birth of *satyagraha*, and would happen thereafter in more occasions than one – the inspiration occurred as a stroke of genius (23 November 1919).

One month before the December 1919 session of the Indian National Congress, Gandhi mentioned the word 'non-cooperation' for the first time in public at a Muslim meeting in Delhi. Or rather, failing to find the corresponding word in his still rough Hindustani, Gandhi used a single English sentence while addressing the meeting: 'We can respond with non-cooperation.'

He was suggesting an alternative to the boycott of British goods demanded by a Muslim leader. Admittedly, non-cooperation was to be the call and strategy of Gandhi's new kind of nationalism and the name of his rebellious campaign to be launched on 1 August 1920. But in November 1919, Gandhi obviously had no plan to offer, and his listeners were only voicing protests and advocating a waiting policy. Not only could he not find a corresponding word in his listeners' tongue – which showed that he had had little time to think the suggestion over – but, one month later (December 1919), at Amritsar, at the very place of the infamous massacre in April 1919, he was still supporting (with Jinnah's help) the Government's political agenda and the elections due in November 1920.

The volte-face therefore did not take place in 1919. The nationalist protest against the Rowlatt Act – the first of its kind on an all-India scale and the shortest (30 March–18 April 1919) – was not rebellion, nor the trigger to rebellion. The ensuing Reforms Act was acceptable to him. Seconded by Jinnah, he moved the resolution in its favour at the session of the Amritsar Congress in December 1919. This was about the last time these two political figures (who had had politically so much in common so far) worked hand in hand, Jinnah using the deferential term 'Mahatma Gandhi.'

The point of no return, therefore, clearly took place in the first half of 1920, that is, between the Amritsar Congress, when Gandhi supported the Government's policies (December 1919) and the launching of the Non-cooperation campaign on 1 August 1920.

The launch was preceded by the usual, and by now familiar, procedure of petitions, the filing of complaints, representations to the authorities, and negotiations with the administration and the government's departments in a kind of give-and-take that stopped at what was considered essential. These preliminary steps had the merit of allowing for time to organise further and more radical opposition.[3] If no satisfactory settlement could be reached, a written warning would then be issued to the authorities.

In this case, the challenge to the government was officially conveyed to the Viceroy in June of that year. Gandhi wrote him a threatening letter, which sounded like the tolling of a past brand of nationalism:

> Your Excellency,
>
> As one... who claims to be a devoted well-wisher of the British Empire... I hope Your Excellency will give those who have accepted my advice and myself the credit for being actuated by nothing less than a stern sense of duty.

And the letter asked for a repeat performance of a Viceroy leading

> the agitation yourself as did your distinguished predecessor at the time of the South African trouble. But if you cannot see your way to do so... non-cooperation becomes a dire necessity.[4]

The *Casus Belli*

That was in June 1920. But what Indian cause was it that demanded – in 'dire necessity' – the withdrawal of cooperation from the powerful Empire?

The cause was not Indian – but Turkish, or rather, Ottoman. Moreover, it did not concern India, but the Middle East. Rather amazingly, Gandhi was trying to save from dismemberment the temporal jurisdiction of the Ottoman Caliph over Arabia, Mesopotamia, and Palestine for an empire that had chosen the wrong side in the war. Polak and Kallenbach, his two main allies in the last political *satyagraha* in South Africa, must have been aghast at the news. Polak, living now in England, openly said so (March 1920); the other held his peace, but failed to join Gandhi in India as had been intended in 1914, and settled instead in South Africa. Both were Jews and, therefore, ill at ease with the whole idea of some kind of non-violent jihad to perpetuate Muslim rule over Jerusalem.

Gandhi was now happy to use the word 'duty' in Hindi, conveying perhaps a new sense, a new direction of what this duty might be. *Dharma*, indeed, means not just doing one's duty in one's own life, but encompasses righteousness and religion, moral law, and personal and social morality, all in one: 'If I had not joined the Khilafat movement, I think I would have lost everything. In joining it, I have followed what I especially regard as my *dharma*... I am uniting Hindus and Muslims.'[5]

However, in spite of calling the Caliphate issue 'the question of questions,' Gandhi was not thinking of the Turks or of the defence of their interests in the Middle East. He was concerned only about the feelings of Indian nationals, namely, Indian Muslims, for their

Caliph. Unlike many Muslims from Arabia and Palestine, who were relieved by the lifting of the Ottoman yoke, the Indian Muslims were incensed by the 'danger to Islam' and the Sultan's loss of temporal power over Jerusalem and other pilgrimage sites. Gandhi had made his motivation clear: 'If I were not interested in the Indian Mahomedans, I would not interest myself in the welfare of the Turks.'[6]

Spelling out the cause of the Muslim chagrin seemed of little consequence to Gandhi, except that it was of religious importance (a plus with Gandhi), and he was not prepared to argue the pros and cons of the Caliphate issue. He was anxious only to side with the Indian Muslims: 'The Muslims claim Palestine as an integral part of *Jazirut-ul-Arab* [Arabia, Mesopotamia, Syria, and Palestine]. They are bound to retain its custody, as an injunction of the Prophet.'[7]

Why should Gandhi come to the succour of the Sultan of Turkey? It was only too obvious, as Gandhi had emphasized: for both Hindus and Muslims, it was the opportunity of a lifetime which would 'not recur for another hundred years.'[8]

The Critical Period of January–June 1920

At this juncture, Gandhi had the motive: Hindu–Muslim unity. He also had the inspiration about the way to fight: non-cooperation. But did he have worthy allies?

He met them unexpectedly at the Amritsar Congress session as he was asking for the endorsement of the Reforms proposals. As it happened, to entice the Congress to approve the Reforms, the Government had offered a Christmas gift: the timely amnesty of political prisoners.

Three Maulanas were thus released on the eve of the Amritsar Congress, including the two brothers Ali, who were soon promoted by Gandhi as his own 'blood brothers.' The third Maulana was equally concerned about the fate of the Caliphate, but while the Alis were believers in jihad, Maulana Abul Kalam Azad favoured *hijrat*.[9] Years later, he was propped up as the Muslim figurehead of the Congress party when the blood link with the two Alis was severed.

The brothers, Mohamed and Shaukat Ali, who had been interned since 1915, attended the Amritsar Congress (December 1919). Gandhi felt attracted to their religious determination and youthful enthusiasm, and they reciprocated the friendship. They became very close friends in 1920. Gandhi started advising them, and they, in the absence of any useful alternative, agreed to shed their violent tactics – such as fomenting an invasion of India by Muslims from Afghanistan.[10]

Instead, Mohamed Ali followed the by now well-established Gandhian practice of leading a deputation to England. In March 1920, he pleaded the cause of the Caliph in London and reminded Lloyd George of his promise 'not to deprive Turkey of the rich and renowned lands of Asia Minor,' made on 5 January 1918 while recruiting Muslim Indians to fight other Muslims.

As Gandhi succumbed to the extremist views of his Ali brothers, he fell under the spell of Saraladevi Chaudhurani, 'who had trained Bengali youth in militant patriotism.'[11] This episode took place from January to mid-June 1920, when, on the eve of launching his *satyagraha*, he renounced the idea of a 'spiritual marriage' with her, under the pressure of his entourage. A strong nationalist pull from these sentimental sources made him reconsider his position in relation to the British Empire.

Gandhi now had the impulse – the strong link with the Muslim Khilafatist leaders – and the unique opportunity to enrol Muslim forces behind a Hindu leader. But where was he to find the organisation necessary to sustain the campaign? This Muslim line of thought and argument could hardly go very far in persuading Hindus to join the Khilafatists in order to save the possessions of the Caliph of Turkey. The Congress had yet to be convinced to join the fray.

The Ali brothers relied on their Khilafat Committees for support, but Gandhi had no secular nationwide organisation worth the name to rely on – although he was busy at writing a new constitution for the Indian National Congress after the Amritsar session. That constitution would give the party a strong organisational framework with a powerful Working Committee of fifteen members and a network of provincial, district, and rural and urban committees, changing profoundly the party's middle-class debating character.

Meanwhile, after failing to get a full grip on the Congress, he accepted the presidency of the All India Home Rule League at the end of April 1920, changing its name to Swarajya Sabha (Assembly) and its creed to '*swaraj*' instead of 'Self-government within the Empire.' But we already know from this incident that Gandhi did not exclude the possibility of staying in the Empire. Explaining his decision in a letter to Jinnah, who had strong objection to the change of words, Gandhi had stressed that it left open the question of India's link with the Empire.[12] Indeed, when the Congress adopted the new constitution, the words 'within the Empire' were included – thereby avoiding the contentious issue.

The Turning Point (May 1920) and the End of Allegiance

The turning point came on 14 May 1920. The Treaty of Sèvres, mimicking the part played by the ticket collector in Pietermaritzburg, evicted the Indian Muslims' claim from the peace settlement. Conveniently, the Hunter Enquiry on the Punjab disturbances produced its report at the end of the same month. Rejected as unsatisfactory by Gandhi, it became the 'Punjab wrong' to be added to the 'Khilafat wrong,' thus putting the weight of the offended Hindu community behind the leader of the Khilafatist movement.

On a different tack, Gandhi fully exploited the Punjab agitation in the wake of the Jallianwalla Bagh outcry to force the Congress's hand. At Allahabad, on 9 June 1920, he further secured the formal approval of the Khilafat Committee meeting to start a campaign of Non-cooperation.

To put pressure on the Congress to endorse, in turn, this policy, he offered it as a fait accompli and decided to launch the *satyagraha* on 1 August 1920, before the special Calcutta session convened in September. The Congress was then invited to adopt 'gradual' non-cooperation, including a boycott of the coming November elections, elections that Gandhi had approved of at the 1919 Amritsar Congress. His tactics worked, and Gandhi's strategy was endorsed.

The Calcutta decision had to be confirmed by the regular 1920 December session. It was. To the redress of the 'Khilafat wrong' and the

'Punjab wrong' (and to win the Congress over to his views), Gandhi had added a demand for *swaraj.* A promise to the delegates to get '*swaraj* in one year' if they followed him behind the non-cooperation banner that made him, in December 1920, the undisputed Congress leader in charge of the Hindu–Muslim nationalist movement for independence.

The year 1921 did not bring *swaraj*, only its promise. But this promise was a major stepping stone on the path to independence. By the beginning of 1922, Gandhi had organised a no-tax campaign, ready to be launched in Bardoli (with special emphasis on non-violence), that could later be extended to the rest of India. Expectation of a great surge to come made the non-cooperators hold their breaths.

At the annual session in Ahmedabad in December 1921, the Congress decided to launch the Bardoli campaign in January 1922, in Gandhi's native Gujarat. The League held its own December session, as usual at the same time and place as the Congress meeting; Jinnah attended the League meeting. On his urging, Gandhi followed him to an All Parties Conference in Bombay to consider the 'Bombay proposals,' asking the Viceroy to release all prisoners and convene a Round Table Conference, and asking Gandhi to call off the Bardoli exercise. The reluctance of both the Viceroy and Gandhi to clinch a deal ended Jinnah's meaningful effort.

An ultimatum was sent to the Viceroy on 1 February, announcing that the Bardoli campaign would start in eleven days. But unexpectedly, Gandhi suspended the movement on 10 February 1922. A police station had been set on fire in the remote place of Chauri-Chaura, and twenty-two policemen had been hacked to death as they tried to escape the flames (5 February 1922).

It was no easy decision for Gandhi. His son Devadas focused his attention on the incident and on the necessity of responding to the violence of the non-cooperators. He hesitated, but did not consult before he suspended the campaign. Violence, as in the Rowlatt agitation, was once more the reason of the suspension, this time shocking into disbelief and resentment the leaders of the campaign, in and out of prison, and, most of all, the Muslims expecting the final push. The discrepancy between the small number of victims of the Chauri-Chaura mob and the disproportionate confrontation due to start at Bardoli seemed to hang in the air. Ink was spilled over the momentous decision. The Mahatma explained that in the same way that you can judge whether the rice is cooked by tasting just one grain in the cooking pot, he could ascertain from the isolated Chauri-Chaura incident the violent potentiality of the situation. Indeed, judging from the events of partition days, it did not take much to cause a riot in India, and Gandhi may well have been right in taking that view (although riots in 1922 might have prevented the wholesale massacres of 1947). His grandson Rajmohan Gandhi, though, points to a more truly relevant explanation, which has been so far overlooked: 'Gandhi had suspected that the suspension was going to be inevitable before long, for Mustafa Kemal [who would soon expel from Turkey the Sultan, for whom he had no use] had knocked the bottom out of the Khilafat issue. To suspend out of moral necessity made political sense.'[13]

Turkey's Caliph had shaken India's nationalist vigour. Turkey's Kemal Ataturk shattered India's nationalist dream. Gandhi was arrested for inciting disaffection for the Government, and sentenced to jail for six years, he joined 30,000 non-cooperators behind bars (10 March 1922). At the trial, Gandhi said:

> I hold it to be a virtue to be disaffected towards a Government which in its totality has done more harm to India than any previous system . . .
>
> I am here to invite and cheerfully submit to the highest penalty that can be inflicted upon me for what in law is a deliberate crime and what appears to me to be the highest duty of a citizen.[14]

Gandhi had pleaded guilty to the crime of disaffection, which is the best term to describe the state of his nationalism at the end of the loyalty period. Yet the issue of *swaraj* within – or without – the Empire had not been settled. As in April 1920, when Gandhi changed the creed of the Home Rule League, explaining to Jinnah in writing that the Empire was still an option, the independence issue was conceived of as the achievement of self-government rather than promotion to Dominion status. Dominion status or no Dominion status – the severance of constitutional links with Britain was to be the topic of the next decade.

Thus in 1920, the 'constitutional' means to *swaraj* in the Congress constitution had been replaced by 'peaceful' and 'non-violent' means, supposedly anti-constitutional. In South Africa, Gandhi had behaved in a similar fashion: while proclaiming loudly his allegiance to the Empire, he chose to disobey some of its laws; in 1920, the nationalist in him had gone only one step further, asking for *swaraj* within or without the Empire.

The emphasis in 1920 was not yet on the end – complete independence outside the Empire – but only on the constitutional means to an unspecified objective. Gandhi easily shifted from one to another, from means to end and from end to means, as he experienced and believed in the cohesion of one to the other. Only the means had to be non-violent; the end would follow like a plant from a seed: 'The Khilafat movement is a great churning of the sea of India. Why should we be concerned with what it will produce? All that we should consider is whether the movement itself is a pure and worthy cause.'[15]

The green metaphor did not always bring out the results intended. With hindsight, we can see that the seed of the Caliphate agitation matured into the tree of Pakistan. And we shall see Gandhi, the sower, shuddering at the result of his well-meant endeavours.

PART III

NATIONALISM AND REBELLION

Figure 7: Gandhi and Rebellion

6

THE WAIT-AND-SEE INTERLUDE

With *swaraj* receding from view after the suspension of the non-cooperation movement, Gandhi's nationalism entered a new phase. Previously, his loyalty had engendered disaffection, disaffection had engendered rebellion, and rebellion had engendered arrest. Now his release engendered political competition among the nationalist leaders, with the Congress in disarray, the Caliph in flight, and the Muslims in grief. Gandhi, the rebel, had lost the first round of his fight in the liberation movement. Now a fighter out of jail after his release from prison, he prepared for the second. He entered a struggle of a different sort, to prevail over the policies of other nationalist leaders, and he could achieve that objective only through compromise. His first task would be to reclaim the Congress as his own.

Henceforth, still bent on *swaraj*, but having lost substantial power in the Congress, Gandhi set about regaining both, *swaraj* and the Congress – *swaraj* through the Congress. The reconquest of the Indian National Congress was pursued over the period extending from his release from imprisonment in 1924 to the next political campaign of 1930.

That half-decade could be compared to the trough between two high sea waves. Mahatma Gandhi had been riding powerfully on the crest of the Hindu–Muslim Non-cooperation movement (1918–22). He would be surfing the mighty surge for independence in 1931. But between the end of one campaign and the beginning of the other, he plunged into an abyss of opposition to his policies.

It is well worth analysing how he recovered his leadership of Indian politics, since the process throws a new light on Gandhi's nationalism. The interlude brought out some interesting political features and tactics. His belief in non-violence, his thirst for independence, and his reliance on the party as the indispensable tool to that end moved him to lead the country relentlessly forward in his own personal way.

The Three Prongs of Gandhi's Policy

To recover his political fortunes, he relied through that period on a three-pronged strategy. The first and foremost prong was aimed at maintaining, at all costs, his party's cohesion, even to the detriment of his own political desiderata: his trump card had been his conquest of the main political party. The second endeavoured to safeguard Hindu–Muslim unity, which had made the Congress such a formidable organisation: an ace up Gandhi's sleeve. The third concentrated on building up his own political strength in rural India through the policy of the spinning wheel: the Congress party was being transformed from an elitist body into a populist organisation, reaching out to the countryside for the first time. The political manoeuvrings of his nationalist recovery were built on these three requirements.

Indeed, at his release, Gandhi picked up all three major political threads that had contributed to his dominant political role in 1919–22. But obstacles blocked his way in every direction. First, he had to accept, very unwillingly, the different views of two revered leaders, Motilal Nehru and C. R. Das, who had been elected to the new Legislative Councils, and flouted his non-cooperation policy. Second, he wrestled with the grievous consequences of the abolition of the Caliphate, which soon ended the Hindu–Muslim alliance so dear to his heart. Third, he could not prevail in imposing his spinning requirements on his reluctant party.

He wanted to achieve progress on these three fronts equally, but circumstances and the loss of his political leadership at his release from jail made him review his priorities, and the party came undoubtedly at the top of the list.

Thus, even as he was regaining control of his party, he shrank from making a deal with his former Khilafatist friend, Mohamed Ali, and with Jinnah as well, for fear of disrupting the fragile cohesion of the Congress – an unfortunate aggravation to these Muslim leaders. It is worth noting that the priority he gave to the cohesive force of his party over other considerations date from the failure of the Non-cooperation campaign. Thereafter, the unity of the party prevailed over other interests on many important occasions.

Gandhi targeted his efforts on the Indian National Congress because that organisation was his all-India ladder, the tool for the realisation of his dream to speak for every Indian in the country. To that end, he showed great adaptability and compromise, great patience, and skilful handling of his party. Flexible on some issues and stubborn on others, he managed to achieve his purpose.

His strategy was not always easy for others to follow or to understand. His co-workers showed incomprehension at the sudden shifts on particular issues. In a letter to Gandhi dated 11 January 1928, Jawaharlal Nehru wrote:

> I admire action and daring and courage and I found them all in you in a superlative degree... During the N.C.O. [non-cooperation] period you were supreme; you were in your element and automatically you took the right step. But since you came out of prison something seems to have gone wrong and you have been very obviously ill at ease. You will remember how within months or even weeks you repeatedly changed your attitude – the Juhu statements, the AICC meeting at Ahmedabad and after, etc. – and most of us were left in utter bewilderment. That bewilderment has continued since then.[1]

For health reasons, Gandhi served only two years of his jail term. Diagnosed with acute appendicitis, he had been operated on in a British hospital and then released. As Gandhi convalesced at Juhu Beach, on the Indian Ocean, he reflected on how to tackle three issues: the split in his party on the issue of cooperation or non-cooperation, the threat to Hindu–Muslim unity from the secular reforms in Turkey, and his hold on rural India for the advancement and reform of 'indianity.' Physical recuperation and political prudence made the respite welcome.

The Challenge of the Congress Pro-changers

Gandhi had probably expected to resume his political work from where he had left it in 1922. For in the first interview given after his release (5 February 1924), he declared: 'I shall resume my activities for the attainment of *swaraj* just as soon as I am restored to complete health.'[2]

Re-assuming activities for the attainment of *swaraj* was not going to be a simple matter. The word 'activities' even suggested the hope and possibility of resuming civil disobedience. On 14 February 1924, he expressed his 'belief in the efficiency and righteousness of civil disobedience.'[3]

After the arrest of its leader in March 1922, the Indian National Congress had been torn by a choice of tactics: either to seek power through elections or persevere in boycotting them. Boycotts had been at the heart of the Non-cooperation campaign, now suspended. Institutions such as government offices, courts, schools, and universities had been targeted with some success, as well as liquor shops and foreign cloth, with a biting decrease in the Lancashire trade in cotton and in the Government's revenue from its monopoly on alcohol. An extension of the boycotts to service in the army and the payment of taxes had had no time to materialise, but had threateningly been kept in abeyance.

Did the suspension of the campaign mean a reversal to the *status quo ante*? Gandhi seems to have understood his decision that way: suspension was no termination. However, being chivalrous, he was bound to feel ill at ease at the prospect of harassing a Government that had shown him leniency.

On the political front, new elections were held in November 1923, in implementation of the Montagu-Chelmsford Reforms of 1919. These were the Reforms that Gandhi had approved of before he started the

Non-cooperation movement, since the Government's proposals, 'inadequate as they were, marked a new era of hope in the life of India.' On this issue, the party came to be divided between the so-called Pro-changers and No-changers. The Pro-changers wished to lift the existing boycott on elections, the No-changers wanted to maintain it. The Pro-changers took the view that it was advisable at this stage to enter the Councils, even if only to boycott them once inside. The No-changers refused to abandon the policy of non-cooperation to gain what they considered illusory power.[4]

These Pro-changers were led by Motilal Nehru – Jawaharlal Nehru's father – and Chitta Ranjan Das, who had been released from prison in June and August 1922, respectively. A debate between the Pro- and the No-changers took place in Gaya, in December 1922. The Pro-changers were defeated, but they formed their own faction inside the Congress, calling themselves – rather defiantly – the Swaraj Party (called the 'Congress-Khilafat Swaraj Party' before the Caliphate was abolished in March 1924). A compromise was reached with the No-changers, which allowed the candidates to try their luck in the November 1923 elections, provided they did not claim to be speaking for the Congress.

The electoral results were encouraging, and the Swaraj Party became firmly rooted inside the Congress. But the sense of unity was lost with the contest between No-changers and Pro-changers. Could Gandhi heal the rift?

Time had moved on: in the country, the yearning for a fight with the Government had gone. The Pro-changers having done reasonably well in the elections, M. Nehru and C. R. Das, now leaders in the Central Legislative Assembly, took their seats on 31 January 1924, just a few weeks before Gandhi's release. In combination with M. A. Jinnah and the group of Independents, they constituted a majority. The forty Swarajists and the twenty-three Independents called themselves the Nationalist Bloc. They could outvote the thirty-six official members, even if they were powerless to enforce a change of policy. This coalition was, however, short-lived.

Ironically, *swaraj* and the road to independence meant different things to different people: non-cooperation for some, cooperation for others, or non-cooperation once inside the Councils. But the word had a power of its own. The '*swaraj* in one year,' promised by Gandhi at the 1920 Congress in Nagpur if non-cooperation were adopted, had made a new and powerful appeal to Indian nationalist sentiments.

A few visits by Motilal Nehru in March 1924 to Juhu Beach, where Gandhi was convalescing – one visit lasting several days – confirmed the divergence of views of these two main political leaders. In an undated letter to Mahadev Desai, his secretary, written within the month of his release, Gandhi confessed that Motilal Nehru could not convert him, and that he too could not convert him.'[5]

Nursing his wound, Gandhi decided to wait and see for three months. It was not the first time that prudence had dictated restraint on his part. In 1915, returning from South Africa, he had followed the advice of Gokhale, his political guru (who had helped him in his dealings with General Smuts), by taking a vow of 'political' silence for a year while testing the political waters. This time he would rest for three months in the breezes off the Indian Ocean, recovering from both his operation and the anguish caused by the Pro-changers' shift of policy. The preface to the relevant volume of the *Collected Works of Mahatma Gandhi* discusses 'the burden of making correct decisions in a situation which seemed beyond control that probably taxed the inner resources of Gandhiji.'

Tensions within the Hindu–Muslim Alliance at Gandhi's Release

The Congress suffered another irretrievable loss. Muslims were now drifting away from the party, and from Gandhi. Understandably, the Muslim-Hindu alliance, forged for the defence of the Ottoman Caliphate, was being undermined by the process of secularisation in Turkey. Gandhi expected the Muslim friendship to endure longer, however, because of the warm and brotherly entente prevailing between himself and the two leaders of the Khilafatist Party, the brothers Mohamed and Shaukat Ali, and because of the devotion he had shown to their cause.

Truly, Gandhi, embarrassed by their impatience and carelessness with non-violence, had constantly striven to rein them in, insisting on a no-tolerance policy on violence: 'not even a single murder by any of us.'[6] He knew too well what they thought and preached openly, namely, that Gandhi's adherence to non-violence was 'for reasons of principle and [theirs] for reasons of policy.'

In May 1921, Gandhi had saved the Ali brothers from arrest by persuading them to send the Viceroy an apology for praising violence. Nonetheless, in July 1921, the brothers tried to force Gandhi's hand on the question of the boycott of the army, stating in public that it was wrong to serve in the forces. This time, Gandhi felt he had to defend them, and the unapologetic brothers were arrested. On 5 October 1921, the Working Committee of the Indian National Congress at Bombay congratulated the Ali brothers on their prosecution and called for the withdrawal of all government employees, military and civilian. As a later recompense and approval, Mohamed Ali was, on release, proclaimed President of the Indian National Congress for the year 1924, only a few months before the abolition of the Caliphate by the Turks.

From 1921, Hindu–Muslim relations suffered repeatedly from an increase of tensions between these two communities. Rioting intensified. In 1921, the Muslim Moplah community rose up against the Government in a very serious and armed confrontation, the Muslim peasantry murdering its Hindu landlords.

Another reason for the break with the Alis was the difference of religious outlook between Gandhi and the two Muslims. Gandhi's tolerance in religious matters could not extend to stoning as punishment for adultery, or to forcible conversions. The latter became a practical issue with the steadily increasing number of riots between Hindus and Muslims, and forced conversions to Islam and reconversions to Hinduism.

Gandhi was faced with another fateful decision, one of prime interest to Muslims. 'Problems are far more perplexing today,' Gandhi wrote to the Khilafatist leader Mohamed Ali. The very existence of the Ottoman Caliphate was in question, since it was no longer in the hands of the European powers, as in 1920 (Treaty of Sèvres), but at the mercy of the Turks themselves. In pursuit of his policy of making

Turkey a secularist state, Ataturk had the Caliph deposed and the Caliphate abolished in March 1924. Gandhi, recently released, but still in the Poona hospital, wrote enigmatically to Mohamed Ali from his hospital bed (11 March 1924): 'The future of Islam rests in the hands of the Mussalmans of India.'

What did he mean to say? In an interview in March 1924, he rejected the possibility of the King of Hedjaz replacing the Ottoman Caliph, on the grounds that Indian Muslims considered him 'a stooge of the English.' Answering a question about the deposition of the Caliph, Gandhi concluded: 'The King of the Hedjaz won't do. All Islam feels he is a British representative.'[7]

What was he then to do? He thought of the setback to the Khilafatist movement from an Indian perspective. He advised the Alis to concentrate on the 'quality' of their supporters rather than on the 'quantity' of their workers: 'I know your own difficulties about the *khilafat* work. As for the *swaraj* movement so for the *khilafat,* I think we shall find we shall have to rely upon the quality of a few workers than the quantity of many.'[8]

Mohamed Ali, as President of the Indian National Congress, decided to go to Turkey with his brother to alter the course of history, as he had tried to do at with his unsuccessful meeting with Lloyd George at the beginning of 1920 on the same issue. But the brothers failed to obtain the necessary documents to enter Turkey, and the visit had to be dropped.

The Khilafatist conferences, offices, and committees persevered ineffectively in their work. Accusations of embezzlement marred the reputation of the organisation, large funds collected in the name of the Caliphate having disappeared inexplicably. Three months of the 'wait and see' policy were to prove a great relief to Gandhi. It gave him time to wash his hands off the *khilafat* issue.

The Hold over the Country, or the Pursuit of Indianity

Gandhi benefited from the veneration shown to sages and ascetics in Hinduism. He looked the saintly man he was, an iconic figure scantily dressed in a loincloth and shawl, looking unmistakenly Indian.

He had spun his own white garments, setting an example for others, since his recent rediscovery and promotion of the spinning wheel.[9] Unflaggingly, he taught the millions two lessons.

The first lesson, on non-violence, or *ahimsa*, was preached day in and day out, but was too often ignored and sidelined.[10] The other lesson lauded the duty of spinning for the sake of the poor. The promotion of *khadi* (cloth made of spun cotton) was now associated with Gandhi and his political party as a sort of party trademark. Delegates displayed their allegiance to the Mahatma by wearing 'the livery of freedom,' as Jawaharlal Nehru described it once.[11] Because *khadi* was so strongly associated with Gandhi and India, the promotion, production, and wearing of spun-yarn was in itself the best publicity for the Mahatma and his political work.

The spinning wheel unobtrusively highlighted the cultural identity of the nation and was far from being the fad it appeared to be. It became a means to an end: the affirmation of the anti-Western, anti-modern civilisation praised in his 1909 pamphlet *Hind Swaraj*. His support of the teeming millions made political sense while also promoting the strong and traditional eastern identity of his beloved nation.

But many in the party had different views and expressed firm objections to spinning as a policy. Such leaders as Motilal Nehru and C. R. Das had no time for plying the *charkha*, a simplified version of the spinning wheel. This new, economic Gandhian requirement of spinning became another strongly divisive issue in the Indian National Congress.

At the time, Gandhi spoke of a 'special bond' between himself and the masses. This bond can be identified as 'indianity': 'Between the masses and myself there is a bond which defies description, but is nevertheless felt alike by them and by me.'[12] How best was Gandhi to preserve and strengthen that bond, the basis of his political appeal and power? He set about restructuring the Congress in order to consolidate his own position in the party. For the three months of his wait-and-see policy, the Mahatma concocted 'drastic and definitive views on Congress for an [early] future.'[13] He found the solution in spinning, an activity both practical and symbolic. The poor could clothe themselves, working during the season when they stayed idle under the scorching heat. The leaders and their supporters were to spin as a sign of solidarity with rural India, showing thereby their adherence to the Gandhian way to *swaraj* and, therefore, connecting spinning to the main political source of power, the Congress party.

Hopeful, Gandhi looked forward to the meeting of the All-India Congress Committee in Ahmedabad in June 1924 to resume his leadership of the national movement on these terms.

7

STOOPING TO RECONQUER

There is a striking contrast between the Mahatma released from prison in 1924 and the Mahatma of 1931. Picture him recovering from an operation for acute appendicitis, and then walking briskly at the head of a crowd of devotees for some twenty miles a day to break the salt laws. Hear the ridicule poured on him for suspending a campaign that looked so promising, and then the acclamation that greeted the theatrical setting of the 'salt march' to the sea. Compare the harsh criticism he suffered in his party for failing it in its hour of need, and then its willingness to let him once again decide, on its behalf, what to do, how to do it, and when. Measure the step taken from reacting to a small outburst of not unusual Indian violence in a remote village, to his promising (in 1930) that unavoidable violence would not curtail any future non-violent campaign.

The Mahatma did not leave the British hospital cured of enthusiasm for more political work, nor was he bent on devoting all his time to social issues only – such as the eradication of untouchability. Nor did he want an honorary backseat in politics, a position better suited to his spiritual halo. This Mahatma would not give up politics. From his release, Gandhi worked unrelentingly to regain his political ascendancy.

When, in 1931, Gandhi managed to reach the pinnacle of political power for the second time, he was treated with great reverence not only by his followers, but by the Viceroy himself – to the disgust of

Churchill, who described disparagingly the 'alarming and nauseating' scene of 'Mr Gandhi, a seditious Middle Temple lawyer, now posing as a fakir of a type well-known in the East, striding half-naked up the steps of the Vice-regal palace . . . to parley on equal terms with the representative of the King-Emperor.'[1]

The road to political recovery, in the case of Gandhi, was not straight, but sinuous, and its meanders are of special interest because of his non-violent methods and integrity. How did he do it? The Mahatma wanted political power, as we shall see, although he appeared indifferent to it. Or rather, he was both detached and indifferent, yet he fought stubbornly for it, faithful as he was to his interpretation of the Gita, his favourite spiritual book, which counselled detachment from the fruit of one's actions.

Thus he stooped to reconquer. The mechanisms of his strategy unfurled, one by one, the previously selected items of Gandhi's relations: with the Congress, with India as a whole, and with his Muslim partners in particular.

From May 1924 to December 1925, Gandhi wrestled unsuccessfully with the Pro-changers intent on cooperation with the Government They called themselves Swarajists, entrenched as they became, in Gandhi's absence, inside the Congress. He also turned aside from the Muslim alliance put in jeopardy by the end of the Caliphate, a breaking-up adding to the disunity and destabilisation of his party. Nonetheless, he kept firmly to two convictions.

The first was the belief that as a convinced non-cooperator, he could not stay in the Indian National Congress alongside the cooperators. This explains two contrary moves on his part in this period: first, he tried to neutralise the Swarajists inside the Congress; failing that, he left the party to them, in a move he described as making the Congress 'a predominantly political body.'[2]

The second unshakable conviction was the need to maintain good Hindu–Muslim relations after the abolition of the Caliphate, now a lost cause. The Khilafatist leaders had adopted non-violence solely ad hoc, and not as a matter of principle: the two Ali brothers always took a light-hearted view of Muslim violence. As the number of riots increased between the Muslim and Hindu communities, so did suspicion and distrust. In April 1924, many were shocked by what seemed to be a derogatory remark about the Mahatma from Mohamed Ali, who was then President of the Indian National Congress. He was reported to have said that Gandhi was 'lower than the most wretched Muslim.' Gandhi brushed aside the sting of the controversial statement, claiming that Mohamed Ali had meant to say he considered 'the religious principles of an adulterous Muslim to be better than Mahatma Gandhi's religious principles.'[3]

The Mahatma never lost sight of another consideration, one capping the problems of unity in his party and unity with the Muslims: how to impose a policy of *khadi* (hand-woven cloth) and spinning as proof of, and testimony to, India's allegiance to his constructive programme. Failure to make headway on these three fronts was to provoke a stalemate, with Gandhi exiting politics proper for a full year during 1926.

The Primacy of the Party's Unity

By May 1924, Gandhi had made up his mind. He would try to expel from the party the Pro-changers with the help of the No-changers. In an open contest, he would defeat – and oust from the party's leadership – the partisans of entering the Councils on the one hand, and on the other, refurbish, with his faithful party colleagues, the policy of non-cooperation. He stood firmly on his nationalist ground, confident in the outcome.

However, as we shall see, he had mis-assessed their relative strength. This made him first change tactics after the Ahmedabad vote on his resolutions in June 1924, then sign on to the Calcutta Agreement (6 November 1924) with his political opponents, and, later still, offer another compromise at the Belgaum Congress in December 1924. Entering this political labyrinth is an interesting experience.

In a first tactical move, Gandhi, after the three months of reflection he had allowed himself, resumed consultations with Motilal Nehru and C. R. Das. When they failed to reach any agreement, their break was made public. On 22 May 1924, Gandhi and the Pro-changers explained their differences in separate statements before the All-India

Congress Committee (AICC) meeting in Ahmedabad, which was to take place in June.

Gandhi, in his own statement given to the Associated Press of India said *inter alia*: 'Council-entry is inconsistent with non-cooperation as I conceive it... To be out {of the legislative bodies} is far more advantageous to the country than to be in them.' A week later, he was looking forward confidently to the AICC meeting: 'I feel that both parties can effectively help each other only if they work separately.'[4]

On the same day, the Pro-changers also issued their statement on Council-entry. They set out their policy on entering the Councils:

> We remain unconvinced by his {Gandhi's} reasoning... Council-entry is and can be thoroughly consistent with the principle of non-cooperation as we understand that principle to be...
>
> Within the Legislative bodies we must continue:
>
> (1) to throw out budgets
> (2) to throw out all proposals for legislative enactments by which the bureaucracy proposes to consolidate its power
> (3) to introduce all resolutions, measures and bills which are necessary for the healthy growth of our national life... {including resolutions} in support of the constructive program of the Congress
> (4) to prevent the drain of public wealth from India.[5]

As a sweetener to Gandhi, the statement mentioned a return to the policy of civil disobedience with the Mahatma if their policy was seen to be 'impossible to work.' In short, there were two parties in the Congress, but there was also an 'abiding and fundamental unity amongst both parties in the Congress.'[6]

Gandhi went to the All-India Congress Committee meeting in Ahmedabad well prepared for the fight. He planned to maintain the unity of the Congress, but he wanted to exclude the Pro-changers from its executive organs. And how could he do that? He had been thinking about it for months, and now he tried to restructure the Congress by making the holding of a responsible position in the party conditional. The – admittedly odd – condition was such office holders were to spin for half an hour each day and thus contribute 2,000 yards of well-spun yarn to the *khadi* association each month.

The Ahmedabad Congress, instead of being the resounding victory Gandhi expected, saw his humiliation. The four resolutions he submitted, including the resolution on spinning, were approved, but by a narrow majority. He knew he had failed in his hope of excluding the Pro-changers from 'the elective organisations of the Congress.' The strong opposition had taken him by surprise. He cried in anguish at the meeting and wrote in *Young India* that he felt 'defeated and humbled' (3 July 1924).

Deeply hurt, Gandhi then changed tack. Once more, he showed resilience and tried to compromise. Since he could not deprive the Swarajists of executive responsibilities in Congress committees, he adapted to the new circumstances. His strong relations with M. Nehru and C. R. Das helped forge an entente between the three of them before the end of the year. This loving relationship allowed him, for instance, to gently rebuke the senior Nehru for enjoying his glass of wine, and to press the reluctant Das, insistently, to learn how to spin. To the ailing Das, he wrote only three days before the latter's death: 'Do learn the thing and spin religiously for half an hour for the sake of millions and in the name of God.'[7]

In August 1924, Gandhi was discussing afresh with Motilal Nehru their differences. He intimated that if the Pro-changers stayed in Congress, he, Gandhi, might walk out of it – and then give them no support. But he would give him any help he could if they left the Congress. On 15 August 1924, Gandhi wrote to M. Nehru: 'With me in the Congress, the Councils, etc, should remain out of it . . . Or with them in the Congress, I must be practically out of it. I would then gladly occupy the place I did from 1915 to 1918.'[8]

The Swarajists could only decline Gandhi's generosity and refuse to bear the responsibility of his having to leave the party. India would not have forgiven them. Negotiations went on and on in hopes of finding a compromise before the Congress session of December 1924 at Belgaum, when the presidential successor to Mohamed Ali would be elected – an open question in the circumstances. The political situation in Bengal, where anarchists and Swarajists had recently been arrested, demanded concessions for the sake of unity.

The Calcutta Agreement of 6 November 1924 between Gandhi and the Swarajists allowed the Pro-changers to work in the Councils on behalf of the Congress. In return, as members of the Congress, they would ply the *charkha* (spinning wheel) for at least one year – the year Gandhi was elected president of the Congress. It was a give-and-take agreement. Non-cooperation would definitely be given up, with the exception of the boycott of foreign cloth: 'Non-cooperation as a national programme must be suspended' (23 October 1924).[9]

This meant the formal end of the Non-cooperation movement started in August 1920 and suspended in February 1922. Gandhi, however, still clung to the idea of individual non-cooperation, and said so, saving face – or rather, making a final point.

On 23 November 1924, the AICC meeting at Bombay was asked to endorse the new decision, to the dismay of the No-changers. 'We must stoop to conquer,'[10] Gandhi had advised on 23 October 1924. And so they did. Non-cooperation was dropped for good.

And the way was clear for Gandhi's presidential election at Belgaum (December 1924). He had previously, before the election, written to Motilal Nehru that he did not want the job unless the senior Nehru insisted that he, Gandhi, should take it. The letter was dated 9 August 1924 and headed 'Very confidential': 'My idea [is] of not accepting next year's presidency . . . The only condition that will make me reconsider my position would be your desire that I should accept.'[11] The former obliged, and Gandhi was elected the head of his party for the year 1925.

Thus the *khadi* and the spinning policy were salvaged, and even reinforced, because the duty to wear *khadi* now applied to every member of the party. This was called 'the stiffening of the franchise.' Gandhi remained adamant that spinning for half an hour each day and producing 2,000 yards of cloth before the fifteenth of every month was the necessary qualification for party vote. The 'Resolution on Calcutta Agreement and Spinning Franchise' at the Belgaum Congress spelled out the right to vote and candidature for spinners:

1 – vote at the election of representatives or delegates or any committee or sub-committee of any Congress organization whatsoever;

2 – to be elected as such, or to take part in any meetings of the Congress or any Congress organization or any committee or sub-committee thereof.

At Belgaum, Gandhi tried to re-assure the No-changers:

> He continued to be as firm a No-changer now as he ever was... It was absolutely necessary for Congress to adopt the spinning franchise... [He] casually referred to a new plan of giving battle to Government... He was not going to unfold it to them fully... [The] principal condition [was] the boycott of foreign cloth... If that could be done then the time would be for civil disobedience.

The latter remark seems to have been added as a comforting assurance that spinning was going to put a non-violent army into fighting trim. In fact, 'details for working the new franchise' were issued: all members were registered as class A (those who spun personally) or class B (those who obtain the yarn otherwise); receipts books were kept, and receipts were issued in triplicate.[12]

Civil disobedience, however, was not in the cards in 1925. At the end of October 1924, Gandhi had written to Motilal Nehru: 'I see no prospect of any effective direct action.'[13] By the middle of 1925, a disillusioned Gandhi, tired of constant travelling through hot India in third-class compartments, was ready to change his mind once more.

The Issue of Spinning in 1925: Saving the Bond with the AICC

The understanding with the Swarajists was that they were now welcome in Congress, but at a price. Gandhi conceded that they had 'introduced a new spirit into the Indian Legislatures,' but now they were expected to wear *khadi* uniforms at Congress meetings. They would, thus dressed, proclaim their allegiance to the Mahatma, his people, his party, and his 'constructive programme.' As Gandhi said: 'Mass awakening was a tremendous gain.'[14]

The agreement did not work. When Gandhi realised the general dislike for manual work, he changed his mind on the 'spinning franchise,' because, as he said, he was presiding over a democratic party. According to a report dated 17 July 1925:

> He was ready to do away with the pact with the Swarajists and thereby make them completely independent of any obligation regarding the Congress mandate. The pact had made it obligatory to the Swarajists to abide by the spinning franchise for full one year and for this reason only many of them were inclined to observe it for the full term. But if the majority were for abolition, he must dissolve the pact in due deference to their wishes. In conclusion he declared that, if the Congress would abolish the spinning franchise, he would, while remaining inside the Congress, form a separate organization for spinning and would work it up just as Deshbandhu Das and others formed and worked up the Swaraj party.[15]

In talking things over with Motilal Nehru, it was agreed that Gandhi would resign his position as president if and when the AICC meeting dropped the spinning franchise: 'I see that educated people feel it a burden even to buy hand-spun yarn and offer it as a subscription... I had thought that everyone would obey the rule, and, in any case, no one would practise deception. [I was] wrong... [The] rule... must be dropped.'[16]

So it was dropped. The spinning franchise was made optional. Gandhi stayed President of the Indian National Congress, but with a difference. The Congress became a 'political body' in the hands of the Swarajists, and he moved to the side, with a new Spinners' Association.

The situation in July 1925 reproduced that of June 1924, but in reverse. In June, Gandhi had wanted to be in the Congress, and had wanted the Swarajists to be out. One year later, they were in charge, and he had moved not quite out, but to the sideline.

Nonetheless, he was still very much opposed to a Swarajist presence in elected Councils, even if he had left the Swarajists in charge of the 'political body' of the Congress while he was working for the newly formed All-India Spinners' Association. There he could pursue, in the name of Congress, the conversion of India to the spinning wheel.[17]

> Personally I am as much opposed to Council-entry as I ever was. You may depend upon it that my part in the Patna resolution was a matter of necessity and not of choice. Necessity in the sense that I recognize the democratic character of the Congress. And knowing that I could not convince the Swarajists of the error of Council-entry and knowing also that my best friends and co-workers had become Swarajists, I took it that I could not do less than throw my weight with them as against other political parties.[18]

After the All-India Congress Committee at Patna endorsed the July understanding between Motilal Nehru and Gandhi at the end of September 1925, power shifted to the Swarajists. The Mahatma felt confused and frustrated. Interviewed at Ahmedabad early in November 1925, Gandhi confessed: 'My mind is a perfect blank as to what I shall do in the Congress, except that, wherever possible, I shall assist the Swarajists in accordance with my promise, but the Congress program will have to be framed by Mrs. Sarojini Devi [Sarojini Naidu, the next President to be elected] in consultation with Pandit Motilalji [Motilal Nehru].'[19]

Then, deciding to take a year's rest from politics, he retired to his *ashram* at the end of his term of office for another period of wait-and-see in 1926.

The Muslim Question

The sabbatical year was welcome, since Gandhi could unload another political weight from his shoulders. The growing tension between Muslim and Hindu communities was palpable, an aggravation he could not soothe. The Moplahs' rebellion against their Hindu landlords during the non-cooperation campaign did not remain an isolated incident.

The Kohat riots in the summer of 1924 and their repercussions were to seriously damage Hindu–Muslim relations. They brought about a lasting, slow, but ever-growing rift between Gandhi and the Ali brothers. In September of that year, when Mohamed Ali was President of the Congress and Gandhi a visitor in his house, the Mahatma decided to go on one of his famous fasts, in Mohamed Ali's home, without consulting his host. The Alis tried, but could not change Gandhi's resolve. The Mahatma fasted for twenty-one days as a penance in that house, and the brothers were so nice to him, turning vegetarians for the duration of his fast and offering him a cow – cows are sacred to Hindus – at the end of it so that the animal would escapc the butcher's knife and be resettled in a cows' home.

However, when Shaukat Ali and Gandhi went to Kohat to investigate the riots, caused by the publication of a disrespectful poem on the Prophet, they were unable to issue a joint report, because of disagreement on issues such as the resort to violence and the responsibility thereof. Disturbances between Hindu and Muslim communities increased. Music played by Hindu worshipers near mosques or cow slaughterings were usually to blame for the violence.

The number of riots increased. By March 1925, Gandhi was feeling helpless to heal the rift between the communities: 'For the time being I have put away in my cupboard the Hindu–Muslim tangle.' A month later, he repeated that he had given up the Caliphate struggle: 'The work of Hindu–Muslim unity has received a setback... I have washed my hands of [the khilafat].'[20]

The Caliphate question now baffled him. Shortly before his retirement, he confessed to his doctor and Muslim adviser, M. A. Ansari on 26 November 1925 his 'utter incapability to successfully tackle any other problem' than khadi, untouchability and the protection of the cow.[21]

However, he continued unabated to preach Hindu–Muslim unity, handling the problems of Hindu music disturbing prayers in mosques and disrespect – or worse – to the cow. He explained to his co-religionists how Hindu–Muslim friendship could save the cow from slaughter. He explained that for this reason, he had tried to save the cow of the Alis – by which he meant the khilafat: 'I gave all the help that I could for the Khilafat, because I wanted to enlist the Mussalman's sympathy in the matter of cow protection.'

Relations with the brothers Ali were turning sour. Gandhi remonstrated with Shaukat Ali to censure the language of his paper, the *Khilafat* (29 July 1925).[22] Muslim membership in the Congress party had fallen from 11 per cent in 1921 to 3.6 per cent in 1923. From the end of 1924, the Indian National Congress and the Muslim League – then a small party – met at different venues instead of a common one, as they had done in previous years. The Khilafatists followed suit. In January 1926, Gandhi announced that he was retiring from politics for one year.

The 'Personal Deadline' of March 1928

Four main reasons explain Gandhi's virtual exclusion from the mainstream of Indian politics at this stage. Three have been discussed: the unsuccessful struggle with the Swarajists, the aftermath of the Caliphate fight, and the failure to make headway in building Gandhian discipline in the Congress through spinning. There was a fourth factor, not so far mentioned, namely, a chivalrous, discreet, subjacent feeling of restraint, which, nonetheless, weighed heavily on Gandhi's political decisions. It was a self-imposed restraint, but it was the kind of penance that made him feel like 'a caged lion.'

The 'caged lion' feeling was a suppressed desire for active pursuance of the 1920 campaign towards *swaraj*, a resurgence caused by the interference of the Swarajists, converted to cooperation, by the loss of Muslim support, and by his own will to engage India further – not solely in non-cooperation, but in active infringement of laws.

From February 1924 onwards, Gandhi had given the Government – and himself – a respite from active political opposition, that is, from civil disobedience of the kind he had envisaged in January 1922. Since he had chosen not take unfair advantage of his early release for political gains, he now decided to abstain from challenging the Government in civil disobedience until March 1928, which would have been the end of his term of imprisonment.

This self-imposed paralysis from 1924 to 1928 has been too often ignored by commentators. However, the Mahatma's grandson Rajmohan Gandhi is well aware of the 'personal deadline' decision taken on release from prison for health reasons, and of the importance and meaning of the 'not before March 1928' date.[23]

In the meantime the Mahatma kept mostly to himself his plans for the future; but a rare letter to a friend, (Srinivasa Iyengar, who was to be elected President of the Indian National Congress for the year 1927), dated 27 April 1926, gives a clear picture of his state of mind:

> The more I study Councils work, the effect of entry into the Councils upon public life, its repercussion upon the Hindu–Muslim question, the more convinced I become not only of the futility but of inadvisability of Council-entry. I would welcome the day when at least a few of the comrades of 1920 leave the Councils to their fate and work if they like at the *charkha* programme or any other thing they wish. I have not the shadow of doubt that they will be the reserve force ready for mobilization when the time for battle comes. However, this is my view. For the present I bottle it up and keep it to myself except when I share it with friends like you. The time for its public ventilation is not yet come... This, therefore, is only for your eyes. More when we meet.[24]

So, when Gandhi emerged from retirement in 1927, the expiring date of his 'virtual' jail term (virtual, since there had been no release) was getting near. He certainly did not pose any threat to the safely entrenched British Government when he re-emerged on the national scene. Who could have guessed that 1930 would see a victorious Civil Disobedience campaign? Who would have expected that Gandhi, a spent force, had stooped to reconquer?

8

THE DEMISE OF THE PRO-CHANGERS

In 1927, a self-effacing Gandhi, afflicted by debilitating high blood pressure, was thinking more of his succession by a younger man who could shoulder the responsibilities of leading the party forward than of pioneering the way to *swaraj* himself. In this search for an efficient leader, his main concern was to consolidate the unity of the Congress for the struggle to come, even at the cost of his own personal wishes, and to restore the power and appeal of the party – fighting fissiparous forces on the right and left.

The Mantle of Leadership

Das had died in June 1925. Gandhi had rallied his partisans by making the spinning franchise optional. Motilal Nehru's policies were too secular for the Hindu right and too temperate and meek for the left of the party, which was mainly in the hands of his own son. Jawaharlal Nehru had returned in 1927 from his studies in Britain and his travels in Europe and had built a strong friendship with Subhas Chandra Bose, the Bengali leader who was to raise an Indian army corps to fight in the Japanese Army in the Second World War. The Congress needed, in Gandhi's view, a man who could command the allegiance of most, even if not all, groupings in the party.

Gandhi took, at the time, a rather dismal view of his own health. Thinking of his successor, he considered several likely candidates. He knew the importance of the choice. He would want a No-changer. He would have liked a Muslim at the head of the Congress in order to strengthen communal ties. Dr. Mukhtar Ahmed Ansari was his doctor and political adviser on Muslim questions as well as a trusted friend. He was elected President of the Indian National Congress in December 1927. But the Brahmin Chakravarti Rajagopalachari would have been a better choice for the Hindus. He had a strong political base in Madras and in the south. However, the prospect of his becoming the father-in-law of one of Gandhi's sons soon played against his selection. Gandhi, who was not keen on securing jobs for his relatives, dropped the idea, although he had declared in September 1927: 'I do say he is the only possible successor, and I repeat it to-day.'[1]

Another possible candidate was Vallabhbhai Patel, Gandhi's right hand, a reliable Gandhian on the right of the party, faithful, a capable organiser devoted to the Mahatma's views and ways, but a stranger to international politics.

The young Nehru, however, had all the necessary useful connections, grooming, training, knowledge, and drive. Although his political convictions were far too far to the left for Gandhi's taste, they were an asset to attract the leftists and the young. In fact, Gandhi thought that the Marxist views of this heir-to-be would mellow with the responsibilities of office. But at the end of 1927, their conflicting views clashed, and Jawaharlal Nehru grew very critical and rebellious in spite of his affection and admiration for the Mahatma. It came to the point that Gandhi thought of making public their differences. Nehru requested Gandhi not to do so. 'Am I not your child in politics?' he wrote to Gandhi on 23 January 1928.

Indeed, Gandhi's search for a political heir was but an aspect of his drive for *swaraj.* In 1927, with a little more than a year left before reaching the 'personal deadline,' unity had to be forged and found in resistance to the Raj, propelled by a strong leadership – a Gandhian leadership still bent on the demise of the Pro-changers and what they stood for.

The British Government watched the political situation closely, observing Gandhi's unsuccessful challenge of the Swarajists, his temporary exit from the political scene in 1926, and his emphasis on social issues, such as spinning and untouchability. The threat to the political stability of British rule in India that Gandhi might pose in March 1928 – the date of his unreal release from jail – seemed negligible.

Even so, the man was unpredictable. His hold on India was evident. His desire for *swaraj* had not receded. To forestall a political move on his part, the British Government decided to take the initiative in March 1927, giving itself one year of manoeuvring before March 1928, when the Mahatma would feel free from jail shackles.

The Simon Commission

The Government of India Act of 1919, which had put in place the Montagu-Chelmsford Reforms in 1920, was due for review after a period of ten years. Westminster decided to anticipate the date, showing thereby the will to advance constitutional progress in India. Thus, in 1927, the work of planning a further constitutional advance was put in the hands of a parliamentary commission. The Simon Commission was set up to start its enquiry in India in February 1928.

Gandhi was asked to come to Delhi to hear the news from the Viceroy himself on 2 November 1927. Much had transpired unofficially before October. It was rumoured that no Indian would be nominated for the Commission. Gandhi, due to leave for Ceylon, was not keen to confront the political problem, but he accepted the Viceroy's invitation, which was to be his first interview with Lord Irwin. 'What will be your reaction to the vice-regal news?' he was asked. He pleaded incompetence in 'as alien a subject to me as, say the cure of tuberculosis,' adding: 'I have paid no thought to the subject of Royal Commission because it is distinctly outside the sphere of my knowledge, thoughts and activities.'[2]

The question of the composition of the Commission came up at the meeting. There are several versions of Gandhi's reaction to being officially informed that no Indian was to be associated with the work of the Simon Commission, because it would be a parliamentary commission. One version of the interview appears in the *History of the Indian National Congress*, wherein Pattabhi Sitaramayya states: 'When he [Gandhi] saw the Viceroy, the interview was a cold affair.'[3] Rajmohan

Gandhi strikes a similar note: 'Saying to the Viceroy that the information could have been sent in a one-anna envelope, Gandhi returned to his ashram.'[4] But *The Life of Lord Halifax* (formerly Lord Irwin) describes the meeting thus: 'In fact, Gandhi and Irwin had a long conversation with exemplary patience and courtesy. Gandhi was in good humour.'[5] The Viceroy's comment to his father conveys another impression: 'He [Gandhi] struck me as singularly remote from practical politics. It was rather like talking to someone who had stepped off another planet on to this for a short visit of a fortnight and whose whole mental outlook was quite other to that which was regulating most of the affairs on the planet to which he had descended.'[6]

Gandhi's letter to his friend Andrews after the interview (Gandhi had promised to raise the question of *khadi* with the Viceroy) gives the Mahatma's only written reaction to the encounter: 'We did not discuss *khaddar* [home-made cloth] but he [the Viceroy] has promised to invite me again for that discussion specially... He is a good man with no power.'[7] *The Hindu* reported the interview to a fuller and more credible extent. The English-language newspaper, published in Madras, mentioned that the Viceroy and Gandhi had discussed both the non-representation of Indians on the parliamentary Commission and their association in the capacity of assessors only. Gandhi expressed the thought that the country would 'resent' the exclusively white composition of the Commission as a 'deliberate insult' and would boycott it. He added: 'However, to him, the Commission was not of any consequence, however well composed it might be and however liberal its terms of reference.'[8]

This remark – which explains the comment of the Viceroy to his father – confirms Gandhi's own political assessment of himself at the time, that is, the belief that he was not shaping politics in the Congress anymore, but was hovering unpolitically, though expectantly, in the wings. As he had written to his dear friend C. F. Andrews the previous month: 'I have not the slightest sympathy with its [the Congress's] present programme... Nevertheless it is a mighty institution – the only institution with an unbroken record of forty years.'[9]

In that state of mind, he really seemed to have stepped out from another planet: when asked by the Viceroy whether 'he would advise his countrymen, particularly the Swarajists, to cooperate with the Commission in its investigation, Mr Gandhi said that it was *none of his business.*' (We may assume that the reporter meant Gandhi's business, not the Viceroy's.) The Mahatma further re-assured 'his Excellency that he would not himself initiate a movement for boycott of the Commission as he had long since abdicated the political functions of leadership to the Swarajists' (9 November 1927).[10]

The Madras Congress, December 1927

A week later, the Viceroy officially announced the personnel of the Royal Commission, and a month later, the Indian National Congress met in full session at Madras, reacting as Gandhi had foretold the Viceroy, by boycotting the Simon Commission as a first step. A more positive sign of defiance was suggested and adopted: the Indians should issue their own constitutional report to rival the Simon report. Motilal Nehru was entrusted with that task.

Thus, as Gandhi had predicted, far from gaining any advantage from this goodwill gesture meant to forecast constitutional advance for India, the British move was met with incensed criticism from all Indian politicians. A new sense of unity was generated by what was taken – although certainly not meant – to be a slap in the face from an insensitive bully. This new feeling was shared by other political denominations, including Muslims. In the Indian National Congress, it provided the cement for the unity and purpose that had been lacking since Gandhi's arrest in 1922.

Gandhi approved of both political decisions, the boycotting of the Simon Commission and the drafting of a constitution for India. However, in view of his chosen place on the political chessboard, and according to the rules of his own political game – the personal deadline – he had to stay aloof and 'refrained from active association with the boycott.' But this he did in his own particular way: by going to Madras to attend the full session of the Indian National Congress in December 1927, showing himself briefly at the opening session, not taking part in the discussions, yet nonetheless being available for consultation 'if at all it was necessary.' Gandhi 'never attended any of the

Committee meetings except one informal meeting and he attended the Congress at the opening only for a few minutes.'[11]

For 'health reasons,' we are told, Gandhi missed the vote on the Independence resolution – the work of Subhas Bose and Jawaharlal Nehru.[12] He certainly was not pleased to have been sidelined. Therefore, he distanced himself from the call to 'complete independence' that the two friends had asked the Congress to endorse. In a letter to Jawaharlal Nehru, he strongly criticised the 'hastily conceived and thoughtlessly passed' resolution.[13] Gandhi thought Congressmen had behaved like 'prisoners in chains spitting frothy oaths only to provide mirth for their gaolers.' The Mahatma had always complained about the ineffectual passing of resolutions from debating societies. In 1916, his first political speech at the Indian National Congress made that point. The Independence resolution voted almost unanimously at Madras did not mention any sanctions and so, to him, belonged in that despised, ineffectual category. Also, he must have thought that any sanction – which should have become logically the threat of non-cooperation – could not bypass him in this way, he who was the expert and founder of non-violent political action. Although he would say that the country was not ready for it yet, he knew that he was not ready for it either – having still to refrain from active political action until March 1928. 'You are going too fast,' he told Nehru.[14]

Jawaharlal Nehru did not take the reproach lightly. In a long letter to Gandhi, dated 11 January 1928, he strongly disapproved to being treated like a schoolboy: 'You chastise us like an angry schoolmaster, but a schoolmaster who will not guide us or give us lessons but will only point out from time to time the error of our ways.'[15]

Nehru also questioned the wisdom of the *khadi* policy and deplored the present lack of political action: 'Has our boycott of foreign cloth succeeded so remarkably? Has our spinning franchise succeeded? They have not but you do not hesitate to press them on the country and the Congress because you felt, and rightly, that they would be good for the nation even if they did not wholly *succeed*.'[16] And Nehru spurred Gandhi on:

> I have asked you many times what you expected to do in the future... All you have said has been that within a year or

> 18 months you expected the *khadi* movement to spread rapidly and in a geometric ratio and then some direct action in the political field might be indulged in. Several years and 18 months have passed since then and the miracle has not happened ... I am beginning to think if we are to wait for freedom till *khadi* becomes universal in India we shall have to wait till the Greek kalends.[17]

Actually, at this stage, Gandhi needed no reminder. The 'caged lion' prowled prudently out of his den.

The All-Important Bardoli Test, April–August 1928

Once more, the Government obliged. As early as mid-February 1928, Gandhi had talks with representatives of the district of Bardoli in Gujarat about their disagreement with the Government. Bardoli was a very sensitive subject for Gandhi and India because, in 1922 and in the name of *swaraj*, he had planned, announced, and threatened the Viceroy with a no-tax campaign in that *taluka*, which would have been then gradually extended to all India.[18] The campaign was cancelled *in extremis*, but the name 'Bardoli' had been widely publicised, achieving a significance far beyond its regional importance. Bardoli in March 1928 became a test case, although Gandhi avoided direct involvement, rather advising and leading from afar. In the March 1928 issue of *Young India*, he expressed and explained his views:

> The campaign cannot be properly deemed to be a no-tax campaign launched for the attainment of *swaraj* as Bardoli would have done in 1922. The *satyagraha* is limited in scope, has a specific local object ... But though the object of the proposed *satyagraha* is local and specific, it has an all-India implication ... Whatever awakens people to a sense of their wrongs and whatever gives them strength for disciplined and peaceful resistance and habituates them to corporate suffering brings us nearer *swaraj*.[19]

There were four Gandhian *ashrams* in the *taluka* of Bardoli with a nucleus of well-disciplined workers. The 1922 episode had prepared the ground and awakened political awareness in the people. The spinning wheel, humming here and there, testified to the conversion to non-violence and to the influence of Gandhi's teachings. Vallabhbhai Patel, Gandhi's most faithful lieutenant, was put in charge of the resistance movement.

The campaign started in early April 1928. Sardar (chief) Patel – a title earned for his labours and his talent at organising the no-tax campaign – produced a document on the Bardoli case.[20] The process of revising land-revenue assessments had started in March 1924 with a Bombay Legislative Council resolution. A Land Revenue Assessment Committee had then been appointed and had published a report. This had been followed in March 1927 by a new resolution to the Governor in Council to effect necessary legislation and 'pending such legislation to issue orders to the revenue authorities not to collect the assessment in revision after the 15th March 1924.'

Patel objected to the revision settlements having gone on: 'Bardoli is only one of several *taluks* where there should have been no revision and no levying of new rates in the terms of these resolutions.' The enhancement was consequently reduced from 30 per cent to 22 per cent, but was still refused by Patel as

> absolutely arbitrary as it is based on no fresh or accurate data. The *Satyagrahis* of Bardoli have therefore pledged themselves to pay no assessment until either
>
> 1 – the enhancement is cancelled; or
> 2 – an independent impartial tribunal is appointed to examine the whole case. (*Young India*, 14 June 1928)[21]

The Bardoli no-tax campaign lasted from April to August 1928. The Government responded in earnest, arresting defaulters, seizing properties, auctioning land and livestock. On 6 August 1928, a settlement was reached whereby prisoners were released and *patels* (local representatives) reinstated. An enquiry was announced the next day, and lands forfeited were to be restored – except those already auctioned. A well-pleased Gandhi arrived in Bardoli on 2 August 1928 to witness the final stage of the campaign.

The Nehru Report came out in August 1928 as the Congress was basking in the victory at Bardoli. An All-Parties Conference was convened at Lucknow at the end of August 1928 to consider and endorse it. Its terms were agreed to after discussion and compromise from all sections of the Congress, including the Hindu right and the Sikhs. This was a formidable achievement. Gandhi himself was ready to compromise to the utmost in order to achieve unanimity, to weld together an acceptance, however shaky, and to save it from any further change or compromise that might cause it to collapse. The endorsement 'paved the way for constitutional or formal government.'

Gandhi gloated about the meaning of the Bardoli and Lucknow achievements and rejoiced in their providentially simultaneous occurrence: 'If the Bardoli victory is part of history, so will be the victory at Lucknow. Bardoli has shown the way to organic *Swaraj* – to *Ramarajya* [the kingdom of heaven], while Lucknow has opened the gate of constitutional *swaraj.* Both things were essential.'[22] Gandhi had sent a similar message, dated 28 August 1928, to the *Indian National Herald*: 'The way to constitutional *swaraj* may lie through Lucknow, the way to organic *swaraj*, which is synonymous with *Ramarajya*, lies through Bardoli.'[23]

The Calcutta Congress, December 1928: Re-entry into Politics Proper

The opening of the next session of the Indian National Congress was a show of pageantry – rather un-Gandhian, but Gandhi appreciated the enthronement of Motilal Nehru as the new President of the Indian National Congress for 1929, with his 'magnificent ride on a chariot drawn by 34 more or less white horses.' The Mahatma, having been asked to by Motilal Nehru, was there, having forsaken a visit to Europe for the occasion, and eager this time to play a full part in the proceedings. Dr. Pattabhi Sitaramayya, who wrote the *History of the Indian National Congress*, asked him: 'What is it that has brought you again out of your den? Is it again to coquet with the *Swaraj* Party because you were in love with Pandit Motilal Nehru?'[24]

The Mahatma, therefore, explained his position, addressing the Congress:

> I would be guilty of breach of duty to the nation, if after having pressed them to take their share at this critical juncture in the history of the country, I had not responded to his [Motilal Nehru's] call and said: 'I shall come on the day you fix and I shall leave on the day you ask me.' You now understand why I have come here.[25]

The Calcutta session was not plain sailing, but plain to all was the cause of the storm blowing icy winds between the two Nehrus. Father and son were in conflict over the Nehru Report. Dominion Status, envisaged in the document, fell short of the resolution on complete independence that had been endorsed by the Madras Congress the year before. The first reflected the father's view, the second the son's. The Mahatma acted as an intermediary and conciliator, his sight firmly fixed on the absolute necessity to maintain Congress unity. The mediation succeeded. A formula was found to please both sides. Gandhi gave the Calcutta Congress his own hazy definition of independence as 'undoubtedly freedom from British control in any shape or form.' He had just blurred the issue further, saying: 'Friends, I think I warned [you] against drawing any distinction between Dominion Status and Independence.'[26]

A compromise was reached under Gandhi's mediation. Dominion Status was to remain the aim mentioned in the Report, but on the condition that it be granted in the near future. Accordingly, Gandhi drafted a resolution to that effect. The younger Nehru and his friend Bose still objected. They could not and would not wait two years – the time limit fixed by the resolution. Gandhi had to move another resolution, one that would reduce the period of waiting to one year: 'If we want unity, then adjustment and readjustment, a series of compromises honourable to both parties and to a variety of opinions, is to be effected... It is a resolution of compromise between them, of a series of adjustment and readjustments between them.'[27]

It was Jawaharlal Nehru's turn to be absent from the vote, sulking, like Achilles, in his tent. He did not hear Gandhi say:

> One year is nothing. One year will be required to create discipline in our ranks. Our Congress roll today is nothing but a bogus affair . . . It is worth nothing . . . I would expect . . . enhanced subscription and increasing membership. That will take one year and one year more will be required for giving ourselves confidence and courage, and for consolidation of communal unity.[28]

Gandhi's loving relationship with Jawaharlal Nehru survived the crisis at Calcutta, in the same way it had outlived the exchange of letters after the Madras session the previous year. The old man became anxious to please the young man – and himself – by enforcing the demand for independence in a way that suited him.

Thus, the resolution was given a sanction, making it palatable to Gandhi's taste: 'What I am to do – a man approaching his end? . . . [Should I say that] you shall work without my services? I assure you, it is not without a considerable pain that I have taken up this position.'[29] The resolution was adopted, putting Gandhi in a key position in his party. It said:

> whilst adhering to the resolution relating to Complete Independence passed at the Madras Congress, [this resolution] approves of the constitution drawn up by the Committee . . . Congress will adopt the Constitution, if it is adopted in its entirety by the British Parliament on or before December 31, 1929, but in the event of its non-acceptance by that date or its earlier rejection, the Congress will organize a campaign of *non-violent non-cooperation* by advising the country to refuse taxation and in such other manner as may be decided upon.[30] (Emphasis added)

The Bond with India Revitalised by the Lahore Congress, December 1929

March 1928 had liberated Gandhi from any political shackles. The 'victory' at Bardoli under Patel's guidance in 1928 was a reminder of what could have happened sixteen years earlier. The outcome was considered a great success, a taste of greater things to come. It renewed confidence in Gandhi's non-violence at a time it was needed. The Bardoli test had worked satisfactorily, and Gandhi was planning to advance non-cooperation plans after the meeting of the Calcutta Congress, in expectation of an adverse decision by the British authorities.

Thus, Gandhi was getting ready for the new challenge. He said, as reported by the *Hindustan Times*: 'I could still lead India. I shall only lead India when the nation comes to me to be led, when there is a national call. I shall not go before then. I shall not go before I am certain of my power over the masses.'[31]

Two months before the deadline, on 31 October 1929, the Viceroy declared that 'the natural issue of India's constitutional progress is the attainment of Dominion status.' But he would not tie himself down to a prompt delivery. Consequently, the idea of Dominion was shunned at the next session of the Congress, in Lahore in December 1929, and 'complete independence' (*purna swaraj*) was proclaimed. Jawaharlal Nehru succeeded his father as President of the 1929 Congress. Most importantly, a new campaign of Civil Disobedience was to be launched under Gandhi's leadership.

The return of the Mahatma as the commander of the operations in the field was accompanied by non-cooperation revisited. The boycott of schools and courts was not renewed, but the boycott of legislatures was to be immediately implemented. Gandhi had won his fight at last and, at least theoretically, because the implementation of resignation from the Legislatures was met with strong resistance to comply among the elected.

The Indian National Congress was again a powerful tool in Gandhi's hand, ready to act at his bidding. He could now dismiss the Swarajists' pro-change policy for good. He had the last word. All eyes now converged on the old man, on what he was going to do.

For Gandhi, the time had now come to reap the fruit of the *khadi* policy. It had proved not so foolish, in spite of all that was said about it. Jawaharlal Nehru had to reconsider his previous opinion that it was a waste of time, 'almost wholly divorced from politics.' His friend Bose had to comply with Gandhi's insistence that all non-*khadi* items be withdrawn from the Textile Exhibition attached to the Congress venue before he would come.

The Lahore Congress over, Gandhi concentrated on choosing a suitable objective for his non-violent army. It was not to be like the first Non-cooperation campaign, with its insistence on no medals, no honours, no schools, no courts, no army, and no taxes. No outbursts of violence would automatically end the campaign – as had happened to the previous one with the riot in Chauri-Chaura. Gandhi was looking for active disobedience of some law enactment – the old favourite, which would not be criminal, but which would constitute some carefully chosen infringement on the legal corpus, and could thus be called 'civil disobedience.'[32]

On 12 March 1930, the old man, the saintly man, staff in hand, marched briskly to the sea with a chosen band of followers to break the law on salt. He marched to give the poor of India – and the rich – the right to season their rice without paying the salt tax. He marched miles and days as tension mounted in the land and the Government held its breath – and its hand. On the beach, he showed the people how they were to gain their freedom: he picked up a pinch of salt. 'Hail the law-breaker,' cried the poet and past (1926) Congress president, Sarojini Naidu. That pinch of salt paved the way for the Gandhi-Irwin Pact (1931).

PART IV

NATIONALISM AND PARTITION

Figure 8: *Le Jugement de Salomon*, Nicolas Poussin, 1649

9

THE TEMPTATION OF THE ONE-PARTY SYSTEM

After the first all-India campaign against the British Government, Gandhian nationalism had turned against the Pro-changers and their policy to enter the Councils. After the second all-India campaign, Gandhi's nationalism veered towards cooperation with the same Government, and it was decided that the Congress should take part in the next elections. In both cases, the result was the same, yet elections were entered against Gandhi's wishes in the first instance, and on his advice in the second. How is that to be explained?

The Government of India Act (1935) gives the clue. It handed real power down to the provincial level of governance through elections due to take place in 1937. Astonishingly, the same sort of Act that caused the drive for complete independence in 1930 now opened a happy era of cooperation between the Congress and the Government that lasted until the Second World War.

Accepting a Pro-changer stance in 1937 was a major U-turn in Gandhi's nationalism. The consequent electoral success of the Indian National Congress proved the soundness of the decision. But it led the party into further temptation, that of becoming the overlord party, to which political power could be transferred at the end of British rule. Its leaders, Mahatma included, revelled in an inspiring vision of one party representing the whole of India, with the Muslims in a niche. However democratic the frame it envisaged, they looked forward to a transfer of power into their own hands. The temptation of the one-party system, to which the African continent succumbed in the decolonisation era, played a starring role in the last years of the Raj.

To realise that dream, the Congress cold-shouldered the Muslim League. The secular party happily included Muslims in its ranks, but was prone to exclude a political alliance at the centre with a rival party. The Congress tried to undo Jinnah, and Jinnah fought for survival. This chapter summarises their nationalist policies and retraces three stepping stones (from 1928, 1931, and 1937) that were seemingly leading to the one-party system, but actually provoked the Pakistan claim.

Gandhi's Shift of Policies

While Gandhi used well-placed political tendrils to consolidate his leadership inside the Indian National Congress, he had stopped searching for new Muslim allies outside his party after the collapse of the Hindu–Muslim alliance in 1924. He was reluctant to repeat another nationalist venture of a Khilafatist kind, and he kept aloof from the many all-party conferences that tried to bridge the gulf of communal disunity at the end of the 1920s.

What comes out clearly from an analysis of the 1930s is a shift in Gandhian priorities. Although still loudly proclaimed as essential, the search for Hindu–Muslim unity gave way to the necessity of maintaining the cohesion of the Indian National Congress. When conflict arose in this way, the Muslim question took second place. Primacy of the party became the first consideration. The 'Muslim problem' was left to fester.

Gandhi's reluctance to attend Hindu–Muslim conferences had been noticeable for some time. He 'maintained a grieved silence' on the efforts of the all-party conferences to find a common Hindu–Muslim response. His absence from meetings organised in the name of Hindu–Muslim unity in 1927 and in 1928 showed his unease at his worsening relationship with the Ali brothers and their compounding disagreements about the proper analysis of current conditions. His feelings were complex and intricate. He confessed to several people that he had lost faith in the goal of Hindu–Muslim unity: 'I have lost all desire to attend meetings held for achieving unity.'[1]

He excused his absenteeism, claiming 'his services would not be of any use.' Moreover, he further explained: 'I simply say that I hold strange views about the way of bringing about unity which in the present atmosphere cannot get accepted. Therefore, I can only be a hindrance [to Muslim-Hindu] unity rather than a help.'[2]

Did Gandhi express some of these 'strange views'? He wrote to Motilal Nehru on 8 May 1928: 'I have no faith in a legislative solution of the communal question.'[3] The previous month, he had made this astonishing confession: 'My solution of the problem is so different from what is generally expected. I am more than ever convinced that the communal problem should be solved outside of legislation and if, in order to reach that state, there has to be a civil war, *so be it*. Who will listen to a proposal so mad as this?'[4] (emphasis added)

Jinnah's Perseverance at Bridging Political Differences

This Gandhian current of prudence and despondency in the treatment of the Muslim predicament after the 1920 campaign confronted the counter-current of Jinnah and Mohamed Ali, anxious to come to terms with the Congress. The Simon Commission, announced in October 1927, had both Jinnah and the Congress on the same political side – at least until they divided over the Nehru Report in the summer 1928. Jinnah had greeted the forthcoming meeting of minds:

> A constitutional war has been declared on Great Britain... I welcome the hand of fellowship extended to us by Hindu leaders from the platform of the Congress and the Mahasabha. For, to me, this offer is more valuable than any concession which the British Government can make. Let us then grasp the hand of fellowship. This is indeed a bright day. (Calcutta, 30 December 1927)

Jinnah then organised a boycott of the Simon Commission when it landed in India (February 1928), and was sent Gandhi's congratulations for its 'very great success.'

Jinnah was looking forward to the coalition of the two political parties in the search for independence – with himself as leader. But Gandhi was reluctant to repeat with Jinnah some form of his partnership with the brothers Ali, and the Congress current wanted only a tributary.

The Muslim Predicament at Calcutta, 1928

Outside the Congress, the Muslims were divided and weak. The Khilafatists were on a fast-losing course. The Muslim League seemed a mouse next to the Congress lion. Furthermore, the League was divided over the Simon Commission, with Jinnah surviving with his group of supporters. The Muslim League even ceased to exist (1930). Muslim power outside the Congress rested in the Muslim provincial parties, whose outlooks and interests clashed. A secular Jinnah, unrepresentative of this religious kaleidoscope, hovered uneasily at the centre of political power.

So tensions were high in the Muslim camp, riven by the diverging opinions of Jinnah, the Alis, the Aga Khan, the Shafi League, and the Nationalist Muslims who were prepared to accept the Nehru Report (August 1928). They were also strained to breaking point between Shaukat Ali and Motilal Nehru. Differing 'strongly' with Motilal Nehru at the All-Parties Conference in Bombay, Shaukat Ali described the confrontation in a letter to Gandhi on 23 October 1928: 'I had a real quarrel with Panditji [Motilal Nehru's title] at Ambalal Sarabhai's and very nearly came to blows, as my blood boiled when in our face he was heaping abuses on us "No-changers".'[5]

The following month, shortly before the Calcutta Congress, Gandhi disowned his former friend: 'No, the speaker at Cawnpore is not the Maulana [Shaukat Ali's title] with whom I have been so long familiar and with whom I have passed so many happy hours as with a blood-brother and bosom friend. The Maulana of Cawnpore is an utter stranger to me.'[6]

Political India had assembled in Calcutta at the end of 1928 for the All-Parties Conference, for the Muslim League session, and for the Indian National Congress annual meeting. All three events were conveniently placed in the old capital of India. Muhammad Ali Jinnah and Muhammad Ali had convened the meeting at the same place and at the same time as the Indian National Congress session in the hope of joining forces with the Congress if it accepted their amendments to the Nehru Report.

They had made constitutional plans of their own, known as the 'Delhi proposals,' and were eager to form a common front with the main party on the issue of constitutional progress in order to counter the Simon Report.

Separate electorates for the benefit of Muslims dated back to the Lucknow Pact, signed in 1916 by the Indian National Congress and the Muslim League and accepted by the British authorities. Jinnah, who belonged to both parties, had mediated the agreement. The same Jinnah was now ready to give up separate Muslim electorates for the sake of Hindu–Muslim unity. Jinnah was ready to agree 'to abandoning the League's separate electoral foundation stone, which gave Muslims alone the right to vote for Muslim candidates and would have obliged all Muslim politicians to appeal to the entire electorate of their constituency in future contests.'[7]

In exchange, Jinnah asked for a third of the seats in the Central Assembly, instead of the quarter envisaged by the Congress draft document, and for statutory majorities in Punjab and Bengal. But the Congress, while insisting on ending separate electorates for Muslims, refused to concede something as substantial: a meagre increase of 2 per cent in the number of Muslim seats at the centre was offered, an unacceptable pittance. The All-Parties Conference, at the eve of the Congress session, led to no agreement.

Gandhi was dragged into the negotiations at the last hour. Could he barter a compromise and seal unity? He referred to the hopelessness of the task when he addressed the Calcutta Congress the next day. On 28 December 1928, he took his listeners into his confidence. He described his ordeal when Congress and Muslim leaders were trying to reach a deal before the next day's session: 'The whole of last night was spent in trying to bring about communal unity.... It is really a fact that my brain [today] is muddled... I was dragged, not called [to the Convention Committee]... I had to jump in a car... [and] could not leave before half-past two in the morning ... You will now see what I mean when I say I have got a muddled brain.'[8]

Had Jinnah's amendments been accepted, some invaluable Muslim support would have rallied to the Congress and helped put formidable pressure on the British Government. It would have resuscitated in another form and in some degree the defunct alliance with the Caliphate Muslims, which had made the Non-cooperation campaign so powerful in 1920. Concerted action in 1928 might have prevented the surge of interest in a separate Muslim entity, since Jinnah was ready to concede a common electorate for Muslims and Hindus. Jinnah, as he then said, was 'not speaking as a Mussalman but as an Indian': 'What we want is that Hindus and Muslims should march together ... We are all sons of this land. We have to live together.'[9]

In his biography of Gandhi, Rajmohan Gandhi, his grandson, puts forward the view that, in fact, the differences between the Congress and the League were not that great. Gandhi's argument, as given to Jinnah in order to explain the Congress's reluctance to compromise, was that, in spite of Gandhi's own friendly feelings on the matter, any modification of the Nehru Report, at this stage, might shake to the ground the fragile edifice of Congress cohesion. Thus, the Congress, and Gandhi, chose to appease the Sikh alliance and the extreme Hindu right, who were opposed to a deal with Jinnah. According to Rajmohan Gandhi: 'Telling Jinnah that he [Gandhi] was personally prepared to concede the Muslims demands, Gandhi pointed out that the Sikhs had declared that they would back out if changes were made to the Nehru Report.'[10]

Rajmohan Gandhi also raises the point that the Congress – and Gandhi – doubted whether the two Muslim leaders, Jinnah and M. Ali, were sufficiently representative of the Muslim community, and consequently, they believed that an eventual agreement with them might not be endorsed by other Muslims. Jinnah was called a 'spoilt child, a naughty child' and as representing 'a small minority of Muslims.'[11]

Jinnah, feeling despised and rejected, talked of 'the parting of the ways.' Stanley Wolpert stresses Jinnah's efforts at achieving Hindu–Muslim unity and speaks of the 'tragic failure' of 1928: 'For this [Calcutta, December 1928] marked a major point of departure in

Jinnah's life, an even sharper veering off from the road of Congress and all it represented than Nagpur had been eight years earlier. He had delivered his swan song to Indian nationalism.'[12]

He was quick to take offence, but slow to take revenge. As for Mohamed Ali, he felt spurned by his own side, and had left the Congress in anger, calling on other Muslims to act likewise.

The Round Table Conference, September–December 1931

In spite of the 'tragic failure,' the nationalism of Jinnah and Gandhi adhered to a common political purpose. On the one hand, Gandhi was still of the opinion that 'Dominion Status can easily become... independence, if we have the sanction to back it. Independence can easily become a farce, if it lacks sanction. What is in a name if we have the reality? A rose smells just as sweet.' [13] And on the other hand, Jinnah was still openly a convinced secularist and believer in Hindu–Muslim unity – offence and revenge being set aside.

Therefore, the following year, Jinnah made another conciliatory move. He 'arranged' a meeting for Gandhi, M. Nehru, Sapru, and Patel to meet Lord Irwin in December 1929 on the question of Dominion status. It failed on the question of dates because the Congress leaders wanted Dominion status there and then. Wolpert comments:

> Within five years, perhaps India could have taken her place beside Canada and Australia as an independent dominion... And he [Jinnah] had actually brought them all into the same room, though that alone had taken almost two months of 'negotiating.' Then to watch everything disintegrate before the stone wall erected by Gandhi and Motilal as spokesmen for Jawaharlal and his friends – how else could it leave Jinnah but bitter? Tired. Frustrated. Furious. Alone and bitter.

After that meeting, the Congress, rejecting Dominion status and voting for a complete severance of ties with Great Britain, launched the Civil Disobedience movement, but without the cooperation of the Muslim League. Gandhi marched to the sea to pick a handful of salt on the seashore. Jinnah went into a self-imposed exile across the seas, starting a short-lived legal and political career in England which he ended in 1934.

After the Gandhi-Irwin Pact ended the salt campaign in 1931, Gandhi sailed to London to take part in the second Round Table Conference (7 September–31 December 1931), which Jinnah and other Muslim leaders also attended. The conference failed to achieve Hindu–Muslim unity, but revealed Gandhi's and Jinnah's new nationalist demands.

Gandhi, as the voice of Congress – whose sole representative he was at the Conference – claimed in fact the preferential benefit of a one-party system for his own party, and its right to take over power from Britain as a non-communal and secular all-India organisation. Gandhi addressed thus the Conference on 1 December 1931:

> All the other parties at this meeting represent sectional interests...Congress alone claims to represent the whole of India, all interests...And yet I see the Congress is treated as one of the Parties...I wish I could convince all the British public men, the British Ministers, that the Congress is capable of delivering the goods. The Congress is the only all-India wide national organisation, bereft of any communal basis...Believe me...without the problem of minorities being solved there is no Swaraj for India...This [Hindu–Muslim] quarrel is...coeval with the British advent.[14]

Jinnah, at the same venue, talked in terms of four parties: 'There are four main parties sitting round the table now. There are the British party, the Indian princes, the Hindus and the Muslims.' He was rounding up all the divided Muslims into a single party – wishful thinking at the time. But was that not clever? By so doing, he made his case so much stronger. And Wolpert comments: 'This was a new departure and became a major theme of his Pakistan strategy, that is that the Muslims were a "*party*," a distinct bloc, separate from, if not actually equal to, the Hindus, the princes, and the British.'

At the end of the Round Table Conference, Gandhi 'warned that it was "somewhat likely"' that, in his opinion, the two groups had 'come to the parting of the ways,' while Jinnah was still pursuing the old constitutional path he adhered to: 'I hope that within a period of months, rather than years, there will be a new Dominion added to the Commonwealth of our nations, a Dominion of another race, a Dominion that will find self-respect as an equal within the Commonwealth – I refer to India.'[15]

Provincial Governments, 1937

The year 1934 was eventful. It saw the end of the 1930–34 Civil Disobedience campaign, which had been re-ignited after the failure of the Round Table Conference and Gandhi's arrest three weeks later. In that year 1934, Gandhi severed formal links with the Indian National Congress, while Jinnah was promoted to 'permanent' president of the Muslim League. And the devolution of power to the provinces was now on the political agenda, with Gandhi soon anxious to enter the election contest.

All this happened as the campaign of Civil Disobedience ebbed and passed away. Once more, Gandhi had been released before the end of his jail term, August 1934.[16] Once more, he considered himself bound in fairness not to take political advantage of his early release. In April 1934, while on a 'non-political' tour of India, Gandhi sounded the retreat for civil resisters: no one but he alone would bear the responsibility of civil resistance. He wrote to his wife, who was still incarcerated, on 6 April 1934: 'I have now decided to stop all others from going to jail. I alone should offer *satyagraha.* Hence when all of you are released you will not have to offer *satyagraha* again for the present.'

Gandhi had also decided in favour of non-boycotting elections. In the middle of April 1934, he wrote to Patel: 'I feel that [this decision] was absolutely correct. It has been taken neither too late nor too early.'

This coincidence in the timing of both decisions, electioneering and ending civil resistance, was indeed meaningful. So, in the words of Rajmohan Gandhi, 'as July progressed, all eyes were on Gandhi, whose self-imposed abstention from politics was to end on 3 August. Would he exercise the right, now confined to him alone, to defy the Raj and court imprisonment? If he did, could the Congress think of contesting elections?'[17]

In that month, Gandhi took a surprising decision. He would 'retire' in September from the Indian National Congress, but he let it be known that he would still be available for political guidance. By hovering above but out of his party, he would not stifle its right, led by Patel, nor its left, led by Nehru, whose views were reinforced, after March 1934, by the newborn Socialist party. The decision was in keeping with his belief in one party inheriting British rule, and with his ambition to represent all India on a non-partisan basis. His retirement became official in October 1934.

In that same year, Jinnah was named 'permanent' president of the Muslim League. He had spent a few years in London, successful in his legal work but unlucky in his ambition to enter Parliament. In 1935, he had ended his self-chosen exile and returned to his country to re-enter Indian politics. He, too, was going to seize power if he could.

In that year too, the word 'Pakistan' was invented by Chaudhry Rahmat Ali, an Indian student at Cambridge University. 'Pakistan,' meaning 'the land of the Pure,' is an acronym: *P* for Punjab, *A* for Afghania (North-West Frontier), *K* for Kashmir, *S* for Sindh, and *Tan* for Baluchistan. Rahmat Ali tried to convince Jinnah, then in London, of the soundness of his idea, but the lawyer remained deaf to his call.

The Government of India Act (2 August 1935), born of the labours of the hated Simon commission, offered a meaningful devolution of power and an enlarged electorate of thirty million. The governor of each province was entitled to select his executive from the largest party, responsible to the Legislature.

But Jawaharlal Nehru and Gandhi were sharply divided. Gandhi held that non-cooperation was 'not an eternal principle' and that his decision was 'a question of strategy.' Nehru called the Act 'a charter of slavery.' The two compromised. They would contest elections, and given the chance, they would form provincial governments, provided the governors would not interfere. Indeed, Gandhi had reversed himself from holding a non-cooperating position to that of entering the legislatures – as the Swarajists had done in the past. Moreover, he had converted a reluctant Nehru to do likewise – what the Swarajists had not managed to do with him. For not just legislatures but governments in the provinces were on offer, provided the Congress showed its strength in the election contests, and provided that governors agreed to behave as constitutional heads in a democratic game.

The change of tactics was brilliant: Gandhi obtained from the Viceroy a vague but conciliatory statement to the effect that governors would not interfere unnecessarily. The Congress was able to form eight ministries out of eleven, get on satisfactorily with the governors, and manage rather well their first experience in administration.[18] These Congress ministers became responsible to, and were disciplined by a 'Congress High Command.'

Jinnah, too, had looked forward to the contest. The Muslim League, reorganised by him to fight the elections of 1937, did well in the Muslim fold, and he was looking forward to an alliance with the Congress and a share in some provincial ministries. He preached his political creed of Hindu–Muslim unity being the best way to achieve independence, and suggested a common League-Congress policy for that purpose: 'Can we even at this eleventh hour bury the hatchet . . . Nothing will give me greater happiness than to bring about complete cooperation and friendship between Hindus and Muslims.'[19] And he said also: 'It is now the duty of the various leaders to put their heads together and chalk out a definite and common policy with regard to the Constitution.'

But the Congress's strategy had made a full turn, not only on governmental cooperation, but also on Muslim representation. The League had won 29 out of the 35 Muslim seats it contested, but provincial parties kept their hold on the Punjab, Bengal, and Assam. Nehru saw the opportunity to absorb the League by phagocytosis. Muslim Leaguers were ordered to integrate the Congress party, and the Congress started a 'mass campaign' to bring unpoliticised Muslims into its ranks. Basking in Congress's electoral success, Nehru was in no mood to accommodate the Muslim League: 'There are only two forces in the country, the Congress and the government.'

Jinnah did not take Nehru's rebuff well: 'I refuse to line up with the Congress. There is a third party in this country and that is the Muslims.' Jinnah appealed to Gandhi to intervene. But camped in his new political position outside the party, Gandhi declined to interfere with Nehru's policy: 'I wish I could do something but I am utterly helpless. My faith in unity is as bright as ever; only I see no daylight.'[20]

The Parting of the Ways

Jinnah did not retort to Nehru that the third party in this country is the Muslim League, but that 'the third party is the Muslims' – a foreboding of things to come. As Nehru pushed him aside with a campaign of 'mass contact' to conquer Muslim India, Jinnah copied his tactics and mobilised Muslims. Obviously, the religious argument was to make the difference in attracting the Muslim electorate, and so it was used effectively, in spite of Jinnah's dislike. Wolpert concludes: 'More than Iqbal [the poet who anticipated Pakistan], it was Nehru who chartered a new mass strategy for the League, prodding and challenging Jinnah to leave the drawing rooms of politics to reach down to the hundred million Muslims who spent most of each day labouring in rural fields.'

Jinnah sought in earnest the alliance of the Muslim provincial parties. He won the support of the Punjab (Sir Sikander Hayat Khan, Unionist party) and Bengal (A. K. Fazlul Haq) premiers. In October 1937, the Muslim League met at Lucknow. The session marked a break with past policies[21], and in Jinnah's appearance, since he came in a more Islamic style of dress: 'To symbolize the dramatic change marked by this Lucknow session, not only in the League's platform and political position, but in Jinnah's personal commitment and final goal... he changed his attire.'

The Jinnah cap and the Gandhi cap became symbols of allegiance.

10

RETALIATION

'An eye for an eye, and a tooth for a tooth' is the popular understanding of the *lex talionis*, the law of retribution. Jinnah applied the precept, subtly and masterly, to the framework of indianity and to the treasured world of the Mahatma.

Gandhi's nationalism took a hard knock from three well-aimed blows. First, Jinnah hijacked the Mahatma's ideal of representativeness for his own benefit in an extraordinary nation-building exercise. Then having created a new nation, he demanded a territory for its inhabitants. Finally, he claimed a state for his nation on equal terms with a Hindu state. This Jinnah-made congruence was nationalism at its cleverest. The two-nation theory (as it was called) hit at the heart of Gandhi's nationalism, at the very heart of the Mahatma, where it was slowly distilled into a powerful cocktail of revenge.

We work, however, from the hypothesis that Jinnah performed a stunt rather than a conversion. His striking change of clothes at the Muslim League session of 1937 initiated a change of tactics, not a change of ideals. The cloth does not make the saint (indeed, in India, it seems to work in reverse, with saintly men going half-naked). His was a change of clothes, not of heart. Between the cloth and the heart, a smokescreen efficiently hid Jinnah's steady political aims. He therefore became evasive, inscrutable, obdurate, and impenetrable.

The Claim of Being One Nation

By February 1938, 'the Congress High Command,' composed of the few leaders in charge of the party's policy, was confronted by the equivalence of a shadow cabinet devoted to Jinnah and complaining about Congress's partisanship in the provinces. These leaders soon realised their mistake of rebuffing the cooperation of the Muslim League. Nehru approached Jinnah and asked him to let him know what were exactly the points in dispute.

Jinnah's response was unfriendly: he certainly was not going to commit himself, or his strategy, on paper for his enemy. He also knew too well by now that the Congress leaders would only refer the matter to Gandhi, who, while aspiring to represent the nation of four hundred million, continued the pretence of not leading the party he officially left in 1934. So Jinnah replied to Nehru: 'Surely you know and you ought to know what are the fundamental points in dispute.' (17 February 1938)

Gandhi then wrote to Jinnah in that same month, expressing a willingness to talk to him, but only after Jinnah had first discussed matters with the Maulana Abul Kalam Azad, the President of the Indian National Congress and his new guide on Muslim policy after the recent death of his Muslim physician, Dr. Ansari. Jinnah was not fooled by the bait – which was designed to trick him into recognising the legitimacy of the Muslim presence in the Congress. Anyway, he despised the Maulana, who was to be the figurehead of the Congress to the end of the Second World War, and showed it by refusing later to shake his hand.[1]

From this incident in February 1938, notwithstanding the fact that he spoke only for a minority of the Muslim of some eighty million, Jinnah firmly insisted on the League's 'authoritative,' representative capacity to speak for Muslims and, therefore, on denying the right of Muslims to serve in the Indian National Congress organisation; consequently, he affirmed the Hindu character of the Congress. In short, he assumed the right to represent all Muslims, because his (yet dwarf) Muslim League was the only Muslim political party at the centre (the others being anchored and scattered in their provinces). He was thus torpedoing the Congress's claim to represent all India. At the next Muslim League session, on 26 December 1938, Jinnah said:

> The Congress High Command makes the preposterous claim that they are entitled to speak on behalf of the whole of India, that they alone are capable of delivering the goods... We, Muslims of India, have made up our mind to secure our full rights, but we shall have them as rights... The Congress is nothing but a Hindu body... The presence of a few Muslims, the few misled or misguided ones, and the few who are there with ulterior motives, does not, cannot, make it a national body. I challenge anybody to deny that the Congress is not mainly a Hindu body. I ask, does the Congress represent the Muslims?
>
> Who is the genius behind it? Mr. Gandhi. I have no hesitation in saying that it is Mr. Gandhi who is destroying the ideal with which the Congress was started. He is the one man responsible for turning the Congress into an instrument for the revival of Hinduism.[2]

Here Jinnah dissociates the Congress as it had been in his younger days from the Congress as it now was. Though repudiating Gandhi so openly, he did not, however, renounce the ideals of a pre-Gandhian period. He was still, at heart, the secular Hindu–Muslim 'ambassador' of 1916, working for all-India independence. But he wanted his share of the transfer of power, a lion's share, and he decided to prove his mettle. In this contest, he had to cut the Congress's wings down to size, at least the wings of its leaders, mainly Gandhi, Nehru, and Azad.

Jinnah's statement, notably, did not reject the ideals of the pre-1920 period. They remained hidden behind a shield of words and an impervious and obdurate attitude that concealed intimate thoughts. Jinnah's credo was not necessarily the creation of Pakistan, as one is tempted to believe it was. It was to create a device to strengthen his political position *vis-à-vis* the Congress and reluctant Muslim parties. Gandhi had claimed to speak for all India; Jinnah made himself the spokesman of all Muslims. And it had to be a religious device, a religious divide, since it was based on representativeness.

Opinions differ, though. While Ayesha Jalal understands that the Pakistan policy was a 'bargaining counter' (and we follow her insight), Stanley Wolpert offers another credible analysis:

> But Jinnah had long since [in November 1939] decided in favour of a separate and equal nation for Muslim India. Only the precise timing for announcing his intentions remained to be resolved...It would have been too easy to come out flatly for Pakistan...as Rahmat Ali had done in England for the past six years. Indeed Ali, who first publicized the Pakistan demand, was left a lonely man to die in England.[3]

As for Gandhi, he was puzzled. 'Astute politician' that he was, he felt he was being led up the garden path by the true Jinnah. However, the Mahatma, so finely politically attuned, but kept guessing, could never be sure. This goes a long way to explain why he thought later that he could stop partition by asking Jinnah to be the Prime Minister of India. Meanwhile, Gandhi reacted by enthroning a Muslim at the head of the Congress in the person of the Maulana Abul Kalam Azad, a scarecrow to Jinnah. Moreover, the Mahatma stubbornly refused to exclude Muslims from any Congress negotiating team, as demanded by Jinnah in later years as a condition for entering an interim government.

The new policy of the Muslim League appealed successfully to Muslims. In the years 1938–39, Jinnah's political party prospered by leaps and bounds. Muslim League membership soared from a few thousand to more than half a million between the Lucknow session of the Muslim League in October 1937 and that in Lahore in 1940. Soon the figure topped two million. Nehru's 1937 plan of 'mass contact' with the Muslim population had worked not in favour of the Congress, but of the Muslim League, thanks to the rural cadre of devoted imams, immune to infidel propaganda.

In the same breath as Jinnah was planning his new strategy, he obtained in December 1938, at the Muslim League session at Patna, a green light from his subservient party to resort to 'direct action,' a departure from his previous adherence to the use of constitutional means only.

In Jinnah, the Congress and Gandhi were now confronted with their 'mirror image' (to use Wolpert's words). The distorted image had turned against its model, with its 'direct action' threat mimicking the other's non-violent injunctions. The image of the Great Chief (Quaid-i-Azam) was facing that of the Great Soul (Mahatma); his All-India Muslim League was poised against the All-India National Congress. In doing so, whether both commanders liked it or not, the secular character of politics gave way to a religious sort of nationalism – anathema to Gandhi and Nehru, but also to Jinnah. Tooth for tooth was compounded with eye for eye in a tit-for-tat retribution, and more was to come.

The claim to represent all Muslims led inevitably to the idea that they formed a kind of special group, a very special group, one called a nation.

The Claim for Territory

The occasion for the unprecedented claim arose with Jinnah reacting to the Congress's renewed demand for unfettered independence, issued at the Ramgarh Congress on 20 March 1940. The war ended the Congress's collaboration with the British authorities in spite of the party's desire to support Britain – non-violent support on the part of Gandhi, violent support by the party. There was discord on that point, since Gandhi had moved his position from his previous 'help Britain in the war' call to 'it is wrong to help Britain in the war.'[4] But why renew the demand for complete independence at this stage?

The Viceroy had declared that India was at war with Germany in September 1939 without consulting any Indian representatives, causing a break in the smooth relations between the Congress provincial governments and the British leadership. The consequent resignation of all Congress provincial ministries in protest, on the orders of the Congress High Command, was celebrated by a Muslim 'Day of Deliverance' (22 December 1939).

Jinnah reacted strongly and immediately to the Ramgarh Congress's call for independence. In January 1940, he had spoken of the two nations living in India. That contention was now made blatantly at the most famous of all the Muslim League sessions, at Lahore on 23 March 1940. It echoed the resolution of the Ramgarh Congress on the 20th of the same month. Muslim nationalism was turning not against British rule, but against the transfer of power to Congress. In this contest, Britain was an ally, and the Congress the enemy. Time was on the side of this nationalism, making it possible to extract more and more concessions from the Government as well as from the Congress. Jinnah had only to say no – and he did – in order to gather more juicy pickings from his waiting game.

Thus, the claim of Indian Muslims being one nation nursed Jinnah's demand for territory, but the demand was left deliberately vague. By claiming that Indian Muslims were a nation, Jinnah was making a diffuse threat to divide India, but he would not say where he would divide. The General Secretary of the Muslim League, Liaqat Ali Khan (who was to be the first Prime Minister of Pakistan) explained this ambition in this way: 'If we say Punjab that would mean that the boundary of our state would be Gurgaon whereas we want to include in our proposed dominion Delhi and Aligarh, which are centres of our culture... Rest assured that we will [not] give away any part of the Punjab.'[5]

The territory referred to in the Lahore resolution mentioned 'geographical contiguous units' where Muslims were 'numerically in a majority,' and, moreover, 'such territorial readjustments as may be necessary.' Did this include the integration of 'units' other than Muslim? Could one draw the boundaries of 'units' to one's advantage? If and when the principle of self-determination was granted, would it justify Jinnah's claim that only Muslims had the right to vote in a referendum on the division of India?

Political manoeuvring obviously played its part – a starring performance on Jinnah's part. Provinces had become all-important since the devolution of power to provincial ministries, and were even more so with the prospect of a federation as the next constitutional stage. The Muslims had demanded and obtained the separation of Sindh from the Bombay Presidency, the promotion of the North-West Frontier into a province, and the creation of Baluchistan. These, along with the Punjab and Bengal, made up the 'geographical contiguous' provinces, which could then be linked by 'necessary' 'territorial readjustments' in areas where Muslims would be 'numerically in majority,' as in Bengal and Assam.

Such Muslim nationalism not only increased the appeal and status of the League in the provinces, but also led to a growing demand for Muslim rule by Muslims – thus conforming to the *Weltanschauung* of the Muslim heritage, with politics suited to a religious outlook. However, the religious taint was played down by Jinnah, hued as it was by an emphasis on social and cultural divergences: 'They are not religions in the strict sense of the word, but are, in fact, different and distinct social orders and it is a dream that the Hindus and Muslims can ever involve a common nationality.'

The Claim for a State

Such nationalism made for a nation. Such a nation made for a territory. Such a territory made for a state. Ernest Gellner stated the criterion in these terms: 'In brief, nationalism is a theory of political legitimacy, which requires that ethnic boundaries should not cut across political ones, and, in particular, that ethnic boundaries within a given state – a contingency already formally excluded by the principle in its general formulation – should not separate the power-holders from the rest.'[6]

In keeping with the preceding analysis, we understand that Jinnah, with his abrasive strategy in one hand and his secret motives in the other, had to hide his real purpose. This he did by steadily refusing to specify his goal. His March 1940 resolution mentioned the word 'state' in the plural, the end letter *s* creating a baffling situation, since it could apply to either two states (east and west Muslim provinces) – or more than two (and then, how many?).

Patrick French stresses the fact that the Lahore resolution mentioned 'independent [Muslim] states.'[7] It seems that these were to be understood as 'powerful provinces,' and certainly not as a 'state' of Pakistan. 'States' in the plural were, after all, in common usage, as in the 'Princely States' of the Indian Empire. Many were Muslim. Some were of outstanding size, like Hyderabad or Kashmir, the first with a Muslim ruler, the second with a strong Muslim majority.

R. J. Moore suggests that the Lahore resolution can be explained by 'the culmination of eighteen months of controversy' about the separation of Sindh from Bombay: 'The benefits of the separation from Bombay had been squandered by the recourse of its Muslim Premiers to Hindus for survival.'[8] This led Jinnah to stress the separateness in the two-nation theory, not the separatism of partition.

Neither state nor territorial claims were allowed to be closely scrutinised. Thus, they became unassailable from outside while contributing, inside, to the growing enthusiasm of Jinnah's Muslim audience. Just as Gandhi had seduced an indecisive Congress in 1920 with the vagueness – and despite the incredibility – of '*swaraj* in one year,' Jinnah fascinated Indian Muslims with what was a promised land open to their imaginations, a land of Narnia we might call it today, satisfying their wildest dreams, whose real scope and purpose he understandably kept to himself. Like *swaraj*, however, Narnia proved an irresistible concept, creating in time a new political world.

This explains why the word 'Pakistan' was not to be found in the Lahore resolution of March 1940 and, why, moreover, Jinnah initially rejected even the name, which was used by others to refer to his resolution. Addressing the Muslim League, he objected to the name 'Pakistan resolution,' suggesting that the appellation was the work of his enemies, the Hindus, and that it was neither his doing nor responsibility. However, he reflected aloud that if that was what the Hindus wanted to call it, so be it. He would not object to it. This episode lifts a corner of the veil on Jinnah's sprouting ambition to build in the Muslim mind, as well as in the Hindu's, a sense of separateness that made not for a state, but for political clout.

This understanding of the Lahore resolution is in line with the comment of the Viceroy Lord Irwin, who stressed in his book, *Fullness of Days* (1957), the lateness of the partition claim.

> When one looks back over the last few years it is surprising how late in the story it was that partition emerged as a practical and pressing proposition and the fact that it was never seriously put forward in the Round table Conferences debates . . . or indeed in any of the discussions between 1930 and 1940, suggest[ing]

> that Federation, if only it could have been quickly implemented might have saved the situation.[9]

Thus, the vagueness of the Lahore resolution concerned the demand for both a state and a territory – and purposefully so, the emphasis focused on the claim for nationhood, on the two-nation theory.

Reaction to the Two-Nation Theory

The Hindu reaction to the two-nation theory was of disbelief and outrage. Had not Jinnah's grandfather been a Hindu? Had not Gandhi thought Jinnah was a Hindu when he met him, before being told otherwise? Gandhi commented: 'I find no parallel in history for a body of converts and their descendants claiming to be a nation apart from the parent stock.'[10]

Not only apart, but cut off. The threat of the two-nation theory, veiled, undisclosed, potential, and vague as it was, took its strength from these few words: 'geographical contiguous units . . . with such territorial readjustments as may be necessary' in areas where Muslims would be 'numerically in majority.' They suggested partition.

A shocked Gandhi reacted strongly by denying the Muslim League the right to 'vivisect' India. But he was torn by the necessity to concede to others the right of self-determination that he demanded for his own brand of nationalism. He was of two minds: on the one hand, he accepted in April 1940 that nobody should be coerced to stay in India; on the other, he declared in September that he would resist partition.

However, although well aware of the potential of the threat, Gandhi failed to take it seriously enough. When the next stage of negotiations with the British Government took place in 1942, he dealt with it, as usual, as a two-sided issue, rather than as a three-sided contest between imperialism and two nationalisms. When the Cripps Mission came to India in March–April 1942 to offer independence after the war in exchange for collaboration in the war, Jinnah seemed appeased by the constitutional proposition, and was prepared to shelve the 'Pakistan' issue if the Congress accepted the deal.

Reginald Coupland analysed the Muslim League's desiderata at the time of the Cripps Mission:

> (i) it need not be full Dominion status
> (ii) he [Jinnah] has never asked that His Majesty's Government should accept Pakistan, but only that it should not be ruled out of discussion nor the chances of its adoption prejudiced by the form of an interim constitutional system.
> Nevertheless, Pakistanism might triumph as a *counsel of despair*. (emphasis added)

Indeed, on 5 April 1942, Jinnah was reported to have said 'that *Pakistan could be shelved*' (emphasis added).[11]

However, Churchill meant the whole affair as an appeasement gesture to American anti-colonialism, one that was bound to fail, and that Linlithgow, the Viceroy on the job, 'merely intended to uphold the status quo rather than to make constitutional progress.' Gandhi joined the anti-Cripps axis to sink the proposal of 'de facto Dominion Status (or in other words self-determination and the possibility of Pakistan).'[12] He would not be satisfied with an Indian national government, even one supported by Jinnah, as the case was to be, because the defence of India, with the Japanese ready to invade, was to remain firmly in British hands.

Thus, Gandhi and Churchill found themselves on the same political side for the second time in their life – they were once present on the same battlefield in the Boer War, Gandhi in British Army battle dress, Churchill as a war correspondent for the *Morning Post.* Both contributed to the collapse of the talks. One recalled Stafford Cripps to London. The other denounced 'a post-dated cheque on a failing bank.'

The Congress, following Gandhi's lead, did not clinch the deal, and consequently, 'Pakistan' was not 'shelved.' The Congress was not so much interested in post-war schemes as in active participation in the war alongside Britain. It was offered minor tasks in the defence of India, tasks that looked rather despicable, not the grandiose entry into the war that the Congress expected. Thus, the deal failed because the price for it was not delivered. The failure to clinch a deal in turn had another cost, not seen at the time: the rooting of the Pakistan issue.

Gandhi looked elsewhere for an answer to the Cripps fiasco and found it in the Quit India campaign (August 1942). Congress leaders were immediately jailed until the war was over. Meanwhile, the Muslim League filled the political void, and assurance was given to Jinnah that he could veto future constitutional deals.

The two-nation theory emboldened Jinnah to raise the stakes when the war was over. Having claimed nation, territory, and state, he now asked for parity with the Congress party. He added to the claim of being the sole representative Muslim authority in the land that of deserving, as such, the same consideration as the 'Hindu' party. The idea had been brewing in his mind since 1937. Gone were the days when, as in January 1930, he talked about India being 'the common motherland of Muslims and Hindus.' He had watched Gandhi's move, at the Second Round Table Conference, to grant all the Muslims' demands, provided they were unanimous, thereby granting them nothing, since (he knew) they could not agree. Finally, after his rebuff by the Congress leadership in 1937, he realised that 'an honourable settlement could be achieved only between equals.'[13]

The Claim for Parity

On 6 May 1944, one month before the landings in Normandy, Gandhi, dying from malaria, was released from jail. Once more it happened ahead of time, and once more, he recovered, out of jail, the Congress still banned and behind bars (the Working Committee would be released only in June 1945). Once more he observed restraint. Overtures to the Viceroy having been rejected, he thought of converting Jinnah, and asked to discuss the divisive issue of Pakistan with him at the latter's Bombay residence in September 1944. For a week, Gandhi stood firm on a three-fold position: that India was only one nation, even if it was a divided family; that the Congress represented Muslims as well as Hindus (hence the importance of including one Congress Muslim in any Viceroy's Executive Council); and that partition should not come before independence.

Jinnah said no, no, and no to the propositions. However, if the Jinnah-Gandhi talks in September 1944 achieved no settlement, they had side effects. They showed the willingness of Gandhi to compromise on matters related to the division of India, enhanced Jinnah's prestige as the Muslim leader in charge, and procured Gandhi's first offer of a Pakistan formula. Jinnah's 'no' policy was bearing fruit.

Jinnah, however, was still bent on clinching power inside an all-India context, or, as K. Tidrick puts it: 'He had not yet ruled out the creation of "Pakistan" within an all-India federation.'[14]

But Jinnah was simply not interested in Gandhi's Pakistan.

Sir Stafford Cripps was back in India in 1946, one of the three wise men sent to end British rule by the new Labour Government. Up in the cooler air of the Himalayan foothills, they tackled the problem of a shared interim government between the Congress and the Muslim League. But the formation of the Viceroy's Executive Council posed an unanswerable riddle. Jinnah had come up with his claim of equal representation: 'Jinnah's parity demand was another obstacle. Consulted in the wings at Simla, Gandhi gave Cripps his opinion that parity between a Hindu majority and a Muslim minority was unreasonable and undemocratic and "really worse than Pakistan".'[15]

On 16 June 1946, Wavell, the Viceroy, produced a tentative list: six Hindus, five Muslims, one Sikh, one Christian, and one Parsi. Gandhi strongly objected to any parity between caste Hindus and Muslims, and to the exclusion of Muslims from the Congress list. After many amendments and much controversy, a Congress Interim Government was formed on 2 September 1946, to the fury of Jinnah, who had expected to be invited to form the government.

The Cabinet Mission returned to England, having obtained the approval of the Congress and of the Muslim League to its Plan, which allowed for one central government for Defence, Foreign Affairs, and Communications, and for the other subjects, three administrative Groups (roughly the actual India, Pakistan, and Bangladesh) to be in charge of their own governance. The problem of a smooth transfer of power seemed solved, but not for long.

Nehru had voted in favour of the Plan, and Gandhi saw in it 'the best document that the British Government could have produced in the circumstances.'[16] Azad, well pleased, handed down the Congress presidency to Nehru on 10 July 1946, only to regret it bitterly when Nehru, once president, felt free to reconsider the Plan, causing Jinnah's withdrawal (27 July 1946) and subsequent revenge: he announced that he was saying 'good-bye' to constitutional methods and, accordingly, the Muslim League declared 16 August 1946 to be a 'Direct Action Day,' which started the great Calcutta killings (5,000 dead, 15,000 wounded).

To the end, Jinnah pursued the claim of parity. When his Muslim League finally entered a coalition government, on 16 October 1946, it worked like sand in the gears, disrupting the smooth operation of the government. Moreover, to cut the Congress's wings further, Jinnah nominated for his governmental team a Hindu Untouchable from Bengal – thereby marking the territory of future Bangladesh and, most importantly, denying the Indian National Congress the right to represent the mass of the Hindu outcastes, just as he had previously denied its right to represent the Muslim fold. He equated the Congress party with caste Hindus, a shrunken organisation, and an enlarged Muslim League. Parity was made real – or at least, as real and threatening as it could be.

Civil war was now around the corner, and retaliation was complete. Jinnah had to be appeased. Some more time, and a few more noes on his part, and he would checkmate.

11

FROM BRITAIN AS EMPIRE TO BRITAIN AS UMPIRE

The two previous chapters were concerned with the two main nationalist parties' tug of war. This chapter will comment on the Raj's political answer to the call for independence. To sum up in one sentence the complexity of the Indian political problem in 1947, we select thirteen words from Wm. Roger Louis: 'The key to the general problem was the nature of the central government.'[1] He goes on to say: 'Jinnah might have settled for something less than a separate state provided he had parity at the centre.' Judith Brown writes in the same vein: 'What it [Pakistan] meant to Jinnah and other major Muslim politicians is less clear, but it probably signified a Muslim-dominated area in northern India that would be part of a loose all-India federation, rather than a separate, independent state, which made little logistical sense given the scattered location of Indian Muslims.'[2]

'Divide and quit' was the Muslim League's motto. The Congress, with its overwhelming majority, shouted to the Raj: 'Quit' – so that we Indians will be left to decide and divide. Nehru and Patel certainly wanted a strong central government – and no parity. To Gandhi, the League's claim was unacceptable for three main reasons. He rejected the ideology of the two-nation theory. He insisted on the presence of Congress Muslims in any Congress negotiating team or government. He refused any division of India before the transfer of power.

Since Jinnah insisted on all three points, but in reverse order, the political situation turned in a two-side power struggle, with the British looking on. So the British Empire, promoted to umpire, adapted to a changing role – in a welcome change of political skin.

So at the end of the Second World War, Gandhian nationalism entered its third phase, the war serving as midwife. The Mahatma had proved his political mettle in the past. He now had to face a new political environment. His nationalist campaigns had not brought independence, but true to form, he re-enacted, after the rebellion of 1942, what he had done twice before in the 1920s and 1930s: he approached the nationalist problem in a cooperative spirit with the Raj.

Indeed, the victorious and glorious British political establishment had been drained of resources, both money and men. Britain was deeply in debt. The armed forces were looking forward to demobilisation. The Indian Civil Service had stopped recruiting in England for what used to be a choice career. No men, no money, and moreover, anti-imperialistic pressure from its provider and ally, the United States, fed a decolonisation drive, with India in the vanguard. A change of government put Clement Atlee in charge and Churchill in opposition. The Labour Government was sympathetic to Indian nationalist aspirations.

The problem for Britain was how to give India its independence and preserve political and strategic ties. The British Government was looking for an honourable exit from India, under the most favourable conditions. The obvious solution was offered by the institution of the Commonwealth.

The Exemplarity of Dominion Status

Gandhi was born two years after the first Dominion, Canada, became the first colony given self-governing status in 1867, putting it on par with Great Britain in home affairs. More Dominions were created in the next century, which are still in the Commonwealth today: Australia in 1901, as Gandhi was demobilised after the Boer War, then New Zealand in 1907, as he was enmeshed in his first *satyagraha* campaign in South Africa (1906–14). Halfway through that campaign, the Union of Natal, the Transvaal, the Cape, and the Orange Free

State obtained Dominion status (1910). The constitutional promotion of the Union of South Africa had been preceded by the granting of self-government to Natal and to the Transvaal, where Gandhi had resisted the enforcement of anti-Indian legislation regarding the franchise in Natal and the registration of Asians in the Transvaal.

In nationalist terms, the lesson taught by Gandhi's South African experience was plain enough. There were two political stages to independence. The first step was self-government in home affairs inside the Empire, when the Royal Assent, a former requisite for enforcing any legislation, became a formality. The second step – the achievement of Dominion status – took seven years in the case of Natal (1893–1910) after the attainment of self-governance inside the Commonwealth. In his loyalty period (Part II), Gandhi took that lengthy evolution for granted. But in the next, rebellious phase (Part III), his inflamed nationalism grew less and less tolerant of delays in the transfer of power.

Equally plain was another lesson: never believe your fight is over until the very end, for in victory's mantle may lurk your defeat. The Royal Assent was likely to be denied to a racist piece of colonial legislation. In fact, the Government of Natal or the Transvaal had been secretly informed that if the same bill were introduced after self-government had been conceded, the Royal Assent would not and could not be denied.

The exemplarity of the great Dominions was toned down by the experience of Newfoundland and Ireland. Newfoundland joined the company, 'the club,' of the four Dominions – 'white,' 'old,' and 'settler' – in 1907, the year the first Imperial Conference was convened. Watchful Indian eyes – not many of them – might have noticed that Newfoundland lost this Dominion Status in 1934, in the wake of an economic crisis, and was downgraded to a colony. The Irish Free State became a Dominion in 1922, but resented all along the British connection, leading to a new brand of nationalism that was a counter-example to the desirability of Dominion Status. Ireland left the Commonwealth after the Second World War, in 1949.

Plain enough was the allegiance as well as the independence of the Dominions before Gandhi returned to India from South Africa. They still felt politically handicapped under a 'measure of subordination to the British Parliament.'[3] But the Dominions took part in the First World War as separate entities alongside Great Britain and entered the League of Nations independently. By the time of Gandhi's 1920 *satyagraha* in India, the Dominions constituted an informal body that sought not only a constitutional definition, but also unrestricted independence in foreign, military, and financial, as well as home affairs.

The Balfour Declaration of 1926 answered that need and proclaimed formally the full equality of status of the Dominions and the mother country.[4] It fitted perfectly with Gandhi's aspirations of his younger days, with self-governance and yet allegiance to the Crown. It guaranteed that Britain and the Dominions would be 'autonomous communities within the British Empire, *equal in status,* in no way subordinate one to another, in any respect of their domestic or external affairs, though united by a common allegiance to the Crown, and freely associated as members of the British Commonwealth of Nations' (emphasis added). Confirming the Declaration of the 1926 Imperial conference, the 1931 Statute of Westminster gave the Dominions a name and their formal independence from British legislative control, confirming the Declaration of the 1926 Imperial Conference.

The Mirage of Dominion Status

Gandhi watched intently as the procedure for securing Dominion status for South Africa was applied to India. Reluctant, half-hearted constitutional reforms paved the way, under the pressure of war needs and Indian nationalism, but whatever the step forward – and here the case differed from that of the Union of South Africa – no one was ever sure that Britain meant to transfer power, because the Government, although agreeing in principle, would not tie itself to a date. Judith Brown writes: 'It is evident that constitutional reforms in 1919 and 1935 were devices to re-establish the Empire on surer foundations of Indian alliance rather than the manoeuvres of a beneficent Imperial demolition squad.'[5]

To Indian eyes, Dominion status appeared on the horizon like a mirage, ever more temptingly, only to disappear as one approached.

Nationalist thirst, and Gandhi's in particular, could never be quenched in time, and eventually the Indian National Congress dismissed the mirage altogether. Instead of their running after the mirage, it ran after them, never to catch up.

The tragedy – or irony – of it was in the disconnection between demand and offer. What was acceptable at the time it was demanded was turned down as unacceptable at the time of offer. The Congress and the Government were out of step. Like a mirage, agreement receded as negotiations advanced, only to disappear until finally dismissed.

Thus, Gandhi witnessed the nationalist outbidding. In 1916, the Congress had simply asked for 'self-government at an early date,' aiming to become 'an equal partner in the Empire with the self-governing Dominions.' The Montagu Declaration in 1917 responded to the expectations of self-rule and envisaged gradual steps to responsible government inside the British Empire. It announced 'the progressive realization of responsible government in India as an integral part of the British Empire.'

The time and nature of each successive step was left in the hands of the British Parliament.[6] This semblance of a promise of Dominion status was soon downgraded by the explanation that 'full self-governing Dominion status might be a step beyond responsible self-government' – the term used in the 1917 Declaration.[7]

At the special session in August–September 1918, the Congress still expressed its 'most loyal homage to His Gracious Majesty the King-Emperor,' but stated also that 'nothing less than Self-Government within the Empire can satisfy the Indian people and by enabling it to take its rightful place as a free and self-governing nation in the British Commonwealth.' And in 1918, at the end of the war, the Delhi Congress required that 'full Responsible Government should be granted at once... in view of the pronouncement of President Wilson, Mr. Lloyd George and other British statesmen... [that] the principle of self-determination should be applied to all progressive nations.'

The Government of India Act of 1919 was a timid step forward, and the 1919 Amritsar Congress reiterated the demand for 'early steps to establish full Responsible Government in India in accordance with the principle of self-determination.'

The following year, the Nagpur Congress, under Gandhi's guidance, voted for the 'attainment of *swarajya* by the people of India by all legitimate and peaceful means' (article 1 of the new Congress constitution adopted at Nagpur), and for the Non-cooperation campaign.

In 1926, the Mahatma would have appreciated the Balfour Declaration on the equality of status for all Dominions if such status had then been granted to India. The Nehru Report asked for Dominion status in 1928 under threat of a renewed campaign of rebellion. In vain did the vice-regal announcement of October 1929 officially proclaim that India would be granted Dominion status and that a Round Table conference would be convened to consult Indian political parties on the matter. Gandhi and the Congress declined to accept an unspecified timetable and, rejecting Dominion status as their goal, launched the Civil Disobedience campaign (1930–34).

However, in 1937, Gandhi accepted the idea of Dominion status in a letter to his South African friend, H. S. Polak. When the war broke out, the Viceroy, hoping to enlist the cooperation of the Congress, issued the statement of October 1939, which offered Dominion status after the war and, in the present, Indian membership on an advisory war committee. Once more the offer was rejected, in spite of the Secretary of State for India specifying on 7 November 1939 that the Dominion status in question was that of the Statute of Westminster variety. In March 1940, Gandhi declared that Dominion status, even of the Westminster variety, was not suitable to India's case.

Not suitable to India's case? Churchill, Gandhi's main British opponent, gave his own idea of 'suitability,' as reported by Wm. Roger Louis who quotes him as saying: 'British Empire or British Commonwealth of Nations... we keep trade labels to suit all tastes.'[8] L. S. Amery, the Secretary of War for India during the Second World War, had no such association of terms, but wanted 'to make clear that we intend to concede to India... full and unqualified independence within the Commonwealth.' He was, in Roger Louis's judgment, 'fully dedicated to the long-range Dominion Status of a unified India and was willing eventually to accept *two* Dominions.'

Linlithgow, the Viceroy at the outbreak of war, was more dubiously intent on reaching the same goal. He had issued the statement of October 1939, promising Dominion status after the war. But Louis comments that 'perhaps he genuinely subscribed to the idea of Dominion Status – but in the remote future; probably the twenty-first century.'

Linlithgow, though, called the Pakistan scheme 'silly' from the start and failed to take it seriously, except to play up Hindu–Muslim sentiment, while Churchill, in his distaste for the 'Hindoo priesthood,' as he termed the Indian leaders, 'applauded the "Hindu–Muslim feud" as "the bulwark of British rule".' In spite of differences and outlook, these three men worked tirelessly for the Raj and its independence from American interference and Japanese advance. Joined by the Commander-in-Chief Wavell (the next Viceroy), they constituted 'the Churchill-Amery-Linlithgow-"plus Wavell" axis.'[9]

Dominion Status: The End of the Game

Lawrence James, in a witty analysis, compares the succession of events in 1946 to the combination of two games: chess, and snakes and ladders.

> Pure chance would wreck the most carefully-considered gambits and send a player sliding towards an abyss. Escape routes were rare and did not always lead to safety. To further complicate matters, each player followed a different set of rules and pursued different objectives, although partnerships of convenience were sometimes possible.
>
> There were two teams of British players. The first was the Cabinet's India committee, headed by Attlee, which defined Britain's goal as a dignified transfer of power which would end in an undivided independent India within the Commonwealth and a friendly partner in British foreign policy. This was to be accomplished in such a way that it would appear to the world as an act of consummate statesmanship, the natural and wholly admirable conclusion to a Raj which had always placed the welfare of India first. The committee also devised a strategy which

> was implemented by a subordinate team based in India. This comprised the Viceroy, the commander-in-chief, their staff, the administration the police and the garrison of India, whose job it was to keep the peace.
>
> The principal Indian players were the working committee of Congress, dominated by Nehru and another veteran, *sardar* (chief) Vallabhbhai Patel, and the Muslim League, which meant Jinnah. There were also the princes, still rulers of two-fifths of India, but now all but edged out from the political process. Last, there was a miscellany of players, who occupied the periphery, but had the power to upset the moves of the rest... The League demanded Pakistan, an independent Muslim state occupying north-western India and Bengal and embracing sizeable and largely unwilling Sikh and Hindu minorities...
>
> Domestic opposition was muted and confined to right-wing Conservatives, with Churchill uttering sibylline warnings about Britain's decline as a world power.[10]

James goes on to describe the bonds of friendship between Congress and the Labour Party, and to discuss the snakes and the peonage in the chess game, but he unfortunately omits to include Gandhi's name on the list of the game's players. Gandhi may have been a spent political force compared to his efficacy in former times, but his approval of constitutional changes was still a prerequisite of the rules of the game. As described by Mountbatten, his assent to the partition of India was considered essential.

Was Dominion status the end of the Raj game? Dominion status had been officially spurned by the main political party. Skilfully forcing the Commonwealth morsel down the unwilling Congress's throat would be no piece of cake. But Mountbatten rose to a challenge that would have taken another two or three years if the Congress had been willing, instead of crying itself hoarse in favour of an independent, sovereign republic.

Circumstances were changing: Jinnah was expressing interest in Dominion status for his Pakistan and seeking Churchill's favourable opinion.[11] This led the Congress to reconsider its position on the issue. Mountbatten, playing indifference, was shepherding the Congress into the Dominions' barn:

> Although I never once discussed with any Congress leader the possibility of India remaining in the Commonwealth, all the indications are that there is violent discussion going on to this effect... [They] realise Jinnah's game. I feel certain that Congress should be given no inkling as to what H.M.G. attitude will be, since the main hope of bringing them back into the fold lies in the fact that this is the obvious solution for them over the difficulty of Pakistan.[12]

The Acceptance of Dominion Status

Wm. R. Louis states that Mountbatten 'secretly spoke of the Commonwealth as a means of keeping India within the Empire.' The Viceroy had 'emphasized to Jinnah that Commonwealth membership could not be taken for granted.'[13] But Mountbatten also skilfully threatened the Congress with a vision of Pakistan as a Dominion fully supported by the Commonwealth, and with Hindustan left to its own resources, problems, and enemies.

Nehru was slowly shifting his own position. In his Personal Report number one, the Viceroy confided:

> Nehru added that he did not consider it possible for psychological and emotional reasons that India could remain within the Commonwealth; but basically he said he did not want to break the threads tying our two countries together. He actually went so far as to suggest that future relations between the two countries might best be served by some formal common citizenship.[14]

Mountbatten warned Krishna Menon – Nehru's right arm – as well. When Menon asked how to prevent a Pakistan from becoming a Dominion, the Viceroy replied: 'By doing the same.'

Confronted by the threat of a Pakistani Dominion fully supported by the Commonwealth, the Congress leaders were now tempted to reverse their policy to sever all links with Great Britain. Mountbatten was on excellent terms with the Congress leaders. He had Krishna Menon to influence Nehru, who was enamoured of the Vicereine. He had another Menon, V. P. Menon, his Reforms Commissioner, on very friendly terms with Vallabhbhai Patel, the other Congress strong-arm. To quote Mountbatten:

> The Commonwealth meant so much to me. And with this emotional background I began to grasp at every straw in the right direction... Krishna Menon, on the one hand for Nehru, and V. P. Menon, on the other hand, for Patel, who were the two people that mattered... And the important thing about people like Krishna Menon and V. P. Menon is, that they were not leaders in any sense of the word at all, but they were my links with the leaders.[15]

The possibility of the new Dominion of India leaving the Commonwealth at a later stage was not rejected, but served as a device to make the change of policy palatable to those Congress members who had been bent on complete independence since 1930 and were now intent on owing no allegiance to the King-Emperor, and on creating an Indian Republic. Prime Minister Attlee showed himself very accommodating. He wrote in early 1948 that there was 'nothing inherently impossible in a republic forming part of a monarchy.'[16]

On 5 and 6 April Mountbatten warned Jinnah of a change of heart in the Congress leaders: 'determined, he said, to inherit to the full all the powers now exercised by the British in India. They would stoop to anything to gain this object – even to acceptance of Dominion status – rather than any part of India should be handed to the Muslims.'[17]

To counterbalance the heterogeneity of Muslim territories, the Muslim side talked about dividing Hindustan into different '*stans*' in north and south India.[18] With the division of the Princely States along lines of religious affiliation, the balkanisation of India was now plausible, with Dominion status for a possible plurality. Indeed, on 2 April 1947, the Nawab of Bhopal, the Dawan of Travancore, and the Khan of Kalet asked Mountbatten for Dominion status for their states or groups of states. Jinnah made the same suggestion to the Viceroy on the 9th for his Pakistan. More significant was 'his outright rejection of Congress's proposal for immediate Dominion Status': 'Jinnah had to settle for whatever he could while the British remained in India. On 21 May, in what was a clear effort to show that he did not consider the agreement to be final, Jinnah asked for a 'corridor'.'[19]

Gandhi did not have to be persuaded. He had come up with a scheme of his own in order to save India from 'vivisection.' He was going to need Mountbatten to work it out. In fact, Gandhi would need Mountbatten as a 'person' and, more exactly, as an umpire to rule over him and Jinnah. So Dominion status was not to be excluded, thus fulfilling Mountbatten's dream:

> From every point of view, it began to be more and more clear to me that the only way they could develop, was not by – I was going to say by cutting the umbilical cord too soon – but they had to continue to take nourishment and strength from us.
>
> It's the least we could do in return. I came out with this determination, and tried to find the connection. And bit by bit I began to grasp – at every turn I could see, even now, it was an absolute miracle that they could see the point, and wish to keep us. And I think that by far my most lucky achievement was to get that through.[20]

According to Mountbatten, who had promised himself that he 'had to be asked to be ordered to do it,' that is, retain the Commonwealth link, Nehru finally asked:

> 'How can we remain in the Commonwealth?' I [Mountbatten] went to George VI and got him to agree that he would have them in as a Republic...and that there must be a specific link. They must owe some common allegiance to the King...And we between us [Mountbatten and Krishna Menon on the day the King died] thought up that idea of Head of the Commonwealth. And he [Krishna Menon] sold it to India, and we got that title put in, under which republics could remain in the Commonwealth.

12

THE JUDGMENT OF KING SOLOMON

A point of equilibrium has to be found, if only temporarily, when dissenting parties, responding selfishly to a new conjecture of events, rethink their positions.

The parties in question were the British Cabinet, bemused but supportive of Mountbatten's performance, and the Opposition in Parliament, which, under Churchill's leadership, could delay dangerously any constitutional changes. Also included were the Nehru-Patel-Gandhi alliance in the Congress, and Jinnah for the League. As for Mountbatten, he saw himself as a testator.[1] But he was more than a testator. He was a judge reaching a verdict.

His predecessor had been removed from office after having sent to London a 'Breakdown' plan for the evacuation of all British personnel and their families, province by province. 'Operation Madhouse,' it was called. To Admiral Mountbatten, his successor, scuttle was unthinkable. However, the new Viceroy was given only a year, until June 1948, to implement the transfer of power, agreement or no agreement. He thought he had carte blanche to accomplish that. His assessment of the situation can be summed up as follows, in his own terms:

> We had not the means of carrying on. That's the point I want to make to you. We had stopped recruiting for the Indian Civil Service in 1939. We'd stopped recruiting for the Indian Police.

> The people carrying on included a lot of people who were past retirement age. They were running it extremely competently – but . . . that machine that we had . . . had run completely down.[2]

He arrived in Delhi with full pomp and magnificence at the end of March 1947, in the role of governor, umpire, and judge. Like King Solomon of old, he had to rule over the destiny of a newborn. Was he going to cut the nation in two? Or was he going to hand it back whole to the desperate mother? To mother-Gandhi, who would rather give it away unharmed to mother-Jinnah than have it 'vivisected'?

This was indeed the nature of the choice facing him in April–May 1947, as soon as he was enthroned: either a partitioned India or an India governed by Jinnah. The latter was Gandhi's latest solution.

The 'Jinnah Card'

Gandhi came to meet the new Viceroy on 1 April 1947 with his 'Jinnah card': a proposition to hand over India to his political rival.[3] In great secrecy he played his last political ace. Said Gandhi to Mountbatten on April Fool's Day:

> You must say to Jinnah Sahib – I will transfer power to you. I'll ask you to be Prime Minister. I'll ask you to form a government to run a unified India. Get him to form a government, then there will be a strong centre and that will be accepted everywhere. The Muslims will accept and they're the people who are trying to break away. They've got to be appeased.[4]

Stanley Wolpert, Jinnah's biographer, strikes the right note:

> It was a brilliant solution to India's oldest, toughest, greatest political problem. The Mahatma alone was capable of such absolute abnegation, such instant reversal of political position. Gandhi understood Jinnah well enough, moreover, to know just how potent an appeal to his ego that sort of singularly generous

> offer would have been. It might just have worked; surely this was a King Solomon solution.[5]

This last image is insightful, but Wolpert did not develop it further.

The 'Jinnah card' preserved the nation's unity and the integrity of one single state. No other proposition could rival that master stroke in the present circumstances – if only it would be accepted by the Congress, by the new Viceroy, and by Jinnah.

Gandhi's relationship with his own party had changed. It now turned a deaf ear to his discourse, feeling power in its grasp. However, having prevailed before, the Mahatma felt he might still prevail in this last hour. Many of his followers expected him to exert pressure, such as a fast to death against partition – and what a formidable pressure that would be on his own followers. Had he not done so to stop the separation of *Harijans*, the Untouchables, from the Hindu electoral fold?

As for the British Government, it had already announced a date of departure. Thus, it might well welcome a peaceful end to its rule as a demonstration of exemplary trusteeship to the world and a justification of its rule.

Jinnah, his game still concealed, might thus have achieved his secret objective: real power at the centre, and the top political job, to be recorded for posterity. If he failed in that ambition, his intention would not be to promote a religious state, but to foster, in his new realm of Pakistan, the tolerance and secularism of his younger days. Indeed, he proved his intent the following Christmas – his last birthday on earth – by celebrating the Nativity with a Pakistani Christian community.

Three days before the creation of Pakistan, he had made that point clear, and publicly:

> You may belong to any religion or caste or creed – that has nothing to do with the business of the State... In course of time all these angularities of the majority and minority communities, the Hindu community and the Muslim community – because even as regards Muslims you have Pathans, Punjabis, Shias, Sunnis and so on, and among Hindus you have Brahmins, Vaishnavas, Khatris,

> also Bengalees, Madrasis and so on – will vanish . . . Indeed, if you ask me, this has been the biggest hindrance in the way of India to attain freedom and independence, and but for this we would have been free peoples long, long ago.[6]

Antecedents of the Offer

Unthinkable proposition? As V. P. Menon, the Reforms Commissioner, pointed out to the bemused Viceroy, the idea of handing over India to Jinnah was not such a novelty for Gandhi. The novelty was in the new conditions attached to it.

In August 1942, just before he was arrested, Gandhi had made that same proposition to Jinnah: join me in the Quit India campaign, and I shall make you India's Prime Minister: 'Gandhi took time to confirm to a friend of Jinnah that if the Muslim League joined in the Quit India call, Gandhi and the Congress would have no objection to the British Government transferring all the powers it today exercises to the Muslim League on behalf of the whole of India.'[7]

Out of jail, Gandhi pursued the same idea after his week of talks with Jinnah in September 1944. The Mahatma guessed that his old foe was on the warpath for something other than Pakistan: 'The talks produced a thought, filed in a corner of Gandhi's mind that despite his advocacy of Pakistan Jinnah might, in some circumstances, accept a leading role for himself in India as a whole.'[8]

No wonder that the same suggestion came up as well in discussions with the Cabinet Mission in April 1946.

> Pethick-Lawrence (one of the three members of the Cabinet Mission) interrupted Gandhi at this point to note that Jinnah's party had not won a majority of the assembly seats, hence he would be asked to preside over a government, most of whose ministers belonged to 'parties other than his own.' GANDHI SAID THAT WAS 'INESCAPABLE.' The Secretary of State pointed out that 'Jinnah's government' would, in that case, be predominantly Hindu. 'Mr. Gandhi said he did not underrate the difficulties of

> the situation which the Delegation had to face. If he were not an irresponsible optimist he would despair of any solution.'[9]

A few months later, Gandhi lost his patience with Viceroy Wavell, telling that unfortunate man, who was so keen to form a League-Congress government: 'You must make your choice of one horse or the other. So far as I can see you will never succeed in riding two at the same time. Choose the names submitted either by the Congress or the League. For God's sake do not make an incompatible mixture and in trying to do so produce a fearful explosion.'[10]

So, when Gandhi suggested the idea to Mountbatten in April 1947, he gave it credibility. He committed himself and his party to endorse systematically the Muslim League's policy, with the Viceroy as umpire – a different cup of tea from previous years, although the same beverage.

With the Viceroy as umpire, cooperation with the colonial power was resumed. That was now indispensable to fight off partition.

Gandhi's Proposition

The Mahatma arrived in Delhi on the last day of March 1947 after four months spent pacifying the countryside. He submitted to Lord Mountbatten, himself freshly arrived from England on 22 March 1947, the proposition that the Congress might accept Jinnah as the first Prime Minister of India, in replacement of Nehru, who was then head of the Interim government. Jinnah would nominate a cabinet of his own. But this time, Gandhi safeguarded the position of Jinnah by guaranteeing the cooperation of the Congress in the legislature and by giving the British, in the person of Mountbatten, the role of umpire to arbitrate disputes. The viceregal response was: 'I need not say that this solution coming at this time staggered me.'[11]

Gandhi did not play the 'Jinnah card' in order to avoid partition in the eyes of the world, but disclosed it to the Viceroy in secure and complete secrecy, for Mountbatten had to accept his role as umpire to make the scheme workable. Gandhi's political position had suddenly shifted. He now embraced Britain's presence, instead of pressing

Britain to quit. Even if he specified that he wanted the Viceroy as a 'person' – by which he meant, one presumes, not representative of His Majesty's Government – the implications of his choice of personality were obvious. As Mountbatten himself put it on 2 April 1947:

> The essence of the scheme was that it should be put through quickly in order that I might have as many months as possible as Viceroy and President of the Cabinet, and, by retaining the right of veto, continue to exercise complete control in the interests of fair play. The fact that I should be there to see fair play for the first few months would ensure Mr. Jinnah's government not doing anything foolish which would prejudice its reputation in the Assembly or in the country; and he [Gandhi] felt that he could guide them along the straight and narrow path after I left in June 1948.

Gandhi 'convinced [Mountbatten] of his sincerity' and was given that assurance by the Viceroy. But when the Mahatma enquired whether his Excellency was 'in favour of his plan,' he received a diplomatic reply: 'I was very interested by it.'

The Viceregal Staff's Reactions to the Proposed Scheme

The Viceroy took the plan seriously, but according to Rajmohan Gandhi's biography of his grandfather, he 'sought ideas from his staff to scuttle it.' However, it seems that the situation was rather the reverse: scuttling was the staff's idea rather than Mountbatten's, at least to start with. The Reforms Commissioner, V. P. Menon, warned him against it. The umpire position would then really be untenable. It would bring disrepute on the Viceroy and his country. This explains the misunderstanding that followed, about the drafting of Gandhi's proposal.

On 4 April the Viceroy wanted the plan put on paper and asked Gandhi to 'explain it once more for Lord Ismay's benefit . . . and [to] put his scheme in writing.' On that day, his staff (Lord Ismay, the Chief of the Viceroy's Staff; Sir Eric Mieville; Mr Abell; and an Indian, the Reforms Commissioner) came 'to the unanimous conclusion that Mr. Gandhi's scheme was not workable. It would put the Viceroy in an impossible position; Mr. Jinnah's Government would be completely at the mercy of the Congress majority.'

On 5 April, the next day, V. P. Menon sent an enclosure to Miéville entitled 'Tactics to be adopted with Gandhi as regards his scheme.' These included showing the proposals to Jinnah in the hope that he would reject them; making no similar offer to the Congress; and holding no meetings with Gandhi: 'In other words, we must, while keeping Gandhi in good humour, play for time.' A note written by the Reforms Commissioner, undated, would also have influenced the Viceroy:

> There is no reason to suppose that Jinnah will now accept an offer which he had rejected previously...The assurance of cooperation by the Congress is more a wishful thinking...The position of [the Viceroy] will become...one of very great difficulty and embarrassment...[If] Jinnah is at liberty to plan for Pakistan and even to put his plans into effect provided that he is successful in appealing to reason and does not use force, this is asking for the impossible.

As Gandhi complained that no agreement had yet been put on paper, Lord Ismay insisted, on 7 April, at a staff meeting that 'it was important to get out of Mr. Gandhi's mind any idea that the note he had prepared giving the outline of Mr. Gandhi's scheme in any way constituted a preparation for a draft agreement.' The Viceroy agreed: 'I must first be convinced that Pandit Nehru agreed with it.'[12]

Sounding Jinnah's Reaction to Gandhi's Proposition

While the viceregal staff was convinced that the plan could not work, and advised the Viceroy to reject it out of hand before Jinnah did, Mountbatten reminded them on 10 April of his meeting with Jinnah the previous day: 'On the question of the inclusion of Mr. Jinnah in the Cabinet H.E. The Viceroy related that he had made a tentative suggestion to Mr. Jinnah that he might become Prime Minister. This suggestion had had a far greater effect on Mr. Jinnah than he would have thought possible.'[13]

The Viceroy had sounded Jinnah very discreetly but positively on 9 April. He reported this conversation with Jinnah after seeing that 'the offer was likely to tempt Jinnah.'[14] This is what he recalled of that interview:

> I finally said that I found that the present Interim Coalition Government was everyday working better and in a more co-operative spirit; and that it was *a day-dream of mine* to be able to put the Central Government under the Prime Ministership of Mr. Jinnah himself. He said that nothing would have given him greater pleasure than to have seen such unity. Some 35 minutes later, Mr. Jinnah, who had not referred previously to my personal remark about him, suddenly made a reference out of the blue to the fact that I had wanted him to be Prime Minister. There is no doubt that it had greatly tickled his vanity, and that he had kept turning over the proposition in his mind. *Mr. Gandhi's famous scheme may yet go through on the pure vanity of Mr. Jinnah!*[15] (emphasis added)

The reason had certainly something to do with vanity. However, we have suggested that the inquisitive flattery met Jinnah's ambitions with a direct relevance to his secret political ambition. The Viceroy was not far from the truth, as he went on to say about the Pakistan claim: 'Nevertheless, he gives me the impression of a man who has not thought out one single piece of the mechanics of his own great scheme.' Premiership, not Pakistan, was Jinnah's Holy Grail. And Premiership, through Pakistan, was the second choice.

The Viceroy warned his incredulous staff: 'It would not be very easy for Mr. Jinnah to refuse Mr. Gandhi's offer.'[16]

Stanley Wolpert assumes in his biography of Jinnah that Gandhi's plan 'might just have worked,' but also that Gandhi's offer was 'never conveyed to Jinnah.'[17] Jinnah had not been informed of the plan. Or had he? In an interview with Mountbatten some thirty years later, Collins and Lapierre reported him to say, when they asked about

Jinnah's reaction to the plan: 'He never showed much reaction to any idea when you spoke to him, but I sensed he was absolutely astonished. At once he said, "He'll never get it past the C.P. {Congress Party}."'

For ten long days, the Plan seemed alive and possible. But on 10 April, Mountbatten told his councillors: 'Mr. Gandhi has affected to be most disappointed and has taken the line that the object of these talks was to produce a draft agreement and not a mere summary. In other words he was hoping for a Mountbatten-Gandhi pact!' And he concluded that it was 'premature to prepare any cut and dried plan even in a draft form.'[18]

Reaction of the Congress Leaders

Gandhi had hoped that the Viceroy himself would handle his plan. Years later, Mountbatten remembered that on 1 April 1947, Gandhi did not come waving a new plan, but asking whether

> I had a solution in mind. My memory is that we got to it by coming after I explained what difficulty I was having in finding a solution. That introduced it. He said, 'Send for Jinnah, get him to form a government, then there'll be a strong centre and that will be accepted everywhere. The Muslims will accept and they're the people who are trying to break away. They've got to be appeased. I said, 'What about Congress?' He said, 'If Kripalani and Patel and Nehru and I agree with this, it will work' Then I did say, 'I think it's a brilliant idea, I'm terribly intrigued by it, will you put it to them?' 'No,' he said, 'I'd like you to.' 'Ah, no,' I said, 'that won't do... I don't propose to risk my own position by putting up a scheme which they're going to say 'no' to.[19]

Although meeting resistance to his scheme, the Mahatma did not want to give it up. He tried to clear up what he called the 'misunderstanding' about the plan, and wanted the matter to be pursued – if not by himself, then by the Raj. That was his new strategy. He hoped that the Viceroy would pursue the scheme on his own and go against the will of the Congress Working Committee.

For the sake of the 'supreme importance of secrecy' – indispensable to give the scheme a chance of success – only a few were in the know. There were half a dozen of them: Nehru, the Interim Prime Minister (who was to lose his job if the plan worked); Acharia J. B. Kripalani, the President of the Congress; the Maulana Abul Kalam Azad, the former Muslim President of the Congress; Khan Abdul Ghaffar Khan, the 'Frontier Gandhi,' a devoted Gandhian Muslim and believer in non-violence; Krishna Menon, Nehru's right hand man and intermediary; and Vallabhbhai Patel, the trusted, faithful, and level-headed Interim Home Minister, second only to Nehru.

On 3 April, Gandhi had informed the Viceroy that 'those leaders of the Congress he had spoken to had all agreed that it [the scheme] was feasible and would support him, but that he had not yet had time to talk to Pandit Nehru, which he intended to do that evening. He was more than ever intense about his scheme as being the best solution.'[20]

Patel was known to have been converted to partition by this time. He kept out of the negotiations. He had certainly been taken into confidence by Gandhi on 31 March, when he met the Mahatma off the train station. His supposedly unfavourable reaction probably explains Gandhi's pessimism at his prayer meeting the evening after his first interview with the Viceroy. Rajmohan Gandhi quoted the Mahatma's words from that evening: 'Nothing will be according to what I say. My writ runs no more... No one listens to me any more.'[21]

Nehru also would have to be persuaded. He promptly developed an excellent rapport with Mountbatten and his wife. They had met before in unusual circumstances, when he had been of help to Lady Edwina. He called on the Viceroy on 1 April, and part of the conversation was recorded in Mountbatten's Papers.

> Pandit Nehru was not surprised to hear of the solution which had been suggested, since this was the solution that Mr. Gandhi had put up to the Cabinet Mission [in 1946]. It was turned down then as being impracticable; and the policy of Direct Action by the Muslim League, and the bloodshed and bitterness in which it had resulted, made the solution less realistic now than a year ago.

It is not clear from this quote how much of this statement can be attributed to Nehru or to the opinion of the defunct Cabinet Mission or to Mountbatten's views. But it is clear that Nehru, who loved the Mahatma so dearly would not dismiss the plan lightly, and the Viceroy noted: 'He [Nehru] realised that Mr. Gandhi was immensely keen on a unified India, at any immediate cost, for the benefit of the long term future.'[22]

After Gandhi talked to Nehru about his plan, there was no mention of any rejection of the scheme. But one difficulty cropped up, the nature of which was not disclosed. On 5 April, Gandhi wrote: 'I must add that Pandit Nehru has at least one vital objection to the outline [of the plan].'[23] When Mountbatten met Nehru on 8 April 1947, he reported: 'Nehru thought the only way the Gandhi plan could be made use of was by offering the premiership of the Interim Government to Jinnah, with the object of strengthening the central authority until the handing over of power in June 1948.'[24]

Gandhi knew that his son and political heir had still to be convinced, and he persevered in his efforts on all fronts. He had experienced similar difficulties with Nehru at the time of the Simon Commission, the Nehru Report, and the demand for *purna swaraj*. The two leaders had compromised over their differences, avoiding a break in their relationship. Why could they not agree this time? Giving up his premiership for India's benefit was no big deal for Nehru.

Things went smoother with the Maulana Azad, whose first meeting with the Viceroy took place on 2 April. He had learned of the plan from Gandhi that very morning. The Viceroy remembered:

> He staggered me by saying that in his opinion it was perfectly feasible of being carried out, since Gandhi could unquestionably influence the whole of Congress to accept it and work it loyally. He further thought that there was a chance *I might get Jinnah to accept it*, and he thought that such a plan would be the quickest way to stop bloodshed, and the simplest way of turning over power. (emphasis added)

The other Muslim Congress leader, Abdul Ghaffar Khan, talked to the Viceroy in the same vein. The frontier was torn because of the polarisation between Muslim Pakistan and *kaffir*-Congress (unbeliever). On 4 April, he had accompanied Gandhi to one of the interviews with the Viceroy and showed his full support for the plan. When asked by the Viceroy whether 'he really thought that Congress would accept this scheme, and that it would be workable . . . he gave a very definitely affirmative reply. I [Mountbatten] then invited Lord Ismay to take Mr. Gandhi to his room and put his scheme in writing.'[25]

Gandhi's Departure

In mid-April, the Viceroy was still testing the waters and fiddling in a desperate hurry with his other plans – 'Plan We' and 'Plan They,' 'Plan Union' or 'Cabinet Mission Plan,' 'Plan Balkan,' the 'Intermediate Plan' – tentative names and schemes that had in common two features: the desire for lightning speed and the prompt delivery of the new state or states into the bosom of the Commonwealth. On 9 April, Mountbatten had made his decision.

Gandhi's plan had one great fault: it looked like a second Gandhi-Irwin Pact – the agreement 'on equal terms' between the 'naked fakir' and the Viceroy, as Churchill saw it. Mountbatten had no enthusiasm for repeating the procedure that had followed the 'March on the Salt' to the Indian Ocean in 1930, when the 'naked fakir' went to parley on equal terms with the Viceroy – as Churchill had criticised. It sounded too much like a deal with Gandhi because Gandhi had demanded that if Jinnah refused, the Viceroy should then turn over power to the Congress.

Mountbatten had made up his mind that he would neither sign a new Gandhi-Irwin pact nor repeat the procedure of the Cabinet Mission from 1946. Therefore, he had already told his staff on 5 April that his decision should 'not be an agreement which the Indian leaders would publicly accept, but a *unilateral decision* from which there would be no appeal'[26] (emphasis added).

On 11 April, two days after sounding Jinnah, the Viceroy received a letter from Gandhi, conceding defeat. He had failed to convince the Congress leaders, and he was leaving Delhi the next day.

On 12 April, Gandhi had a meeting with Mountbatten before leaving Delhi. The purpose was for him to sign a solemn announcement with Jinnah, under the Viceroy's auspices, that they had both renounced violence for political ends. Gandhi, there and then, suggested, in the Viceroy's words, that 'he regretted his failure very much, but said he thought I [Mountbatten] could still go ahead on the plan myself if I ardently believed in it.'[27] And the Mahatma made a further suggestion to the Viceroy, who recalled:

> He then said that he *advised me* to go on strengthening the Interim Government, and making them function correctly for the next 14 months; after which he considered *I should hand over power to the Interim Government.* This staggered Lord Ismay and myself, and we both pointed out that that meant handing over power to one party, namely Congress.... possibly leading to civil war. (emphasis added)

Referring to the agreement he had come to sign, the Mahatma countered that the possibility of civil war was being removed at this very moment by Jinnah and himself signing the document. Was the Viceroy not asking them to sign a solemn declaration to forsake any resorting to violence? Thus, reported the Viceroy, 'Mr. Gandhi, with a wily smile, pointed out that if Mr. Jinnah indeed signed the paper we were sending round to him he could not again use force for political purposes.' Commenting on that episode, the Viceroy remembered: 'I was speechless at this immoral suggestion, and shook my finger at him. But he only blinked and smiled.'

The Mahatma was being facetious, and Mountbatten enjoyed that side of his personality. But his smile had all the seriousness of a lawyer's statement, and the Viceroy did not quite know how to take it: 'I must say I was speechless to find that he proposed, if Mr. Jinnah indeed meant to sign and stick to the statement, to take advantage of this to impose a Congress Government on the Muslims. Here again I find it hard to believe that I correctly understood Mr. Gandhi.'[28]

On 12 April 1947, the Mahatma then left Mountbatten, after signing the vice-regal document denouncing violence. Next to Jinnah's signature, dated 15 April 1947, he signed in Devanagari and Urdu scripts, adding, in Roman script, 'i.e. M K Gandhi' – a cunning reminder of their past feud on languages.

The Preferred Alternative: Partition

According to Rajmohan Gandhi, Mountbatten applied himself to wreck Gandhi's plan by creating dissension in the Congress leadership. Gandhi's grand-son may be right, indeed, but then, Mountbatten would try to cling to impartiality. As a result, the proposition was not made to Jinnah.

For one, the Maulana Azad changed his mind about the plan, under what influence we do not know. Moreover, Patel was for partition at this stage and would not have agreed with the scheme. Gandhi had unfruitful discussions with Nehru, but made no comment on their content (otherwise, Rajmohan Gandhi would have known about it). Only Abdul Ghaffar Khan sided with Gandhi.

A Patel-Nehru alliance against Jinnah's promotion as the first Indian Prime Minister terminated what seemed at the time a crazy idea, the idea to hand over to the Muslim League the fruit of a hard-won victory. Gandhi explained in his letter of 11 April to the Viceroy:

> I had several short talks with Pandit Nehru and an hour's talk with him alone and then with several members of the Congress Working Committee last night, about a formula I had sketched before you and which I had filled in for them with all the implications. I am sorry to say that I failed to carry any of them with me except Badshah Khan [Abdul Ghaffar Khan].
>
> I do not know that, having failed to carry both the head and the heart of Pandit Nehru with me, I would have wanted to carry the matter further. But Panditji was so good that he would not be satisfied until the whole plan was discussed with the few members of the Congress Working Committee who were present. I felt sorry that I could not convince them of the correctness of my plan from every point of view. Nor could they dislodge me from

> my position... Thus I have to ask you to omit me from your consideration.[29]

Like Abraham, cherished by Muslims, Gandhi had been ready to sacrifice his 'political heir.' Like Abraham's son, Nehru was saved from immolation. The sacrifice that did take place was India's, which was cut in two.

A week after Gandhi's departure, on 20 April 1947, Nehru conceded Pakistan, and the Working Committee reconsidered its position on Dominion status, since Jinnah, advised by Churchill, wanted it for Pakistan. Nehru explained:

> The truth is that we were tired men, and we were getting on in years too. Few of us could stand the prospect of going to prison again. But we accepted. The plan for partition offered a way out and we took it. We expected that partition would be temporary, that Pakistan was bound to come back to us. But if Gandhi had told us not to, we would have gone on fighting, and waiting. But we accepted.[30]

On 2 May 1947, the Balkan Plan, which had not been seen 'in writing' by any of the Indian leaders, was sent to London for approval. In mid-May, the Viceroy took Nehru for a working holiday in the hills and disclosed in confidence his Plan to him. Nehru, emotional and enraged, saw in the Plan the disintegration of India into numerous states. Mountbatten took immediate notice of his refusal, and within a day, V. P. Menon, the Reforms Commissioner, managed to produce yet another and better Plan, which Mountbatten himself flew immediately to London, leaving the British Cabinet gasping for breath at the sudden change. Menon's Plan was to cleverly go back to the Government of India Act (1935) by promoting Dominion status for India.

Menon's glory was to harvest *swaraj* in the form of Dominion status. The Viceroy wrote him a thankful letter:

> It was indeed fortunate that you were Reforms Commissioner on my Staff, and that we were brought together into close association with one another at a very early stage, for you were the first

> person I met who entirely agreed with the idea of Dominion status, and you found the solution which I had not thought of, of making it acceptable by a very early transfer of power. History must always rate that decision very high, and I owe it to your advice given in the teeth of considerable opposition from other advisers.[31]

The 3 June Plan was endorsed and duly announced to the world on that day. Mountbatten commented years later:

> One of the things that Jinnah grossly miscalculated was, he was convinced that I would split India into Hindustan and Pakistan, I didn't know that the Indians had intended to ask me for the continuation of India, inheriting all the previous things, and that Pakistan should be thrown out. It was a must. Jinnah was absolutely furious when he found out they were going to call themselves India. It was a very good idea. The real body blow to Pakistan was *Menon's idea of India inheriting* everything. They were the *successor state* and Pakistan was to leave them and there was no way Jinnah could get around that. Now, that was one of the things that made people begin to think that Pakistan was not going to be viable and would not survive. (emphasis added)

Of his short stay in London in May 1947, Mountbatten remembered: 'Nobody argued with me at all. I had as great control over the Cabinet as I had over the leaders in India at that time, and I had the most frightful, not so much conceit, but a complete and absolute belief that it all depended on me, and they had to do what I said or else.'[32]

A sullen Jinnah nodded consent – he had been warned by Churchill not to refuse. The latter, canvassed by Mountbatten on 22 May, had pledged the help of the Conservative Party to push through the necessary legislation speedily when he knew that Nehru would accept Dominion status if power were transferred that year. Mountbatten 'pointed out that [he] had been unable to obtain a similar written assurance from Mr. Jinnah,' who only the day before had demanded a 'corridor' between East and West Pakistan. (This demand would not only permit communications by land, but also preserve old centres of Muslim culture like Delhi and Aligarh for Pakistan.)[33] Mr. Churchill expressed great surprise:

> 'By God,' he said, 'he is the one man who cannot do without British help . . . ' I then asked him if he would advise me how I should proceed if Jinnah was intransigent. He thought about this for a long time and finally said: 'To begin with you must threaten. Take away all British officers. Give them military units without British officers . . . without Dominion status.' He authorised me to give Mr. Jinnah the following message: 'This is a matter of life and death for Pakistan, if you do not accept this offer with both hands.'[34]

Gandhi, too, shared Jinnah's negative disposition, which Mountbatten described in these terms:

> Since Gandhi returned to Delhi on May 24, he has been carrying out an intense propaganda against the new plan, and although I have always been led to understand he was the man who got Congress to turn down the Cabinet Mission plan a year ago he was now busy trying to force the Cabinet Mission plan on the country. He may be a saint but he seems also to be a disciple of Trotsky. I gather that the meetings of the Congress Working Committee have been most acrimonious in consequence, and I believe the leaders were quite apprehensive on my seeing Gandhi on Monday. I certainly was. Judge then my astonished delight on finding him enter the room with his finger to his lips to indicate that it was his day of silence![35]

The Viceroy had assured Churchill that although Gandhi was 'unpredictable,' Nehru and Patel could deal with any difficulty. However, just before the announcement, Mountbatten was briefed that the old man would object to the birth of the two nations at his 3 June prayer meeting. He immediately asked the Mahatma to call on him before the announcement. Silent Gandhi complied and Mountbatten rejoiced: he could talk, uninterrupted:

> The fact that he let me do all the talking and only intervened with a few remarks on paper, gave me a chance . . . If he, in fact, had not had a day of silence, I don't know how it would have ended. I'm sure it was a tribute to me that he decided to have a day of silence . . . It wasn't his usual day of silence.[36]

The Viceroy took the line that the final plan could be called Gandhi's Plan.

> And I then started off by saying, well, you can tell them it's the Gandhi Plan. And he was very surprised, and I said, 'Well, because you wanted the people to choose. The salient point you want to make is that this plan gives them the right, through their elected representatives to choose what they want.' I said, 'You don't want to impose your will against that, do you?' So, bit by bit, we got the thing round. The main thing, you see, was the voice of God, which I also had access to . . . 'I'm sure you wouldn't wish us to oppose them with the force of arms.'

As the Viceroy's rhetoric worked, Gandhi let things be. Mountbatten confided his secret for dealing successfully with Gandhi: 'Whereas former negotiators had thought the only person they had to placate, and get along with was Gandhi, I came to the conclusion that, really, they were all on my side against him. That gave me a great feeling of strength against him.' After all, India was going to be the 'successor state,' and seceding parts would be cut away from it. But the unity of India that Gandhi cherished would be preserved and saved in legal documents. Gandhi, in fact, as a lawyer, had won.

Alea jacta est: The Die Is Cast

By now, Nehru and his colleagues were exhausted from worry, fatigue, and overwork. They said no to an independent Bengal, and were then refused an independent North-West Frontier. They canvassed for the Princely States, including Kashmir, to join India (helped by a willing Viceroy), and they chose to believe that Pakistan would soon collapse.

It does live on, but Jinnah did not survive long. He was a nervous wreck and terminally ill, but unbelievably, nobody was aware of his condition. Speed, which had haunted Gandhi in 1942 and the Viceroy in 1947, defeated any hope of keeping the whole of India together. For Jinnah's two-nation theory might have died with him in 1948 – had his prognosis been known.[37] But nobody knew.

When asked as to what he would have done, had he known, Mountbatten replied after some thought:

> I assumed that I was dealing with a man who was there for keeps, and had Pakistan as his object on which I could not steer him around. If in fact, we suppose for a moment that Jinnah had died, literally before the transfer of power, I believe the Congress would have been so relieved that their arch enemy was dead – and none of the others were regarded as anything more or less than Jinnah's shadow – we would have been dealing on a basis where Congress would have been prepared to give up much more and the others would have been ready to accept that. It's a horrifying thought that we were never told.

And what would have been Mountbatten's attitude? 'Would I have said, Let's hold India together and not divide it? Would I have put back the clock, and held the position? Most probably.'[38]

Swaraj Accomplished!

Away with the ill winds that blew from Noakhali, Bihar, and the Punjab went the unity of India, torn apart between two nations that hated each other, and into two states soon at war with one another. The cruel cut gave ethnic cleansing a boost. But for the British Government, partition lost its awfulness if it engendered two Dominions in the Commonwealth: 'A request by India to remain in the Commonwealth would enhance British prestige enormously in the eyes of the world. This factor alone was of overriding importance.'[39]

In his role as Solomon, Mountbatten had ignored the plea to hand the infant over to Jinnah, the mother of the dead dream. He could not give it whole to the real mother either. So he decided to partition the child. It would be his own, proud decision, not Gandhi's, that would prevail. Speed, speed, and speed would force the agreement of the dissenting parties. The Viceroy gave his ruling in the first days of June 1947 and transferred power on 15 August 1947 – it took him exactly two and a half months. The final 3 June Plan was accepted by the British Empire and the leaders of the two main political parties. It decided the partition of British India and left the Indian States with no choice but to join either Pakistan or the Indian Union.

Gandhi boycotted the celebration of independence, among riots, massacres, and refugees galore in India and Pakistan. But he congratulated the Viceroy: 'I wanted to tell you how thrilled I am that the Congress Party should have asked you to stay on as the Head of State... Who could have envisaged five months ago that, having got rid of the hated British, we should ask the last Viceroy to be our President?'[40]

He also asked for permission to visit the Pakistani state. His idea, conveyed by the Viceroy to London, was that he would 'spend the rest of his life in Pakistan looking after the minorities.'[41] Was he thus still conspiring against the two-nation theory? He was waiting for an answer to his request when he was assassinated at the end of January 1948. The visit would have been an odd experience if the answer had been 'Yes, you can.'

The Mahatma had not wanted to live to see the division of India. But when partition took place, he did not fast to death. However, he had evidently been well prepared to take that fateful decision, because when the assets of India were being divided and the Congress declined to transfer a huge sum of money due to Pakistan (money then used to buy arms to contest the Kashmir question), he volunteered spontaneously to fast into death in order to force the transfer of funds, as if the idea of a fast to the death had been constantly on his mind.

As the Viceroy testified about Gandhi: 'You know, he is very honourable.' And he proceeded to explain:

> They [the Congress] froze the assets of Pakistan, which they had not yet transferred... 'Are you going to agree to this? Rob them of a hundred million or several hundred million, pounds?' 'No,' he said. I said, 'How are you going to do it?' He said, 'I shall fast to death until they give the balances over.' And I got up and shook him by the hand, and said, 'I congratulate you.' And they [the Congress party] were terribly upset that he'd agreed to this – terribly upset he'd done it with me and not with them... And he got them absolutely by the short hairs; they had to give up. Now that was courage; he was prepared to fast to death. He *knew* it was a dishonourable act. My point is I utilized Gandhi whose power was immense to force him to force the Government of India to dispose of these sterling balances.[42]

My own point is that in 1947, Gandhi was prepared to fast to death for a debt of sterling pounds, but not to protest against the partition of the body politic of India. This pinpoints his nationalism on the scale of his priorities. *Tout est perdu, fors l'honneur:* all is lost, save honour. The two-nation theory was implemented, two new dominions were created, and Mother India lived on, her honour thus saved.

ENVOY

THE TWO BROTHERS

A despotic ruler had two sons

The eldest bore the name Mohan, the younger Moham.[1]

At birth they looked very much alike. They had the same education, shared the same diplomas, and followed the same vocation, respecting their father's wishes. But they inherited different religions. In the end, it made all the difference to their ambitions and careers.

When the older came of age, he resented the paternal yoke and claimed his inheritance as what was rightfully due – in those times – to the eldest son. He asked for the Realm and promised to provide for his brother. The brother objected and asked for his share.

Father and sons fought one another in the name of nationalism. This meant, for the father, the prolongation of his rule; for the elder son, freedom, independence, and power; for the younger, the sharing of the spoils.

Making a deal, the father left them, all too suddenly, to fight it out amongst themselves. To the chagrin of Moham, the Realm went to Mohan, but two chunks were severed for Moham, one to the west and one to the east.[2] However, Moham soon died, for he was terminally ill. Had his brother and father known of his state of health, this story would have ended differently.

In fairy tales, the end invariably should be: 'And they lived happily ever after.' Happily, because lovingly.

Imagine a world without love. It would be hell. Nationalism without love is hell. Gandhi's message in this world is love – as the Mahatma had said, in his *Letters to the Ashram*: 'God is Love, Love is God.' Shantidas,[3] the Mahatma's disciple in the West, had sung the same vibrant message in the Gandhian Community of the Ark:

> *Ubi caritas et amor,*
> *Deus ibi est.*[4]

GLOSSARY

Ahimsa	non-violence
Ashram	community: Gandhi founded his first *ashram* at Sabarmati, near Ahmedabad, and the second twenty years later at Sevagram, near Wardha in Central India
Bapu	father, the term often used to address Gandhi
Brahmacharia	chastity
Charkha	spinning wheel
Dharma	religious duty
Dhoti	loincloth
Gandhianity	the world of Mahatma Gandhi, namely the basket of economic, social, and political beliefs, and the practices he promoted. It has two dimensions of global relevance: an inner conviction expressed in a way of life, and the creative political experiments of his faith in non-violence
Harijan	child of God as Gandhi called the untouchables
Hartal	day of strike and shop closures as a form of protest
Hijrat	exit from the land of the infidels as an alternative to fighting them *(Jihad)*
Indenture	contracted servitude, referring to Indians shipped to plantations or mines usually for a period of three years
Indianity	awareness of the identity and specificity of the Indian nation
Khadi	handspun cloth
Khilafatists	defenders of the Caliph, Sultan of Turkey, at the end of the First World War
Mahatma	great soul

Maulana	honorific title to learned Muslims
Nai talim	Gandhi's views and work on education
No-Changers	congressmen opposed to taking part in elections, after 1924
Panchayat	village council of elders
Pro-Changers	congressmen favourable to the elections and standing for office
Purna Swaraj	complete independence
Quaid-e-Azam	great leader
Ramarajya	kingdom of heaven
Rowlatt Act	act to prolong in peace time the powers of the Defence of India Act in the First World War in case of unrest
Sarvodaya	the welfare of all
Satyagraha	adherence to truth: a composite of two Indian words woven together by Gandhi: a way of life and the political weapon of non-violence
Swadeshi	self-sufficiency
Swaraj	self-rule or independence
Varna	caste

NOTES

Gandhian Nationalism in One Song and Three Cartoons

1. A. S. Hornby, *Oxford Advanced Learners Dictionary of Current English,* 4th ed. (Oxford, 1989).
2. *Petit Robert, Dictionnaire de la Langue Française* (1986), p. 1257.
3. E. Kedourie, *Nationalism*, 4th ed. (Oxford: Blackwell, 1993), p. 1.
4. J. Brown, 'Gandhi and Human Rights: In Search of True Humanity,' in R. L. Johnson, *Gandhi's Experiments with Truth* (Oxford: Lexington, 2006), p. 237.
5. M. K. Gandhi, *An Autobiography: The Story of My Experiments with Truth* (Ahmedabad, 1927), p. 212.
6. R. Gandhi, *Gandhi: The Man, His People And The Empire,* (London: Haus Books, 2007), p. 180. Gandhi had discarded the smart European suit after entering his first political fight in South Africa.
7. Two years later, in a similar incident, Gandhi was chairing a conference in Godhra, north Gujarat (November 1917). The anglophone Jinnah had to comply 'unwillingly' with Gandhi's request that he should speak in an Indian language and he 'stammered out a speech in Gujarati.' (Quoted in R. Gandhi, 2007, p. 194). Gandhi pursued the delicate matter further in 1920, a few months before the break with Jinnah at the launch of the Non-cooperation Campaign (Nagpur Indian National Congress, December 1920). He wrote to Jinnah's wife (30 April 1920): 'Please remember me to Mr. Jinnah and do coax him to learn Hindustani or Gujarati. If I were you, I should begin to talk to him in Gujarati or Hindustani...

   Will you do it? Yes, I would ask this even for the love you bear me.' (*Collected Works of Mahatma Gandhi* (New Delhi, Publications Division, 2007), vol. 20, p. 258.

8. Raphael painted two versions of this biblical scene (1510–11 and 1518–19); both are in the Vatican. In *Jinnah of Pakistan* (1984), Stanley Wolpert makes a fleeting allusion to the symbolism of Solomon.
9. Quoted in Johnson, *Gandhi's Experiments*, p. 157.
10. See the negotiations with the INC at the time of the Simon Commission (1928) and the 1937 endeavours to form coalition ministries with the Congress party.
11. Quoted in L. Mosley, *The Last Days of the British Raj* (London: Weidenfeld and Nicholson, 1961), p. 239.
12. Mountbatten interviewed by L. Collins and D. Lapierre, *Mountbatten and the Partition of India* (Singapore: Trans-East, 1982), p. 46.
13. This well-known phrase occurs in Jalal's assessment of Jinnah's tactics; see *The Sole Spokesman* (Cambridge: Cambridge University Press, 1994).
14. *The Concise Oxford Dictionary* (1982).
15. M. K. Gandhi, *Collected Works of Mahatma Gandhi,* GandhiServe Foundation (New Delhi: Publications Division Government of India, 1999), vol. 1, p. 9.
16. Ibid., vol. 1, p. 1. This is taken from Gandhi's diary in English, in which he reported also his stammer and difficulties with public speaking: 'My head reeled . . . my whole frame shook.'
17. Referring to a movement in South Africa aiming at isolating Indians from Africans, he said in April 1928, in a different political context: 'Indians cannot exist in South Africa for any length of time without the active sympathy and friendship of the Africans. I am not aware of the general body of the Indians having ever adopted an air of superiority towards their African brethren, and it would be a tragedy if any such movement were to gain ground among the Indian settlers of South Africa.' *Collected Works,* vol. 41, p. 365.
18. *Collected Works of Mahatma Gandhi,* vol. 1, p. 19.
19. J. Brown, *Gandhi: Prisoner of Hope* (New Haven: Yale University Press, 1989), p. 175.
20. 'Gandhian' is first featured in *The Oxford English Dictionary*, Second Edition, vol. VI, citing from the *Daily Telegraph* on 7 March 1921; then in the 1950s from the title of J. V. Bondurant's analysis of non-violence: *Conquest of Violence: Gandhian Philosophy of Conflict* (Princeton: Princeton University, 1958); and much later in the *Hindustan Times Weekly* (New Delhi) on 4 April 1971.
21. The French politician and writer André Malraux favoured the word '*gandhisme*.' He said in October 1973: 'Gandhism is the only example in the world of a revolutionary thought that has triumphed without shedding

blood.' Quoted by Marie-France Latronche, *L'Influence de Gandhi en France de 1919 à nos Jours* (L'Harmattan: Recherches Asiatiques, 1999) from Yves Beigbeder, *Malraux et l'Inde*, doctorate thesis, Sorbonne, Paris IV, 1983.

22. September 1944, *Collected Works,* vol. 78, pp. 62–64.
23. K. Mantena traces the 'genealogy' and 'lineage' of Gandhi's political thought; see 'On Gandhi's Critique of the State: Sources, Contexts, Conjunctures' (*Modern Intellectual History*, 2011). This lineage stresses the ideological Influence of the Victorian age on his political thought, mainly with non-Indian writers like Tolstoy, Thoreau, and Ruskin.
24. This group is not related to the well-known welfare association of the same name.
25. The author was staying at the Ark at that time.
26. Jacques Sémelin, *La Liberté au Bout des Ondes. Du Coup de Prague à la Chute du Mur de Berlin* (Paris: Belfond, 1997) and *Non-Violence Explained to my Children* (New York: Marlow & Company, 2000).
27. Oxford: Oxford University Press (2009).
28. Edited by J. Brown and A. Parel (Cambridge: Cambridge University Press, 2011), p. 261. Hardiman also published *Gandhi in His Time and Ours: The Global Legacy of His Ideas* (New York: Columbia University Press, 2003).
29. P. 261.

1 *Swaraj*, the Objective

1. M. K. Gandhi, *Collected Works,* vol. 96, p. 311, August 1947.
2. Quoted in Johnson, *Gandhi's Experiments*, 2006, p. 134.
3. Ibid., pp. 134–135. A panchayat is an ancient structure composed of a village committee of five.
4. Brown, 'Gandhi and Human Rights,' p. 247.
5. M. K. Gandhi, *Collected Works of Mahatma Gandhi,* vol. 43, p. 467 and p. 466 under the caption 'What is in a name?' (29 December 1928).
6. Gandhi, quoted in Johnson, *Gandhi's Experiments*, p. 90. Gandhi said this in a speech given 29 August 1925.
7. Lawrence James, *Raj: The Making and Unmaking of British India* (London: Little, Brown, 1997), p. 359.
8. Quoted in Johnson, *Gandhi's Experiments*, p. 86; the quotation is from chapter 17 of Gandhi's *Hind Swaraj* (1909). Gandhi's resistance, or *satyagraha*, was first called 'passive' for lack of a better word.
9. 'Civil Disobedience' is the name given to the 1930 campaign.
10. *Hind Swaraj*, ch. 10; quoted in Johnson, *Gandhi's Experiments*, p. 85.

11. R. Gandhi, *Gandhi: The Man, His People, and the Empire* (London, Haus, 2007), p. 144.
12. *Young India*, 26 January 1921; quoted in Johnson, *Gandhi's Experiments*, p. 88.
13. *Hind Swaraj*, chapter 8; quoted in ibid., p. 84.
14. See S. Panter-Brick, *Gandhi contre Machiavel* (Paris: Denoël, 1963), ch. 1.
15. Jinnah speaking at the provincial War Conference in Bombay, June 1918.
16. Gandhi to Jinnah, 4 July 1918, *Collected Works,* vol. 17, p. 116.
17. Official estimates for casualties from the massacre were 379 killed and 1,000 wounded.
18. Quoted in R. Gandhi, *Gandhi: The Man*, p. 233.
19. In a letter to Gandhi, the great poet Tagore objected strongly to this deceptive promise.
20. Quoted in R. Gandhi, *Gandhi: The Man,* p.232.
21. Quoted in R. Gandhi, *Gandhi: The Man*, p. 294.
22. M. K. Gandhi, *Collected Works,* vol. 41, pp. 105–106.
23. M. K. Gandhi, *Collected Works,* vol. 53, p. 364.
24. Muslims were 55 per cent of the population in the Punjab, 53 per cent in Bengal.

2 The Voice of India

1. E. Gellner, *Nations and Nationalism* (Oxford: Blackwell, 1983), p. 6.
2. Collins and Lapierre, *Mountbatten*, p. 71. Answering the question 'Would it be reasonable to say Congress exercised a veto over the creation of an independent Bengal?' Mountbatten answered: 'Yes, I think it would be fair.'
3. Abdul Ghaffar Khan, a prominent Congress leader, raised his own semi-military but non-violent organisation, the Red Shirts. The relation between India and the North-West Frontier Province (NWFP) was a tit-for-tat situation. Said Mountbatten: 'They [Congress] wouldn't let me do it [creation of an independent Bengal] when it made sense in Bengal: how could they expect me, therefore, to let them have whichever way suited them in NWFP? Jinnah couldn't have accepted, it would have completely blown the agreement. Congress wouldn't accept an independent Bengal which made perfect sense. Why should Jinnah hand over an independent NWFP when a straight vote would give it to him?'
4. Quoted in D. G. Tendulkar, *Mahatma: Life of Mohandas Karamchand Gandhi* (New Delhi: Publications Division), vol. V, p. 139.
5. M. K. Gandhi, *Collected Works,* vol. 2, p. 364.
6. M. K. Gandhi, *An Autobiography: The Story of My Experiments with Truth*, p. 175.

7. Letter to Dadabhai Naoroji, 'the Grand Old man of India' (died in 1917), 5 July 1894, *Collected Works*, vol. 1, p. 155.
8. M. K. Gandhi, *An Autobiography: the Story of My Experiments with Truth*, p. 142.
9. Ibid., p. 187. Two bills, on trade and immigration, were passed in this way.
10. M. K. Gandhi, *An Autobiography: The Story of My Experiments with Truth*, p. 178.
11. In 1895, 1896, 1898, 1900, 1901, 1904, 1905, 1906, 1908, 1909, 1910, 1911, 1912, 1913 (thanking the Viceroy for his help), 1914, and 1915, the year Gandhi returned to India. See A. M. Zaidi, *Indian National Congress* (New Delhi: Indian Institute of Applied Political Research, 1987–89), vols. I and II.
12. M. K. Gandhi, *An Autobiography: The Story of My Experiments with Truth*, p. 216.
13. Both became Crown Colonies, and within a few years, the Crown Colony of the Transvaal was granted responsible government (1 January 1907).
14. He actually came back specially from India (November 1902), where he had returned in October 1901.
15. Quoted in R. Gandhi, *Gandhi: The Man*, p. 172.
16. *Collected Works of Mahatma Gandhi*, vol. 69, p. 192.
17. Quoted in Veena Choudhury, *Indian Nationalism and External Forces*, 1920–1947 (Delhi: Capital Publishing House, 1985), p. 25.
18. Quoted in G. Shimoni, *Gandhi, Satyagraha and the Jews: A Formative Factor in India's Policy Towards Israel* (Jerusalem: The Leonard Davis Institute for International Relations, Hebrew University, 1977), p. 25.
19. Read the story in full in S. Panter-Brick, *'Gandhi and the Middle East: Jews, Arabs, and Imperial Interests'* (London: I.B.Tauris, 2008).
20. Ibid., p. 31.
21. Some years after Gandhi's assassination, she moved to Switzerland, where she spent her last days trying to resume her study of Beethoven.
22. M. K. Gandhi, *Collected Works,* vol. 74, p. 196. See also Gandhi to Mirabehn, 15 October 1938, ibid., vol. 74, p. 108.
23. Ibid., Gandhi to Mirabehn, 5 November 1938, vol. 74, p. 195.
24. He wrote two letters to Hitler. After the debacle of 1940, he wrote 'To every Briton,' and after the fall of Burma, 'To every Japanese.' This period in Gandhi's life has attracted little attention and much undeserved criticism. Panter-Brick's *Gandhi and the Middle East* contributes to a better understanding and a more balanced assessment of the Mahatma's contribution to world peace.
25. However, a telegram had been sent by the Congress president, asking Gandhi to come. But Gandhi was on his way to Bihar, having answered: 'Send messenger Bihar.' See R. Gandhi, *Gandhi: The Man*, p. 577.

3 The Defence of Indianity

1. Quoted in J. M. Brown's essay 'Gandhi and Human Rights: In Search of True Humanity': she insists on the fact that Gandhi was no activist for human rights (p. 239), but that 'his essential search for Truth could only be through the pursuit of duty or *dharma* and *dharma* was learned through tradition modified by reason or conscience' (p. 240). Ed. by Richard L. Johnson, *Gandhi's Experiments with Truth: Essential Writings by and about Mahatma Gandhi* (Lanham, Lexington Books, 2006).
2. M. K. Gandhi, quoted in Johnson, *Gandhi's Experiments*, p. 108.
3. Brown, 'Gandhi and Human Rights,' p. 251.
4. M. K. Gandhi, *Non-violence in Peace and War* (New York, Garland edition, 1942), vol. I, pp. 27–28. Gandhi's arrest and trial followed his suspension of the Non-cooperation Movement in February 1922.
5. M. K. Gandhi, *An Autobiography: The Story of My Experiments with Truth*, p. 212.
6. Ibid., p. 264.
7. Especially the Jain tradition, which was very influential in Gandhi's Gujarat province.
8. A. Read and D. Fisher, *The Proudest Day: India's Long Road to Independence* (London, Jonathan Cape, 1997), pp. 159–160.
9. Gandhi to the Viceroy, 29 April 1918, *Collected Works,* vol. 17, pp. 7–8.
10. Quoted in Read and Fisher, *Proudest Day*, p. 138.
11. He was thus acclaimed by the poet and leading Congresswoman, Sarojini Naidu, at the time of the Lucknow 1916 Agreement between the Congress and the Muslim League.
12. Brown, *Prisoner of Hope*, p. 185.
13. S. Wolpert, *Jinnah*, pp. 339–40, reporting Jinnah's discourse at some length.
14. M. K. Gandhi to T. B. Sapru, 25 January 1941.

4 War and Non-Violence

1. M. K. Gandhi, quoted in Johnson, *Gandhi's Experiments*, p. 120.
2. Johnson, *Gandhi's Experiments*, pp. 154–55.
3. Ibid., p. 155.
4. Ibid., p. 155.
5. Read the document in S. Panter-Brick, *Gandhi and the Middle East,* pp. 163–168.

6. 'To every Briton,' *Collected Works,* vol. 78, p. 387.
7. See Panter-Brick, *Gandhi and the Middle East*, pp. 163–168.
8. M. K. Gandhi, *My Experiments with Truth*, p. 264.
9. Gandhi, as an Indian, was referred to as the 'coolie-barrister.'
10. M. K. Gandhi, *My Experiments with Truth*, p. 141.
11. Ibid., p. 212.
12. Ibid., p. 264.
13. M. K. Gandhi, *Collected Works*, vol. 5, p. 268.
14. Quoted in R. Payne, *The Life and Death of Mahatma Gandhi* (London: The Bodley Head, 1969), p. 154.
15. M. K. Gandhi, *My Experiments with Truth*, p. 383, p. 384.
16. Ibid., p. 386.
17. M. K. Gandhi, *Collected Works,* vol. 5, p. 179.
18. M. K. Gandhi, *An Autobiography: The Story of My Experiments with Truth*, pp. 427–429.
19. Ibid., p. 425.
20. Ibid., p. 400 and p. 433.
21. Ibid., p. 430.
22. The Government of India was aware of Gandhi's willingness – he was 48 years old – to serve on the battlefields of France or Mesopotamia. The Home Member, Sir William Vincent, suggested to the Private Secretary to the Viceroy, in answer to a letter dated 17 April 1918:

    'I notice that Mr. Gandhi is anxious to be employed on war service in Mesopotamia or France, and if he could be sent to Mesopotamia in any capacity, it would save a lot of trouble' (from the official correspondence quoted in B. R. Nanda, 1981, p. 193).
23. Quoted in R. Gandhi, *Gandhi: The Man*, p. 200.
24. M. K. Gandhi, *My Experiments with Truth*, p. 543.
25. Gandhi to the Viceroy, 29 April 1918, *Collected Works*, vol. 17, p. 9.
26. R. Gandhi, *Gandhi: The Man*, pp. 202–204.

5 Volte-Face

1. In 1939, Gandhi declared his non-violent support for Great Britain. In 1940, he organised an individual *satyagraha* against the war. In 1942, he was about to launch an All-India Quit India campaign against the Government when Congressmen were locked behind bars until the end of the war.
2. R. Gandhi, *Gandhi: The Man*, p. 206 cites Gandhi recalling the incident on 29 December 1946.
3. For instance, the August 1942 campaign could not be organised, because of the swift and widespread arrests. Gandhi complained that the Government

should have given him the time to negotiate. But the Government had learnt its lesson from previous *satyagraha* campaigns.

4. In November 1914, Lord Hardinge had openly criticised the Government of South Africa for not looking after Indian interests.
5. Quoted in R. Gandhi, *Gandhi: The Man*, p. 229.
6. M. K. Gandhi, quoted in Panter-Brick, *Gandhi and the Middle East*, p. 55.
7. M. K. Gandhi, *Collected Works,* vol. 22, p. 429: this *Bombay Chronicle*'s interview is about Gandhi's objections to the Treaty of Sèvres.
8. Quoted in Panter-Brick, *Gandhi and the Middle East*, p. 5.
9. Maulana Abul Kalam Azad, after his release, favoured a policy called *hijrat*, whereby Muslims were to leave the land of the infidels for the country of their Afghan brothers. The emigration of thousands ended disastrously when they were refused sanctuary and were turned back in the winter cold to India. Khan Abul Ghaffar Khan, later to be called 'the Frontier Gandhi' for his involvement in *satyagrahas* and his strong friendship with the Mahatma, crossed over to Afghanistan in the *hijrat* temporary exodus.
10. Gandhi objected that 'the duty of every Hindu [would be] to resist any inroad on India' (*Young India*, 23 June 1920). *Collected Works,* vol. 20, p. 419.
11. See R. Gandhi, *Gandhi: The Man*, pp. 213–217, on their spiritual relationship.
12. Jinnah's answer was: 'I am afraid I cannot accept [your methods and your programme], for I am fully convinced it must lead to disaster.'
13. R. Gandhi, *Gandhi: The Man*, p. 250.
14. M. K. Gandhi, *Collected Works*, vol. 26, p. 384.
15. M. K. Gandhi, *Collected Works,* vol. 20, p. 283.

6 The Wait-and-See Interlude

1. The letter that Nehru wrote to Gandhi on 11th January 1928 is part of a critical exchange of diverging opinions on independence between the two leaders. See *Collected Works,* vol. 41, pp. 101, 104–107, 120–122, and *Jawaharlal Nehru: A Biography,* (Bombay, Allied publishers Limited, 1993), pp. 52–53.
2. M. K. Gandhi, *Collected Works,* vol. 27, p. 7.
3. Ibid., p. 13.
4. The Montagu-Chelmsford Reforms of 1919, which Gandhi was still defending at the Amritsar Congress of 1918 before changing his mind in 1919, provided for elections to the Councils on a restricted suffrage every four years.
5. See M. K. Gandhi's Draft Statement on Council-entry (11 April 1924), in *Collected Works*, vol. 27, pp. 220–223 and Motilal Nehru's counter arguments in ibid., Appendix VIII.
6. M. K. Gandhi, *Collected Works*, vol. 20, p. 318.

7. M. K. Gandhi, interviewed by the *Liverpool Post,* 21 March 1924, in *Collected Works,* vol. 27, p. 104.
8. M. K. Gandhi, (11 August 1924), *Collected Works*, vol. 28, p. 470.
9. See Gandhi (1927), *An Autobiography: The Story of My Experiments with Truth.*
10. Instances of mob violence marred and compromised the success of his campaigns.
11. Gandhi commented: 'Your calling *khadi* "livery of freedom" will live as long as we speak the English language in India. It needs a first-class poet to translate into Hindi the whole of the thought behind that enchanting phrase. For me it is not merely poetry but it enunciates a great truth whose full significance we have yet to grasp.' *Collected Works,* vol. 72, p. 75.
12. M. K. Gandhi, *Collected Works,* vol. 33, p. 378.
13. M. K. Gandhi, *Collected Works*, vol. 24, p. 111.

7 Stooping to Reconquer

1. Quoted by Roy Jenkins, in *Churchill* (London: Macmillan, 2001), p. 436.
2. M. K. Gandhi, 1 October 1925, *Collected Works*, vol. 33, p. 463.
3. Ibid., vol. 27, p. 207.
4. M. K. Gandhi, *Collected Works*, 22 May 1924, vol. 28, pp. 14–17 and 29 May 1924, ibid., p. 65.
5. Swarajists' Statement on Council-Entry, *Collected Works,* vol. 28, Appendix I, p. 499 (22 May 1924).
6. Ibid., *Collected Works,* Appendix I, vol. 28, p. 500.
7. Gandhi to C. R. Das, 13 June 1925, *Collected Works*, vol. 31, p. 467.
8. Ibid., vol. 28, pp. 492–493.
9. Ibid., vol. 29, p. 274.
10. Ibid., vol. 29, p. 274.
11. Ibid., vol. 28, p. 449.
12. Speech to the No-changers at the Belgaum Congress, 21 December 1924, *Collected Works,* vol. 29, p. 466. And Agreement between Gandhi, Motilal Nehru and Das, 26 December 1924, ibid., vol. 29, p. 509: the resolution was voted by show of hands on the same day.
13. Ibid., (30 October 1924), vol. 29, pp. 284–285.
14. Quoted in R. Gandhi, *Gandhi,* p. 268.
15. M. K. Gandhi. *Collected Works*, vol. 32, p. 146.
16. Ibid., (26 July 1925), vol. 32, p. 180.
17. It was to be a great disappointment when the wheel of Asoka, rather than Gandhi's simple spinning wheel, the *charkha*, was chosen for the Indian flag at independence.

18. M. K. Gandhi, *Collected Works,* explaining his position in 'My Duty' (26 July 1925), vol. 32, pp. 179–183.
19. M. K. Gandhi, *Collected Works*, vol. 33, pp. 207–208.
20. Ibid., 15 April 1925, vol. 31, p. 160.
21. Ibid., vol. 33, p. 262.
22. Ibid., vol. 32, p. 201.
23. See R. Gandhi, *Gandhi: The Man*, pp. 262–95.
24. M. K. Gandhi, *Collected Works*, vol. 35, p. 151.

8 The Demise of the Pro-Changers

1. M. K. Gandhi, *Collected Works,* vol. 40, p. 155 (on or before 25 September 1927).
2. M. K. Gandhi, *Collected Works*, vol. 40, p. 331 (on or before 30 October 1927).
3. Gandhi-Irwin Interview, *Collected Works,* vol. 40, Appendix V, p. 496.
4. R. Gandhi, *Gandhi: The Man*, p. 294.
5. Quoting *The Life of Lord Halifax*, in M. K. Gandhi, *Collected Works*, vol. 40, Appendix V, p. 496.
6. Quoted in *Collected Works*, vol. 40, p. 352, note 1.
7. M. K. Gandhi, *Collected Works,* 11 November 1927, vol. 40, p. 352.
8. Gandhi-Irwin Interview, *Collected Works,* vol. 40, Appendix V, p. 497.
9. M. K. Gandhi, *Collected Works,* vol. 40, p. 192 (1 October 1927).
10. Ibid., Gandhi-Irwin Interview, vol. 40, Appendix V, p. 497.
11. M. K. Gandhi, *Collected Works*, Interview to *Indian Daily Mail*, 30 December 1927, vol. 41, p. 72.
12. M. K. Gandhi, Interview to Indian Daily Mail, 30 December 1927, ibid., vol. 41, pp. 71–72.
13. *Collected Works,* Appendix II, vol. 41, p. 488.
14. Gandhi to Nehru, 4 January 1928, *Collected Works,* vol. 41, p. 79.
15. Nehru to Gandhi, 11 January 1928, *Collected Works*, Appendix II, vol. 41, p. 489.
16. Nehru to Gandhi, 11 January 1928, *Collected Works,* Appendix II, vol. 41, p. 489.
17. Nehru to Gandhi, 11 January 1928, *Collected Works,* Appendix II, vol. 41, p. 490.
18. A *taluka* is an administrative unit between a village and a district.
19. M. K. Gandhi, *Collected Works*, *Young India,* 8 March 1928, vol. 41, p. 264.
20. *'What is the Bardoli Case?'* by Mahadev Desai, *Collected Works,* vol. 42, Appendix I, p. 462.

21. *'What is the Bardoli Case?'* by Mahadev Desai, *Collected Works,* vol. 42, Appendix I, p. 464.
22. M. K. Gandhi, *Collected Works*, vol. 42, p. 453.
23. Gandhi to B. G. Horniman, *Collected Works*, vol. 42, p. 414.
24. Gandhi speaking at the Calcutta Congress, 28 December 1928, *Collected Works,* vol. 43, p. 460.
25. Ibid., *Collected Works,* vol. 43, pp. 460–461.
26. Ibid., *Collected Works*, vol. 43, p. 461.
27. Ibid., *Collected Works*, vol. 43, p. 456.
28. Ibid., *Collected Works*, vol. 43, p. 463.
29. Ibid., *Collected Works*, vol. 43, p. 457.
30. Gandhi moving his Resolution, 28 December 1928, *Collected Works*, vol. 43, p. 458.
31. Interview to *The Hindustan Times,* 3 November 1928, *Collected Works*, vol. 43, p. 174.
32. 'Civil' should not be understood as 'civic,' but, as Gandhi explained, as 'non-criminal.'

9 The Temptation of the One-Party System

1. M. K. Gandhi, *Collected Works,* 1 December 1927, vol. 40, p. 476.
2. Interview to the Press, 29 October 1927, ibid., vol. 40, p. 329.
3. M. K. Gandhi to Motilal Nehru, 8 May 1928, *Collected Works,* vol. 42, pp. 8–9.
4. M. K. Gandhi to C. Vijayaraghavachariar, 29 April 1928, vol. 41, p. 474.
5. Shaukat Ali to Gandhi, 23 October 1928, *Collected Works,* vol. 43, Appendix III, pp. 524–526.
6. Gandhi to Shaukat Ali, 30 November 1928, *Collected Works,* vol. 43, p. 297.
7. Wolpert, *Jinnah*, p. 94. Wolpert estimates that 'Jinnah's proposals would... have given Muslims elective majority control in five provincial governments,' and that the Nehru Report of summer 1928 was but the 'Hindu position' in answer to Jinnah's constitutional proposals.
8. M. K. Gandhi, Speech at the Calcutta Congress, 28 December 1928, *Collected Works*, vol. 43, p. 458.
9. Quoted in Wolpert, *Jinnah*, p. 101.
10. R. Gandhi, *Gandhi: The Man*, p. 297.
11. By Tej Bahadur Sapru, a Liberal leader, who was advocating, however, a deal with Jinnah.
12. Wolpert, *Jinnah*, pp. 101–102.
13. M. K. Gandhi, 6 September 1928, *Collected Works,* vol. 42, p. 438.

14. M. K. Gandhi, Speech at Plenary Session of Round Table Conference, 1 December 1931, *Collected Works,* vol. 54, p. 219.
15. Quoted in Wolpert, *Jinnah*, pp. 121–122.
16. The Government had not wanted Gandhi to die in prison after he decided on 16 August 1933 to fast for twenty-one days.
17. R. Gandhi, *Gandhi: The Man*, p. 367.
18. Until their resignation en bloc at the outbreak of the Second World War.
19. These quotations can be found in Wolpert, *Jinnah*, pp. 136–152.
20. Gandhi to Jinnah, 22 May 1937, *Collected Works,* vol. 71, p. 277.
21. Gandhi called Jinnah's speech at Lucknow 'a declaration of war': see Gandhi to Jinnah, 19 October 1937, *Collected Works,* vol. 72, p. 353.

10 Retaliation

1. In April 1938, Jinnah refused Gandhi's request to break his train journey from Calcutta to Bombay in order to talk to the old man. Gandhi then had to go to Bombay, but he failed to change Jinnah's mind.
2. Quoted in Wolpert, *Jinnah*, pp. 165–166.
3. Ibid., p. 175.
4. Gandhi led a campaign of individual civil disobedience in 1940–41 against the war, with *satyagrahis* courting imprisonment by shouting that slogan.
5. Quoted in R. Gandhi, *Gandhi: The Man*, p. 432.
6. Gellner, *Nations and Nationalism*, p. 1.
7. French, *Liberty or Death: India's Journey to Independence and Division* (London: Flamingo, 1998), p. 124.
8. R. J. Moore, *Endgames of Empire: Studies of India's Britain Problem* (Oxford: Oxford University Press, 1988), pp. 112–117.
9. Quoted in ibid., p. 37; the 'Federation' refers to the implementation of the Government of India Act (1935).
10. Quoted in ibid., p. 126.
11. See *India: A Re-statement* (London: Oxford University Press, 1945).
12. W. R. Louis, *Ends of British Imperialism* (London: I.B.Tauris, 2006), p. 398.
13. R. J. Moore, *Endgames of Empire*, p. 110. Such a settlement was based on Chakravarti Rajagopalachari's formula, which was at first turned down by Gandhi.
14. K. Tidrick, *Gandhi: A Political and Spiritual Life* (London: I.B.Tauris, 2006), p. 301.
15. Quoted in R. Gandhi, *Gandhi: The Man*, p. 524.
16. Mosley, *Last Days of the Raj*, p. 24.

11 From Britain as Empire to Britain as Umpire

1. Louis, 'The Dissolution of the British Empire,' in W. R. Louis and J. M. Brown, eds., *The Oxford History of the British Empire*, vol. IV: *The Twentieth Century* (Oxford: Oxford University Press, 1999), p. 335.
2. Brown, 'India,' in ibid., p. 436.
3. See Moore, *Endgames of Empire*, p. 12.
4. This was the second Balfour Declaration. The first, in 1917, had promised a national home in Palestine for the Jews.
5. Brown, 'India,' p. 437.
6. See Moore, *Endgames of Empire*, p. 10.
7. Statement to the Indian Legislative Assembly by the Home Member of the Government of India.
8. Wm. Roger Louis, *Imperialism at Bay: The United States and the Decolonization of the British Empire, 1914–1945* (Oxford: Oxford University Press, 1977), p. 16.
9. The quotations are from Louis, *Ends of British Imperialism*, p. 397, p. 398, and p. 399.
10. L. James, *Raj: The Making and Unmaking of British India* (London: Little, Brown, 1997), pp. 587–588.
11. Jinnah used to correspond secretly through Churchill's caretaker letter-box. Churchill thought the Commonwealth could not deny entry to Pakistan and advised him to go ahead.
12. Quoted in N. Mansergh and E. W. R. Lumby, eds., *The Transfer of Power*, 12 vols. (London: Her Majesty's Stationery Office, (1970–1983), 1981, pp. 541–542.
13. Louis, *Ends of British Imperialism*, p. 408 and p. 418.
14. Quoted in Mansergh, 1981, p. 92.
15. Quoted in Collins and Lapierre, *Mountbatten and Partition*, pp. 53–54.
16. Quoted in Louis, *Ends of British Imperialism*, p. 417.
17. Mansergh, 1981, p. 138.
18. French, *Liberty or Death*, p. 124 and p. 127.
19. Jalal, *The Sole Spokesman*, pp. 277–278.
20. Quotations from Collins and Lapierre, *Mountbatten and Partition*, pp. 53–55, including this reminiscence of a conversation between the King and Mountbatten. The King said to the Viceroy: 'I know I have to take the "I" out of G.R.I.' [George, Rex Imperator].

12 The Judgment of King Solomon

1. Mansergh, 1981, p. 144: 'His idea was that he should tell the Indian leaders of his decision – there should be no written agreement nor would he ask

for their acceptance... He was in the position of a testator on behalf of His Majesty's Government.'

2. Quoted in Collins and Lapierre, *Mountbatten and Partition*, p. 14.
3. R. Gandhi, *Gandhi: The Man*, p. 588.
4. Read more about this episode, interviews and documents collected in the 1980s by Collins and Lapierre, in *Mountbatten and Partition* (1982), and in Mansergh, *The Transfer of Power* (1970–1983).
5. Wolpert, *Jinnah*, p. 317.
6. Quoted in A. von Tunzelmann, *Indian Summer: The Secret History of the End of an Empire* (London: Simon and Schuster, 2007), p. 237.
7. From notes of correspondence dictated by Gandhi to Mahadev Desai on the day of his arrest (8 August 1942) in M. K. Gandhi, *Collected Works*, vol. 83, pp. 186–187. Gandhi goes on to say: 'Provided the Muslim League co-operated fully with the Congress demand for immediate independence without the slightest reservation... the Congress will have no objection to the British Government transferring all the powers it today exercises to the Muslim League on behalf of the whole of India... And the Congress will not only not obstruct any Government that the Muslim League may form on behalf of the people, but will even join the Government in running the machinery of the free State. This is meant in all seriousness and sincerity.' (ibid.)
8. R. Gandhi, *Gandhi: The Man*, p. 507.
9. S. Wolpert, *Jinnah*, p. 257.
10. Gandhi to Wavell, 13 June 1946, *Collected Works*, vol. 91, p. 56. The situation was complicated by the fact that, according to governmental promises, Jinnah should have been asked to form an interim government because of the Congress's reluctance to endorse the Cabinet Mission Plan of 16 June Offer. He talked of 'broken pledges' and was 'thoroughly shocked.'
11. 1 April 1947 from Mountbatten Papers, N. Mansergh, 1981, p. 69, where further quotations are also to be found (pp. 120–129).
12. N. Mansergh, 1981, p. 145.
13. Mansergh, 1981, p. 177.
14. R. Gandhi, *Gandhi: The Man*, p. 585.
15. Mansergh, 1981, p. 163.
16. Mansergh, 1981, p. 127.
17. Wolpert, *Jinnah*, p. 316 and p. 317.
18. Mansergh, 1981, p. 168.
19. Quoted in Collins and Lapierre, *Mountbatten and Partition*, pp. 34–35.
20. Mansergh, 1981, p. 103.
21. M. K. Gandhi, Prayer meeting, 1 April 1947, *Collected Works*, vol. 94, p. 216–217.

22. The two last quotations are in Mansergh, 1981, p. 70.
23. Letter to Lord Ismay.
24. Mansergh, p. 155.
25. Mansergh, 1981, p. 86, p. 121.
26. Mansergh, 1981, p. 128, from Uncirculated Record of Discussion no. 3.
27. This quotation and the two following are from Mansergh, 1981, pp. 211–213.
28. Mansergh, 1981, p. 212. The original idea had been that the president of the Muslim League and the president of the Congress, Kripalani, would sign the declaration. But Jinnah objected, refusing to sign the joint appeal with anybody but Gandhi. Gandhi agreed, on the condition that the word 'peoples,' used in the appeal to refer to Muslims and non-Muslims (an implied consent to the two-nation theory), should be changed to 'communities.'
29. Mansergh, 1981, p. 197.
30. Quoted in Mosley, *Last Days of the Raj*, p. 248.
31. Quoted in ibid., p. 127. Mountbatten changed his mind after V. P. Menon received too much prestige from the event, and criticised him for his pride and for not sharing the glory with him.
32. Quoted in Collins and Lapierre, *Mountbatten and Partition*, p. 60 and p. 70.
33. Liaqat Ali Khan, Jinnah's right arm and future Prime Minister of Pakistan, had previously expressed the view that 'we want to include in our proposed dominion Delhi and Aligarh, which are centres of our culture.' In R. Gandhi, *Gandhi: The Man*, p. 432.
34. Mansergh, 1981, p. 944.
35. Quoted in Collins and Lapierre, *Mountbatten and Partition*, p. 103 (Viceroy's Personal Report no. 8, 5 June 1947).
36. This quotation and the following two are in Collins and Lapierre, *Mountbatten and Partition*, pp. 66–68.
37. Mountbatten: 'I am absolutely convinced and ready to stake everything on the fact that the time will come when it will be recognized that I couldn't have gone any slower. I only just held the position by going as fast as I did... It was because the thing was breaking up under my hands. The reason was that neither side would cooperate with each other. I could feel the damn thing simmering. It's like standing on the edge of a volcano and feeling the moment of explosion' (Collins and Lapierre, *Mountbatten and Partition*, p. 50).
38. Ibid., p. 39, p. 40.
39. Ibid., p. 114 (Minutes of Viceroy's Staff Meetings, 9 May 1947).
40. Ibid., p. 75. Jinnah refused to do the same for Pakistan, naming himself Governor General.
41. A. Von Tunzelmann, *Indian Summer: The Secret History of the End of an Empire*, 2007, p. 236.
42. Quoted in Collins and Lapierre, *Mountbatten and Partition*, p. 36.

Envoy: The Two Brothers

1. The Mahatma's full name is *Mohan das* Karamchand Gandhi and *Moham* is a diminutive for Muhammad Ali Jinnah.
2. Pakistan and Bangladesh in the 'Realm' of India.
3. Name given by Gandhi to Lanza del Vasto (1901–1981), the founder of the Gandhian Community of the Ark.
4. Literal translation of an old Christian hymn: Where (there is) charity and love, God there is.

BIBLIOGRAPHY

Bondurant, V. Joan. *Conquest of Violence: The Gandhian Philosophy of Conflict.* Princeton: Princeton University Press, 1958.

Brown, M. Judith. 'Gandhi and Human Rights: In Search of True Humanity.' In R. L. Johnson, *Gandhi's Experiments with Truth*, pp. 237–252. Oxford: Lexington, 2006.

—— *Gandhi: Prisoner of Hope.* New Haven, Conn.: Yale University Press, 1989.

—— *Gandhi's Rise to Power in Politics, 1915–1922.* Cambridge: Cambridge University Press, 1972.

—— 'India.' In Wm. Roger Louis and Judith M. Brown, eds., *The Oxford History of the British Empire*, vol. IV: *The Twentieth Century*, pp. 421–446. Oxford: Oxford University Press, 1999.

—— *Nehru: A Political Life.* Oxford: Oxford University Press, 2003.

Brown, M. Judith and Parel, Anthony, eds. *The Cambridge Companion to Gandhi.* Cambridge: Cambridge University Press, 2011.

Choudhuri, Veena: *Indian Nationalism and External Forces,* 1920–1947. Delhi: Capital Publishing House, 1985.

Collins, Larry and Lapierre, Dominique. *Freedom at Midnight: The Epic Drama of India's Struggle for Independence.* London: Harper Collins, 1975; repr., 1997. Singapore: Trans-East Distributing Company, 1982.

Coupland, Reginald. *India: A Re-statement.* London: Oxford University Press, 1945.

Del Vasto, Lanza. *Le Pèlerinage aux Sources.* Paris: Denoël, 1942.

Fisher, Louis. *The Essential Gandhi: An Anthology.* London: Allen and Unwin, 1961.

French, Patrick. *Liberty or Death: India's Journey to Independence and Division.* London: Flamingo, 1998.

Gandhi, Mohandas Karamchand. *Collected Works of Mahatma Gandhi.* (Electronic Book), 98 vols. New Delhi: Publications Division, Government of India, 1999.

—— *An Autobiography: The Story of My Experiments with Truth.* Ahmedabad, 1927.

Gandhi, Mohandas Karamchand. *Non-Violence in Peace and War.* New York: Garland Edition, 1942.

Gandhi, Rajmohan. *Gandhi: The Man, His People, and the Empire.* London: Haus, 2007.

Gellner, Ernest. *Nations and Nationalism.* Oxford: Blackwell, 1983.

Ghose, Sankar. *Jawaharlal Nehru: A Biography.* Bombay: Allied Publishers Ltd, 1993.

Gopal, Sarvepalli. *Selected Works of J. Nehru.* 3 vols. London: Jonathan Cape, 1975–1984.

Hardiman, David. *Gandhi in His Time and Ours: The Global Legacy of His Ideas.* New York: Columbia University Press, 2003.

—— *'Gandhi's Global Legacy.'* In M. Judith Brown and Anthony Parel, eds., *The Cambridge Companion to Gandhi,* pp. 239–257. Cambridge: Cambridge University Press, 2011.

Jaffrelot, Christophe, ed. *Pakistan: Nationalism without a Nation?* New Delhi: Manohar, 2002.

Jalal, Ayesha. *The Sole Spokesman: Jinnah, the Muslim League, and the Demand for Pakistan.* Cambridge: Cambridge University Press, 1994.

James, Lawrence. *Raj: The Making and Unmaking of British India.* London: Little, Brown, 1997.

Jenkins, Roy. *Churchill.* London: Macmillan, 2001.

Johnson, Richard L., ed. *Gandhi's Experiments with Truth: Essential Writings by and about Mahatma Gandhi.* Oxford: Lexington, 2006.

Kedourie, Elie. *Nationalism.* 4th ed. Oxford: Blackwell, 1993.

Khan, Yasmin. *The Great Partition: The Making of India and Pakistan.* New Haven, Conn.: Yale University Press, 2007.

Latronche, Marie-France. *L'influence de Gandhi en France de 1919 à nos Jours.* L'Harmattan: Recherches Asiatiques, 1999.

Louis, Wm. Roger. 'Dissolution of the British Empire.' In Wm. Roger Louis and Judith M. Brown, eds., *The Oxford History of the British Empire,* vol. IV: *The Twentieth Century*, pp. 329–356. Oxford: Oxford University Press, 1999.

—— *Ends of British Imperialism: The Scramble for Empire, Suez, and Decolonization.* London: I.B.Tauris, 2006.

—— *Imperialism at Bay: The United States and the Decolonization of the British Empire, 1941–1945.* Oxford: Oxford University Press, 1977.

Mansergh, N. and E. W. R., eds., *The Transfer of Power,* 12 vols. London: Her Majesty's Stationery Office, 1970–1983.

Mantena, Karuna. 'On Gandhi's Critique of the State: Sources, Contexts, Conjunctures.' *Modern Intellectual History*, 2011.

Moore, R. J. *The Crisis of Indian Unity, 1917–1940.* Oxford: Oxford University Press, 1974.

—— *Endgames of Empire: Studies of Britain's Indian Problem.* Oxford: Oxford University Press, 1988.

Mosley, Leonard. *The Last Days of the British Raj.* London: Weidenfeld and Nicolson, 1961.

Nanda, B. R. *Mahatma Gandhi: A Biography.* Oxford: Oxford University Press, 1981.

Panter-Brick, Simone. *Gandhi and the Middle East: Jews, Arabs, and Imperial Interests.* London: I.B.Tauris, 2008. Translated into Arabic by Abu Dhabi Authority for Culture and Heritage: Kalima, 2011.

—— *Gandhi contre Machiavel.* Paris: Denoël, 1963.

——*Gandhi against Machiavellism: Non-violence in Politics.* Translated from the French by P. Leon. Pondicherry: Asia Publishing House, 1966.

—— 'Gandhi et la création du Pakistan.' In Marie-Pierre Bovy, ed., *Gandhi: L'Héritage.* Nantes: Siloë, 2001.

Read, Anthony and Fisher, David. *The Proudest Day: India's Long Road to Independence.* London: Jonathan Cape, 1997.

Roberts, Adam and Garton Ash, Timothy. *Civil Resistance and Power Politics: The Experience of Non-violent Action from Gandhi to the Present.* Oxford: Oxford University Press, 2009.

Sémelin, Jacques. *La Liberté au Bout des Ondes: Du Coup de Prague à la Chute du Mur de Berlin.* Paris: Belfond, 1997.

—— *Non-Violence Explained to my Children.* New York: Marlow & Company, 2000.

Sitaramayya, Pattabhi. *The History of the Indian National Congress, 1935–1947.* Bombay: Padma, 1947.

Shimoni, Gedeon. *Gandhi, Satyagraha and the Jews: A Formative Factor in India's Policy Towards Israel.* Jerusalem: Leonard Davis Institute for International Relations, Hebrew University, 1977.

Tendulkar, Dinanath Gopal. *Mahatma: Life of Mohandas Karamchand Gandhi.* 8 vols. New Delhi: Publications Division, Government of India, 1954.

Tidrick, Kathryn. *Gandhi: A Political and Spiritual Life.* London: I.B.Tauris, 2006.

Von Tunzelman, Alex. *Indian Summer: The Secret History of the End of an Empire.* London: Simon and Schuster, 2007.

Wolpert, Stanley. *Gandhi's Passion: The Life and Legacy of Mahatma Gandhi.* Oxford: Oxford University Press, 2001.

——*Jinnah of Pakistan.* New York: Oxford University Press, 1984.

Zaidi, A. M. *Indian National Congress: The Glorious Tradition.* Texts of the Resolutions passed by the INC, the AICC and the WC. 5 vols. New Delhi: Indian Institute of Applied Political Research, 1987–1989.

INDEX

Abbreviations: INC: Indian National Congress; MAJ: Muhammad Ali Jinnah; MKG: Mohandas Karamchand Gandhi